LIFE'S A PITCH

MUSINGS ON FOOTBALL PAST, PRESENT & FUTURE

BY STEVE MASSEY

WITH RODNEY MARSHALL

FOREWORD

In 2022, I agreed to help ex-player, manager and director of football Steve Massey write his autobiography, *Where's My Towel?* The completed book was the result of a series of recorded conversations which we conducted face-to-face. *Life's A Pitch* has been created in a similar manner, with me throwing in the questions and sometimes playing devil's advocate, drawing out Steve's observations and opinions about a wide range of football topics. We chose a threefold formula for each chapter: reflecting on English football's past; examining the current state of the game, including constructive criticism; finally, offering a blueprint for the future. The topical nature of the book's content and the ever-evolving world of both football and society mean that some details or comments will, inevitably, soon be out-of-date.

In creating the historical timeline, located near the front of the book, I have drawn on Simon Inglis' *The Football Grounds of England and Wales*, in addition to numerous websites, including the official ones for the FSA, FA, PL and EFL, the PFSA, *Football Stadiums*, English Heritage, and *Football History*. The timeline is selective, mostly relating to the topics explored in the subsequent chapters.

Finally, I am acutely aware that *Life's A Pitch* is not an original title. There are at least half a dozen other books carrying the same one, from several guides to business sales methods, a novel centring on camping, a collection of essays by football journalists, and a book of memoirs written by an EFL groundsman. Nevertheless, we both felt that the popular title perfectly matched the content. Any factual inaccuracies are down to me as editor.

Rodney Marshall
Suffolk, UK, June 2023

"Behind every kick of the ball, there has to be a thought."
(Denis Bergkamp)

"Football is played with your head. Your feet are just the tools."
(Andrea Pirlo)

"Success isn't owned, it's leased. And rent is due every day."
(JJ Watt)

"Football is the ballet of the masses."
(Dmitri Shostakovich)

"That's the beauty of sport. Sometimes you laugh, sometimes you cry."
(Pep Guardiola)

"Keep the passion and lose the poison..."
(Jurgen Klopp)

"You can overcome anything, if, and only if, you love something enough."
(Lionel Messi)

PREFACE

It is more than thirty years since Nick Hornby's *Fever Pitch* was published. Like Simon Inglis' emotive portrait of football grounds, a decade earlier, it immediately struck me as a rare book, written by someone who was something of a 'football anorak', an obsessive who understood both the raw passion and some of the pitfalls of following 'the beautiful game'. Today the market of football-related books is, arguably, saturated. Autobiographies or biographies of players; volumes dedicated to the history of the game, to a specific club, or single campaign; books which explore a topical issue such as Michael Calvin's *Living on the Volcano* (managers), *The Nowhere Men* (scouts) and *No Hunger in Paradise* (youth football); books such as Daniel Gray's fascinating *Stramash* and *Hatters, Railwaymen and Knitters* which explore football as social history... On one level, *Life's A Pitch* simply adds another pebble to the football book mountain. However, its broad canvas hopefully offers up a series of intriguing debates about the sport's past, present and future: what has been lost, what has been gained and where we might go from here. Equally, it is interested in exploring football from top to bottom, from the professional top-flight down to the grassroots of the game.

It has often been suggested that football is a microcosm of life itself. There is an element of truth in there, although it is a difficult claim to fully justify. Nevertheless, the sport can hold a mirror up to society, reflecting both the beauty and the ugliness. In addition, like the human world around us, it is in a constant state of evolution. Those are two themes at the heart of this book's project.

Football has a long pre-history, stretching back to sports such as the Chinese *cuju* – which involved kicking an air-filled ball into a net without the use of hands – and the more violent contact sports found in Ancient Greece (*episkyros*) and Rome (*harpastum*) which both used leather balls. Each of these games – played more than 2,000 years ago – includes pre-echoes or elements of today's codified, global sport. In Britain, various types of 'mob football' were popular in the Middle Ages. However, one might argue that football's official history began in mid-Victorian England, with the formation of the FA in 1863, when the previously conflicting laws of the game were discussed, some rules rejected, others ratified, and the new laws codified. [1] These thirteen FA rules included players being able to catch the ball, but not allowed to run with it in their hands, nor to halt an opponent by 'hacking', tripping or holding him.

In many respects, that embryonic Victorian sport now seems like something from a vanished age – there were no crossbars and goal height restrictions, nor were there any referees, for example – and yet the raw passion it clearly evoked in players and spectators alike in the mid-nineteenth century does not feel alien or remote at all. Football is, essentially, a fascinating paradox, in that it must be seen within its historical and cultural context and yet there are aspects of it which appear 'timeless'.

One of these constants, sadly, is the hooliganism which has blighted the sport ever since the late-Victorian period, with a noticeable peak in the 1970s and 1980s. If football does hold up a mirror to society, what do we see in it? The ugliest prejudices we encounter daily in society – such as male violence, xenophobia, racism, sexism, homophobia, extreme nationalism and tribalism – are continually reflected in football's mirror. And yet, that mirror also reflects the ways in which football can bring seemingly disparate people together. Just as it can divide, it can also connect, if not unify. The

Football Supporters' Association – with its 500,000 plus membership – is an example of fan empowerment and a collective spirit involving supporters from a wide range of clubs in terms of level and size. Within a specific club and town, this spirit can be equally powerful. As Football Trust pioneer Brian Lomax once memorably commented, it is closely connected to the twinned notions of community and belonging:

"I believe there are certain very important values in life and that football support embodies them. There is a sense of pilgrimage, of going to a sacred place; there is loyalty, sticking with something through good and bad times. It's about emotion, about caring and comradeship, about the whole thing being greater than the sum of its parts. These are very deeply rooted human needs and I believe that that is at the root of people's love for football and loyalty for their clubs." [2]

Brian was writing this in a now vanished era before social media, at a time when many fans travelled more in hope than expectation. The latter is not necessarily a negative, but the general mindset has, arguably, shifted; patience is at a premium nowadays with more people demanding instant success, from club owners to supporters. Nevertheless, I still think that many of us can identify with his passionate belief. Lomax understood that football remains *the* one sport which can bring a community together. In an age where there appears to be less and less to differentiate one town or city from another – the disappearance of traditional local industries, the tendency for the same chain stores, supermarkets and restaurants to pop up in every high street or out-of-town shopping complex – a football club can still play a powerful role in terms of regional identity, marking out one place as being distinct from another. In a world of bewilderingly swift technological and cultural change, it also offers a sense of continuity, a bridge between the past and present. Increasingly, professional clubs are not simply magnets on a match day but are involving themselves in community projects with a cross-range of the area's population, including 'extra-time hubs' for older people, out-reach programmes, disability sports provision and PE education providers.

I described both society and football as constantly evolving, but evolution should never be simplistically equated with 'progress'. Things tend to be both lost and gained along the way. Rather than putting on rose-tinted glasses and viewing the past with misty-eyed nostalgia, *Life's A Pitch* examines football's evolution with an objective, critical eye, putting the sport under the proverbial microscope: the ever-changing laws of the game; the Premier League; football's pyramid structure; the 'magic' of the FA Cup; artificial pitches; club ownership; the managerial hotseat; stadiums; media coverage in print, radio, television and online, including social media and podcasts; player pathways; finally, in our conclusion, we provide a discussion/debate on where we find ourselves now and how we can move forward to a brighter future.

Taking us on this football journey from the 1970s to the present day, and beyond, is former professional footballer and non-league manager Steve Massey. His CV credentials for being our 'tour guide' include half a century immersed in the game. He has experienced life as a raw apprentice, a tiny cog in a machine, but he has also overseen an entire club – from the men's first XI to youth and women's teams – as its Director of Football. He has ridden the professional roller-coaster, from the highs of European cup football to the lows of being released by clubs. He has witnessed the FA Cup from its grassroots Extra Preliminary Round – in front of a smattering of spectators – through to a third-round match against the European Cup holders watched by millions on *Match of the*

Day. Over the course of five decades, he has seen the myriad changes which have taken place, many no doubt improving the sport, others arguably undermining the reputation of football as both 'the people's sport' and 'the beautiful game'. *Life's A Pitch* offers the reader an insider's view, insights and opinions seasoned with both humour and honesty.

In Charles Dickens' *A Christmas Carol* (1843), Ebenezer Scrooge is visited by the spirits of Christmas Past, Present and Yet to Come. The story is, on one level, a cautionary tale, even if it leaves its protagonist feeling transformed and wiser. By musing on football's (recent) past, present and the 'yet to come', the aim here is threefold: to revisit and evaluate the past – the good, the bad and the ugly – examine the present day state of the game at all its levels and, finally, both anticipate its potential future developments and offer a vision of what, arguably, needs to change in order to make the sport better: fairer, more attractive and more inclusive for the millions who play or watch matches, for whom football is more than just a game.

Rodney Marshall
Suffolk, June 2023

1. Association football, in 1863, offered a 'unifying' code which took elements from both the Cambridge rules (1848-63) and the Sheffield rules (1857-77).
2. Brian Lomax interviewed by David Conn for *The Football Business* (Mainstreaming Publishing, 2002).

SELECTIVE TIMELINE

1857: Creation of the world's oldest club, Sheffield FC.

1863: The founding members of The Football Association meet to finalise the laws of football at Lincoln's Inn Fields in London. Thirteen original rules of the game. Pitches marked off with flagpoles.

1865: Tape stretched across the goal posts at a height of eight feet.

1866: Offside – 'three opponents' rule – formally introduced. Before then, players could not pass the ball forward at all apart from when kicking behind the goal line.

1869: Goal kicks introduced.

1870: Eleven-a-side matches including a goalkeeper introduced by FA. Outfield players no longer allowed to handle the ball.

1871: Club umpires introduced to help captains keep order.

1871: Inaugural FA Cup tournament is launched. Only 12 of the 50 member clubs compete in the competition. Two neutral umpires and a mediator/time-keeping referee were to officiate each match.

1872: The nomadic Wanderers win the inaugural FA Cup at Kennington Oval.

1872: Corner kicks and indirect free-kicks for handball introduced.

1874: Indirect free-kicks introduced for foul play.

1874: Club umpires first mentioned in the laws of the game.

1878: Officials allowed to use whistles.

1878: Bramall Lane stages first ever floodlit match.

1882: Crossbars, allowed by FA since 1875, become obligatory.

1882: Pitch markings introduced for the boundaries.

1885: FA legalises professionalism.

1885: "Howling roughs" at Deepdale attack both sets of players with stones, sticks, punches and kicks.

1886: Preston and Queens Park fans fight at a railway station.

1887: Centre circle and six-yard semi-circles introduced.

1888: Twelve-club Football League introduced. North and Midlands teams only.

1889: Preston North End's The Invincibles' complete the (inaugural) League and FA Cup double, remaining unbeaten all season.

1891: FA decide that neutral referees should be the sole decision makers. Club umpires banished to the side-lines, in effect becoming linesmen.

1891: Penalty kicks (concept invented by a goalkeeper!) and twelve-yard line introduced.

1892: FA approve goal nets.

1892: Everton buy a field, Mere Green, and swiftly develop a stadium, Goodison Park, beginning the first wave of purpose-built football grounds.

1892: Second Division of Football League introduced.

1893: Accrington FC, one of the 'original twelve', resign from the Football League.

1893: FA Amateur Cup introduced.

1893: Creation of the 'retain-and-transfer' system which tied players to a club.

1894: Southern League introduced as a rival to the FL.

1898: Promotion and relegation introduced.

1898: Neutral linesmen introduced.

1902: Penalty areas marked out.

1903: Direct free-kicks introduced.

1905: Scottish Engineer Archibald Leitch designs and remodels several English football grounds, beginning his thirty-year body of stadium work south of the border.

1907: Players no longer offside in their own half.

1907: PFA trade union formed, looking to challenge both the £4 maximum wage and transfer restrictions.

1908: FA Charity/Community Shield launched.

1909: Herbert Chapman takes Northampton Town to the Southern League title and the Charity Shield, the beginning of a remarkable career in which he revolutionised many aspects of football management.

1912: Goalkeepers only allowed to handle in their box and forced to wear a different colour shirt.

1920: Division Three introduced, mainly Southern teams.

1921: Divisions Three North and South formed.

1921: Players no longer offside from a throw-in.

1923: First FA Cup Final at the newly opened Wembley Stadium ('Empire Stadium') with chaos amongst an estimated 200,000 crowd.

1924: Departmental Committee on Crowds examines policing, advanced booking, stadium design and safety etc., following crowd chaos at Wembley.

1924: Goals can now be scored direct from a corner.

1925: Onside modified to two opponents in front, rather than three.

1927: BBC radio broadcasts first live match, the FA Cup Final.

1929: Sports Turf Research Institute set up.

1930: FA places ban on member clubs playing in floodlit matches.

1937: Ten-yard distance for opponents from a free-kick replaces previous six-yard rule; penalty arc introduced.

1937: BBC television broadcasts its first football match, Arsenal v Arsenal Reserves.

1938: BBC broadcast the FA Cup Final in its entirety, at a time when there were fewer than 10,000 television sets.

1945: Maxwell Ayrton designs a revolutionary stadium for Derby which would have doubled up as a revenue-generating community hub health care system during the week. It was never built.

1946: BBC broadcast first live post-war televised match, Barnet v Wealdstone.

1946: 33 people die in crush at over-crowded Burnden Park, Bolton.

1946: Hughes Enquiry recommends tighter ground inspections, safety licences and scientific measuring of ground capacity.

1948: BBC radio launches its Saturday 5pm *Sports Report* programme, with its 'Out of the Blue' opening theme tune.

1954: BBC television covers the World Cup finals for the first time.

1955: BBC start showing brief highlights of a single match – maximum five minutes – on its Saturday night *Sports Special* programme.

1955-56: Several train-wrecking incidents take place involving Everton and Liverpool fans.

1956: First floodlit FL match played at Fratton Park.

1958: The Munich Air Disaster results in 23 fatalities, including eight Manchester United players.

1958: ITV join BBC in covering the World Cup finals.

1958: First cantilever stand is constructed, at the Old Show Ground, Scunthorpe.

1958: Fourth tier of Football League introduced.

1960: Football League Cup introduced, originally conceived as the Football League Floodlight Cup. (Twenty-four FL clubs still without floodlights.)

1960: *The Big Game*, a short-lived venture by ITV into broadcasting live FL matches.

1961: Maximum wage of £20 abolished.

1962: Alf Ramsey's Ipswich Town crowned champions in their first-ever season in the top-flight.

1962: Anglia Television launch local football highlights package *Match of the Week*, with Tyne Tees Television launching *Shoot*.

1962: The original Accrington Stanley resign from the FL mid-season.

1964: *Match of the Day* launched on (London only) BBC 2, in a bid to prepare cameramen for the forthcoming World Cup.

1965: Substitutions added to the English game.

1965: ATV launches its London-based highlights package *Star Soccer*, Southern Television offering *Southern Soccer*.

1965: Several clubs attempt to block the BBC moving *Match of the Day* to BBC 1, fearing that it would affect attendances at the game. As a compromise, the BBC agree not to reveal the match covered until after the games have been played.

1966: *Match of the Day* moves to BBC 1 after England's World Cup success.

1967: Launch of BBC Radio Leicester heralds the dawn of BBC local radio stations.

1968: John Moynihan's *The Soccer Syndrome* explores, amongst many other topics, football hooliganism in the English game.

1968: First colour transmission of *Match of the Day*, on BBC 2 as BBC 1 was still transmitting in black-and-white. Newly formed LWT launches London-based *The Big Match*, with alternative shows in most ITV regions.

1969: Laing report into ground safety and policing, in the light of increasing football hooliganism.

1969: FA Trophy introduced for semi-professional clubs.

1970: Penalty shoot-outs introduced.

1971: First slow motion replays on *Match of the Day*.

1972: Non-league Hereford United beat top-flight Newcastle United in the FA Cup, a victory which arguably helped secure them a place in the Football League.

1974: A Blackpool fan is stabbed to death at Bloomfield Road in the year when Manchester United's 'Red Army' hooligan firm causes chaos at a number of Second Division grounds. Crowd segregation and fences are introduced at many grounds. The 70s seen as the era where many hooligan firms emerge.

1974: FA abolishes official amateur status. FA Vase replaces the FA Amateur Cup.

1974: BBC launch Ceefax, world's first teletext information service.

1975: Safety of Sports Grounds Act includes legal requirement for safety certificates for 'designated' grounds. Football Grounds Improvement Trust set up by Labour government (with assistance from Football League and pools companies) to provide grants to help clubs implement the Act.

1976: Goal difference replaces goal average.

1976: Colour coded yellow and red cards introduced in UK. (Dropped between 1980-87).

1977: FA allow shirt sponsorship.

1977: Watford chairman Elton John appoints Graham Taylor as manager. Taylor's ten-year tenure would see the club rise from the fourth tier to the top division in five years, a runners-up position in the top-flight and an FA Cup Final.

1978: Full-scale riot at the Den during an FA Cup quarter-final match between Millwall and Ipswich.

1978: Viv Anderson becomes England's first black player at senior international level.

1981: QPR introduce the first artificial surface into the FL.

1981: Coventry's Highfield Road converted into England's first all-seater stadium.

1981: Three points awarded for a League win, rather than the previous two.

1983: *Match of the Day Live* and *Big Match Live* both launched.

1983: ITV's regional-based Football League coverage ends.

1983: Football League Trophy introduced.

1985: Riot at Kenilworth Road leads to Luton banning away fans for four years and introducing a membership scheme.

1985: Valley Parade fire kills 56 people. Subsequent Popplewell Inquiry leads to new legislation.

1985: Charlton leave the Valley due to financial issues and safety concerns. They would return in 1992.

1985: Thames Television broadcasts a documentary *Hooligan* focusing on the Inter City Firm associated with West Ham United.

1985: Heysel Stadium disaster sees 39 people killed and English clubs given an indefinite European ban by UEFA.

1986: Football League and PFA launch 'Football in the Community' organisation.

1986: Manchester United appoint Alex Ferguson as manager; he would go on to win a record-breaking 38 trophies during his time in charge.

1986: Independently published fanzine *When Saturday Comes* is first published.

1987: Play-offs introduced for promotion. Relegation from FL replaces re-election system.

1987: Two substitutes permitted.

1988: Scunthorpe United become the first 'modern era' FL club to relocate to a purpose-built stadium, Glanford Park, anticipating a new wave of ground building.

1989: Hillsborough disaster leads to 97 deaths.

1990: Taylor Report issued. FL requires clubs in top two divisions to have all-seater stadiums by 1994, leading to an exodus from traditional grounds for new ones, often located out-of-town.

1990: Walsall relocate to a new purpose-built Bescot Stadium.

1990: Dorchester Town FC move into their new Avenue Stadium home, specially designed by the Duchy of Cornwall to evoke traditional Edwardian football grounds.

1990: Onside modified as being 'level' with the second-last opponent.

1990: BBC Radio 5 launched, offering football content.

1991: Radio 5 begins its *606* football phone-in show.

1991: *A Stadium for the Nineties* 'vision document' launched in Birmingham, inspired by the eye-catching new stadia at Italia 90.

1991: Top-flight bans artificial pitches.

1991: First use of Wembley for an FA Cup semi-final.

1992: Nick Hornby's *Fever Pitch: A Fan's Life* is published.

1992: Premier League introduced.

1992: BSkyB outbid both BBC and ITV to acquire live and exclusive TV rights to the new PL, in five-year £304 million deal.

1992: Sky launches *Soccer Saturday* with score updates.

1992: Back pass rule introduced to deter time wasting and tempo-killing territorial play.

1992: Northampton Town's Brian Lomax helps establish the first modern era Supporters Trust.

1993: *Kick It Out* set up to tackle racism in football.

1994: *Radio 5 Live* launched as a repositioning of Radio 5.

1995: Huddersfield's new stadium named the Royal Institute of British Architects Building of the Year.

1995: FA bans artificial pitches from the professional game.

1997: *Kick It Out* expanded to cover all forms of discrimination in football.

1997: Talk Radio makes its first foray into football broadcasting.

1997: Bolton move six miles out of town to Horwich to a new purpose-built stadium.

1997: Afewee community project founded in Brixton; Urban Academy division set up in 2004.

1997: The sale of the Goldstone Ground to property developers leaves Brighton homeless and playing 'home' games 70 miles away in Gillingham.

1997: BBC News website launched, including online football coverage.

1998: MUTV launched, initially as a joint venture by Manchester United, ITV plc and BSkyB. Other clubs would follow.

1999: Doncaster Rovers majority shareholder and 'self-styled benefactor' Ken Richardson is jailed for hiring men to torch the club's Belle Vue main stand.

1999-2000: Manchester United do not defend their FA Cup title due to involvement in inaugural Club World Championship.

2000: The Football Foundation is set up. Funded by the PL, FA and Sport England, the organisation awards grants to clubs at grassroots level to provide community sports facilities. This has led to the creation of both the National Football Facilities Strategy (NFFS) and Local Football Facility Plans (LFFP).

2000: *Talksport* launched.

2000: Creation of a Football League-wide website platform.

2000: End to FA Cup Semi-Final and Final replays.

2000: Six-second keeper rule replaces former four-step rule.

2000: Supporters Direct set up to help supporters' trusts.

2001: The National Football Museum is officially opened at Deepdale, Preston.

2002: Wimbledon fans form AFC Wimbledon, in the wake of the commissioners' decision to allow their former club to relocate to Milton Keynes.

2003: Supporters' Trust takes over Exeter City FC.

2003: Manchester City move to the City of Manchester Stadium which had hosted the 2002 Commonwealth Games.

2004: Milton Keynes Dons founded, a year after Wimbledon's controversial relocation to MK.

2004: Arsenal win the PL title without losing a game, matching Preston's record in 1889.

2004: Rebranding of the FL: Championship, League 1 and League 2.

2004: *Match of the Day 2* is launched.

2004: FA introduce the Owners' and Directors' Test, formerly the 'Fit and Proper Test', brought in to combat corruption, lack of transparency and to protect the reputation/image of the sport.

2004: *The Observer* runs an article titled 'The game that ate itself', exploring the drop in PL attendances and a fans' survey which suggested several factors: the growing sense that it is uncompetitive; over-pricing; lunchtime and teatime kick-offs.

2005: The Glazer family complete a 'hostile takeover' of Manchester United.

2005: Fan-owned FC United of Manchester founded by disenchanted supporters.

2006: Online social media and social networking service *Twitter* is launched. (As of April 2023, the official PL account had 40.2 million followers, Manchester United 35.6M, Liverpool 23.6M, Manchester City 15.7M, the EFL 592.5K, EFL Championship 423.1K, EFL 1 216.4K, EFL 2 152.4K)

2006: Arsenal relocate 500 metres from their historic Highbury Stadium to the 'Emirates', Ashburton Grove.

2007: The 'new' Wembley is opened, with its distinctive arch.

2008: Level 8 side Chasetown become the lowest-ranked team to reach the FA Cup Third Round.

2008: 'New' Wembley hosts FA Cup Semi-Finals.

2011: A record 763 clubs enter the FA Cup.

2011: *Match of the Day* moves to MediaCityUK in Salford, allowing for high-definition recording.

2012: English professional football introduces the PL-driven Elite Player Performance Plan (EPPP) with a four-tier academy system. Abolition of the '90-minute' travel time rule. Category 1-3 clubs able to recruit from Under 9 level through to professionals, while Category 4 is a 'late development model' operating from Under 17s upwards. Professional Development League system is introduced, covering Under 18 and Under 21 age groups. The EPPP introduces fixed tariffs for the transfer of Under 18 players and several EFL clubs scrap their academies as a result.

2012: The Football Combination reserve league folds.

2012: Manchester City begin construction of their CFA (City Football Academy), on an 80-acre site, including the 7,000 capacity Academy Stadium, at a cost of more than £200 million.

2012: Football fan-led *YouTube* and website channel AFTV (Arsenal Fan TV) is created by former BBC reggae radio host Robbie Lyle.

2012: St George's Park, the Football Association's state-of-the-art national football centre, opens on a 330-acre site at Burton Upon Trent.

2012: The new National Football Museum opens in Manchester, replacing Preston after funding issues and financial losses led to a relocation. (The original site is now a PNE fanzone.)

2013: Manchester United win a record twentieth top-flight league title.

2013: Launching of *Twenty's Plenty* campaign for £20 cap for away tickets in English football.

2014: FA allows 3G pitches to be used in all rounds of FA Cup.

2016: 5,000-1 Leicester City win PL title.

2016: FL rebranded as the EFL.

2016: *Talksport 2* launched.

2016: PL introduce £30 cap for away tickets.

2016: Brentford close their academy, with one Director of Football describing the academy system itself as "morally bankrupt".

2016: Offside Trust set up to support survivors of childhood abuse and make sport safer for children.

2017: National League side Lincoln City reach the FA Cup quarter-finals.

2017: Just 5.8% of players in PL squads are England-qualified academy graduates.

2017: EFL launches *iFollow*, a digital live streaming and content platform. Findings suggest that 55% of EFL fans live overseas in US, Canada, Australia and New Zealand.

2018: VAR formally written into the Laws of the game by the IFAB.

2018: Football Supporters' Association set up as a result of a merger between the Football Supporters' Federation and Supporters Direct. The FSA are described as "the leading advocates for supporter ownership, better fan engagement, cheaper ticket prices, the choice to stand at the match, protecting fan rights, good governance, diversity, and all types of supporter empowerment." As of 2023, 500,000+ members.

2018: Channel 4 premier *The Real Football Fan Show*.

2019: Subscription-based sports website *The Athletic* expands to include coverage of English football.

2019: Abu Dhabi Investment United Group announces that it is selling a 10% stake in the CFG (City Football Group) to US private equity firm Silver Lake Partners, valuing the group at $4.8 billion.

2020: Elite football suspended due to Covid-19 pandemic, on March 13th.

2020: May 19th sees the first step in the PL's 'Project Restart'.

2020-21: Most of the domestic season sees matches being played behind closed doors (BCD).

2020: Wrexham AFC sold by Supporters' Trust to RR McReynolds Company LLC.

2020: Bury FC – twice winners of the FA Cup – expelled from the Football League after failing to start the new season amidst financial difficulties.

2020: Newly relegated from the EFL, Macclesfield Town expelled from the National League and wound-up in the High Court.

2020: Northampton Town win EFL Project of the Year Award for their 'Tackling Loneliness' initiative during Lockdown.

2021: Research into multi-club ownership reveals that 15 English clubs are part of a multi-club system, including the ten-club City Football Group.

2021: Proposed European Super League with twelve 'permanent' members, including six PL clubs.

2021: Fan-run Exeter City placed top of the Fan Engagement Index for the second consecutive year. The Index rates clubs according to 'dialogue, governance and transparency'.

2021: Trialling of concussion substitutes introduced.

2021: Consortium including PIF, the sovereign wealth fund of Saudi Arabia, complete takeover of Newcastle United, amidst claims by human rights groups of 'sportswashing'.

2021: UEFA club benchmarking report claims that 40% of PL clubs are majority owned by foreign investors, with a further 35% having foreign investors as minority stakeholders.

2021: Clubs in the top two tiers invited by the Sports Grounds Safety Authority to apply to offer 'safe standing' areas from January 2022. In April 2022 the SGSA reported that rail-seating at five clubs had brought "a positive impact on spectator safety" and improved the match day experience.

2022: BBC radio axes its iconic *Sports Report* classified football results, due to its coverage of 17.30 PL matches.

2022: 29 EFL clubs using their own platforms, rather than *iFollow*.

2022: Sheffield Hallam University research indicates that English professional football clubs lost £1 billion in revenue during Covid-19 pandemic. The report recommended a re-think about broadcasting distributions throughout the football pyramid. It also praised the work of football Community Trusts – not only to fans but to the wider community – during the pandemic.

2022: *Portsmouth News* stops publishing its Saturday evening *Sports Mail*, bringing an end to the English football institution of the Pink 'Un.

2023: February. PL and PFA renew call for temporary concussion substitutes, with almost 80% of players backing the trial. FIFA consider that using permanent subs is safer: the 'suspect and protect' principle.

2023: February. UEFA publishes its European Club Footballing Landscape report, highlighting concerns about multi-club investment, including the potential threat to the integrity of European club competitions. Number of teams globally involved in multi-club groups up from less than 40 in 2012 to more than 180 in 2022, including several PL sides.

2023: March. BBC online reports that the PL has charged Manchester City with more than 100 breaches of its financial rules following a four-year investigation.

2023: March. BBC online reports that Manchester United's debt has risen to almost £1bn (£969.6m).

2023: March. PL announces updated owners' and directors' test rules, with Human Rights Abuses added as a new "disqualifying event"; the changes are described by former Sports Minister Tracey Crouch as "smoke and mirrors".

2023: March. FA announces that PL clubs spent almost £320m in agents' fees over the past year.

2023: April. Comparing today's U21s football to "old style reserve football" Ipswich defender Janoi Donacien describes the current matches as "pointless. The football is not real, it doesn't translate to actual men's football and for a lot of these kids it isn't helping them improve."

2023: April. The sacking of Walsall boss Michael Flynn marks an unprecedented statistic: exactly half of the 72 EFL clubs have parted company with their managers during the 2022-23 season.

2023: April. BBC announce that Trent Alexander-Arnold is launching 'The After Academy', a scheme focusing on providing career opportunities for former academy players, to be run in conjunction with the PFA.

2023: May. The sacking of Javi Garcia at Leeds brings the total number of Premier League managers that have been sacked so far during the 2022/23 season to a record-breaking thirteen.

2023: May. Watford appoint Valerien Ismael as the new Head Coach, their 10th Head Coach in the past five years and 19th managerial appointment in eleven years.

2023: May. With Manchester City crowned PL champions, the BBC report that PL investigations are still ongoing into whether the club has breached FFP regulations over an extended period.

2023: May. Luton Town's play-off final promotion to the PL sees the club progress from non-league to top-tier in nine years, with Pelly-Ruddock Mpanza becoming the first ever player to rise from National League to PL with the same club.

2023: May. *Soccer Saturday* presenter Jeff Stelling bids goodbye to Sky Sports.

2023: May. *Match of the Day* pundit Alan Shearer, reflecting on Leicester City's relegation from the PL, warns that at least a dozen other PL clubs are in danger because "the system is designed to make upward mobility very, very difficult."

CONTENTS

CHAPTER 1: TAKING THE LAW INTO OUR OWN HANDS

Human civilisation and societies require laws in order to provide a basis by which we can live alongside each other. A sport is no different in this respect. It requires commonly accepted rules and regulations. Like a nation's laws, these are in a constant state of evolution. Before Rodney passed me the timeline produced near the front of this book and a list of the Football Association's original thirteen laws, ratified in 1863, I would have added that, like human society, football requires officials to 'police' the game, to ensure that law and order on the pitch is maintained. Yet we were both struck by the fact that for the first few years there were no neutral referees; the two captains and 'club umpires' were charged with keeping order. Wow! How did that work? On one level, it adds a genuine charm, suggesting that 160 years ago players were 'gentlemen', able to accept and abide by the rules of the game. And yet the fact that referees were introduced sadly adds a note of realism; it clearly wasn't all sweetness and light and, 'After you, Sir!' [1]

Why not dive straight into the deep end, with VAR, before exploring some of the individual laws of the game? VAR (Video Assistant Referee) – where available – formally became a rule of the game five years ago. It is a perfect example of football reflecting society in the sense of technology playing an ever-increasing role in our lives. The Hawk-Eye technology introduced into other sports such as cricket and tennis has, by and large, worked successfully to reduce human error. It may not be perfect, and some experts are keen to stress that it is far from fool proof; nevertheless, most players and supporters have accepted it. However, the use of VAR has been far more controversial. At the time of writing this chapter, it is used in four areas of decision-making: goals, penalties, direct red cards, and mistaken identity. We sat recording this first chapter in Milton Keynes just a day after two Premier League clubs had received formal apologies for incorrect VAR decisions, one leading to a goal incorrectly awarded, the other to a goal wrongly disallowed. Whether or not VAR comes out of a particular incident smelling of roses, for me one of the major issues is how it affects the raw, instant passion experienced by players and fans when a goal is scored. The delay of up to three minutes while this is reviewed undermines that moment of euphoria and – even if the goal is validated by VAR – the edge has already been taken off the celebration. It is, for want of a better phrase, a passion killer. If VAR was flawless, there would obviously be fewer grumbles. However, given the fact that it has failed to eradicate human error, why not allow the officials in charge of a match to make those key decisions? Football is played by imperfect human beings who make mistakes. Isn't part of the charm of the game that these players are refereed by equally imperfect people, rather than remotely by people sat in front of screens in a VOR (video operation room) at Stockley Park? Why not place our faith in the officials who are in place and, by doing so, cut out these major delays which kill the tempo of playing and cut the unique atmosphere of watching a sport live and in the flesh? Earlier today I was quoted a statistic which reinforced my views: in the Premier League it has been alleged that 98% of the decisions made by assistant referees turn out to be correct ones. If we accept this incredibly high figure, it suggests that most match officials are doing a reasonable job, so do we need VAR?

VAR was never going to be perfect, of course. Unlike the technology used to review major decisions in cricket or tennis, VAR still relies on human judgement. Nor can we simply blame those video officials. First, they are under enormous pressure, psychologically, with a maximum of 180 seconds to make their decisions. If errors are still being made after three minutes of reviewing images, perhaps we should be asking ourselves whether it is VAR which has brought confusion, rather than clarity, or whether it is the laws themselves. Besides, VAR is not going to go away, if only because of the vast amount of money which has already been spent on installing the technology. Instead of smashing up the machinery like 21st century Luddites, we need to explore how we can simplify the rules and do something to counteract the growing disconnect between the players and coaches – on one side of the 'fence' – and the officials. Let's start with the rules...

Offside and handball are two of the biggest bones of contention. Offside was already part of the game before the first FA Cup campaign (1871) or Football League season kicked off (1888). It has been modified many times. I would never suggest getting rid of the general rule. After all, it prevents teams from simply hoofing the ball constantly up to a striker who is 'goal hanging', to use that school playground expression. Nevertheless, what was once in theory a fairly simple rule has gradually become more and more complicated, with more splinters, footnotes – or grey areas – than an insurance contract. 'Interfering with play', 'interfering with an opponent', 'gaining an [unfair] advantage', 'second phase', which parts of the body are not applicable...Part of the attraction of football is that it is a simple game to follow and understand. In theory. In practice I cannot put my hand on my heart and say that I completely understand all the nuances and technical jargon of the offside rules today. If I am sometimes left confused – after almost fifty years in the game as an ex-professional player, former manager, and current director of football – then something must be wrong. In terms of that contentious question of whether a player is 'interfering with play', Rodney reminded me of two famous offside quotes from footballing legends. The great Bill Nicholson once remarked, "If he's not interfering with play, what's he doing on the pitch?" Meanwhile, another Bill, Shankly commented: "If a player is not interfering with play or seeking to gain an advantage, then he should be." As a newspaper columnist suggested back in 2006, these are insights which "today's rule-making suits would do well to listen to and discuss". [2] We need to strip back the offside rule to its simplest level, one where everyone can understand it and where it once more becomes solely part of the 'art' of an attacking player to time his run and beat the trap organised by the opposition. What does and does not constitute a handball offence is another troubling grey area where no one seems sure nowadays what does and does not constitute a foul. Some bafflingly severe handball decisions are given; for me, handball should solely be about intent. A simple game requires simple rules, not increasingly complicated ones which are hard to follow and equally difficult to regulate, as VAR continues to demonstrate.

Today's referees in the top-flight are no longer part-timers combining match day officialdom with a weekday job as a postman or bank clerk. These men and women are now training and studying the art of refereeing on a full-time basis. Clearly this means that they are getting better and fitter. Conversely, there is an increasing sense that referees are no longer in charge of a match; that it is players and managers who are running the game, particularly in terms of time wasting and gamesmanship – a euphemism for cheating – including feigning injuries to get play stopped. In an ideal world, players and managers would respond positively to the general call to clean their act up, as simulation is in danger of ruining the game as a competitive spectacle. In reality, the only way to combat the increasing darker arts will be to change or adapt the rules. For example, if someone goes down with what appears to be a head injury you cannot simply play on; referees aren't trained medics, and, after all, the player *might* be seriously hurt. What you can do, though, is tweak the rules to discourage this form of cheating. If any player going down with a 'head injury' had to be immediately substituted – as a potential concussion victim, as in other sports – it would soon sort out legitimate cases from players simply trying to buy time or a free kick. Rodney offered me the analogy of cheating players being like car thieves: you cannot expect them to stop stealing; you need to make it harder for them to successfully break into the vehicle.

Part of me feels nostalgic for a now vanished age where players tended to stay on their feet and where simulation was not a major part of the game. Realistically though, we cannot return to the past and we must accept that the sport has evolved, in both positive and negative ways. It is a step forward that technical players are better protected both by the laws and by the officials, just as it is great that subjects like mental health are no longer taboo. Conversely, we have seen an increasing number of players looking to 'cry wolf', for example, and by doing so mis-using laws which were brought in to safeguard them on the field of play.

Earlier in this chapter I referred to the growing, worrying disconnect between players/coaches and the officials. This can be seen on a weekly basis, from the Premier League down to grassroots football.

To a certain extent, it is up to the referees, assistants and fourth officials to stamp down on, for example, dissent and foul-and-abusive language by strictly applying the letter of the law. That, after all, is what we have yellow and red cards for. Nevertheless, I think that it would be a cop-out to place all the pressure and onus on them. There are far more radical solutions which could help to build bridges…

First, I would propose that all young players must take the equivalent of a driving test. They would have to study the laws of the game and pass a written exam, in much the same way as I had to for my coaching badges. Believe it or not, most footballers do not have a full understanding of the game's rules and regulations. Indeed, I would go so far as to suggest that the general appreciation of the laws of the game is almost non-existent. By completing their 'theory', it would not only make them better practitioners. It would also give them a better understanding of how difficult a job it is for the man or woman out in the middle with a whistle.

In terms of the 'practice' part of the test, young players would have to officiate some games themselves, thus placing themselves on the other side of the proverbial fence. Their performances would be monitored by an observer. You would not be qualified as a young player until you had passed both sides of the test; we could even have ID cards – like driving licences – as the official stamp of approval. At the moment, young professionals simply have to attend a morning's course run by a referee tutor, with no test, or even the obligation to turn their mobile phones off! With nothing at stake, many players fail to take these sessions seriously. My radical change would hopefully have its most profound effect on PL

Academy youngsters who are currently cocooned in a hermetically sealed bubble.

In addition, I think we need to create a clearer pathway for ex-players to become future referees. I have always believed that it would help enormously if matches were officiated by people who had played the game at a decent level. It would involve an element of 'fast-tracking' which would not go down well with traditional referees. Arguably, we should avoid this emotive term, as it tends to reinforce the sense of an us/them divide between players and officialdom. Nevertheless, the reality is that matches officiated by former players is the norm in other sports such as cricket. You could argue that, for example, my fourteen years as a professional player should have earned me some 'points' towards becoming a professional referee, a pathway I would happily have gone down had it been available to me. A referee known to players as someone who had played the game would already have earned himself a higher status or respect when it comes to refereeing a match. In addition, it would open a potential new career for many lower division ex-pros who are often at a loss of what to do next when the bubble of playing bursts. Rodney threw in a further analogy. If a football match were a jungle, wouldn't you want the person guiding you through it to be someone with survival skills, who has experienced life in the jungle themselves? [3]

Football is under the microscope nowadays as never before. Every game in the PL, EFL and further down the pyramid is officially observed and recorded. Goals and highlights are analysed by so-called experts and watched by thousands online. Nothing like that coverage existed when I started out on my footballing journey. Would I be shocked if I was able to rewatch some of the early games I played in? Would I suddenly be aware of more dissent, simulation etc., than I remember? In the absence of a time machine, we cannot go back and properly review the differences. What we can do though is sift through the present day, pick out what seems to work well, what appears to be broken, and try to fix the latter.

Some rule changes have undoubtedly improved the game. Outlawing the goalkeeper picking up back passes (1992) revolutionised football in terms of tempo, negative play etc. I only wish it had existed when I was a striker, fruitlessly chasing down a succession of time-wasting back passes. It was a brilliantly simple tweak, illustrating how the best modifications are often uncomplicated ones. (As a bonus, it has led to a vast technical improvement from goalkeepers and defenders with the ball at their feet.) [4] In contrast, last night watching an EFL match from the comfort and bird's-eye-view of the director's box illustrated to me how other changes can genuinely detract and, indeed, distract from the spectacle. [5] In my playing days, managers simply sat in a dug-out, but nowadays they tend to stand or restlessly pace about in 'technical areas'. I've been in the technical area as a manager myself, and when you are in 'the zone' you are almost oblivious to your own behaviour. As the game we were watching yesterday moved towards ninety minutes, it became ever more frenetic and nervier, and the coaching staff of both teams were increasingly drawn into confrontation with the fourth official standing in his no-man's-land between them. Through no fault of his own, it was clear that his very presence was acting as a magnet and this side-show was in danger of becoming the main spectacle. I have no doubt that – rather than acting as a deterrent for the respective coaches to behave badly – his proximity was almost encouraging their childlike, pantomime villain actions. Whatever the best solution is in terms of placing and utilising the fourth official, the current zones are not improving the comportment of coaches. You might argue that there should be no interaction between them at all.

Returning to that bugbear of players 'killing time', while it has always been an element of 'game management', it is rightly seen as an increasing issue or problem, a modern malaise. What changes can we make to combat the fact that barely any matches see the ball in play for even sixty of the ninety minutes? Stricter controls over the time taken at throw-ins and goal kicks; combatting the needless delays before restarts after a goal has been scored by introducing a thirty-second limit...[6] These things would obviously help. The FIFA proposal to have rolling subs made with no break in play is an interesting idea; it would surely help in this age where you can replace almost half your side during the course of a match. A giant clock, stopped by an off-field official timekeeper whenever the ball is out of play, would add transparency and also act as a deterrent to timewasters. They would have a constant visual reminder of time frozen. It is a case of changing a player's and coach's mentality and mindset.

You might argue that the stakes are so high nowadays in the professional game – in terms of financial reward, ever-increasing pressure on managers in a 'results business' and the 'instant success/gratification' culture fuelled by social media – that some of the spirit of the game has been lost. It will require a joint effort invested in by everyone involved in football to restore that. Those young player 'driving tests' and a genuine player pathway to refereeing would help to mend some of the rifts between the law-enforcers and the law-breakers. Both measures would only improve the 'stand-off' between players and officials, the 'us versus them' mentality which has always existed in the game during my time in football. [7] The lawmakers need to simplify and streamline the rules and regulations of the game. The referees then need to be strong enough to enforce those, particularly when it comes to the darker arts such as collective swarming around the man with the whistle, diving, or grappling in the box. Instead of a blame culture where everyone looks accusingly at each other, we need to reconnect every part of the football family. Only then will playing, coaching, watching and officiating become a far more enjoyable, rewarding experience.

Unlike goal-line technology, which is a no-brainer, the merits of VAR are eternally debatable. We cannot rely on VAR to solve all the game's issues. People naively thought it would be some superhuman, all-seeing, all-dancing machine. It is only as good as the fallible human operating it. Perhaps, in a strange way, that is a good thing. Football run by 'perfect' automatons would take away the imperfect, human touch.

Ultimately, whatever rule changes are made, there will always remain grey areas. Referees need to apply common sense in what is a contact sport played at speed. No one wants to see the full-blooded clean tackle outlawed, nor the talented flair players 'cleverly' fouled out of a game. This connects to a paradox in the modern game: there is far less aggressive contact in the sport today, compared to when I started playing in the mid-1970s, and yet the number of yellow and red cards brandished is far higher. Part of this might be explained by the evolution of the laws; but clearly part is due to some referees being too trigger-happy. Interpretation of the laws of the game requires a nuanced understanding of the sport and will never be an exact science. Rather than rail against the system or the play acting, we need to seek solutions. It is high time that we took the law into our own hands.

Hotel La Tour, Milton Keynes 14/02/2023

1. As the footballhistory.org website observes, some of those original rules now feel alien, including: no crossbars and no height restrictions for the goals; outfield players able to catch a ball, leading to them being rewarded with a free kick; no forward passes allowed; throw-ins one-handed and taken by whichever player reaches the ball first after it went out of play.
2. 'The Knowledge: Football', *Guardian*, 13/09/2006.
3. Weeks after we put this chapter together, Nigel Clough — speaking at a Mansfield Town fans forum — suggested that the referees' association is reluctant to welcome in former players; he referred to "a closed shop". He went on to suggest that ex-players should benefit from their obvious potential, as experienced 'readers' of the game: "They shouldn't have to start right at the bottom...however, if they go in at a certain level, get all the necessary training, and they are not good enough, then they don't make it. Just like anyone else...It's about the only sport where ex-players don't do it." It is great to hear someone of Nigel's standing in the game echoing what have been my own thoughts for years, the need to break down the us/them divide or mentality. Instead of adding further bricks to the wall, we need to knock it down.
4. To be fair to the then Northampton manager Graham Carr, I remember going there with Wrexham, five years before the back pass rule was brought in and saw first-hand that he had coached his goalkeeper Peter Gleasure to bring the

ball out like a sweeper. In those days, the centre backs would normally stand 25 yards from their goal, but they were already up at the halfway line. I had to run further that day than any other before, chasing the ball. The footballing goalkeeper was already being 'groomed', something which is standard practice nowadays.

5. Northampton Town v AFC Wimbledon, 14/02/2023.

6. If the team which has scored and – understandably – celebrated their goal has not regrouped behind the halfway line after thirty seconds, the opposition would be entitled to restart the game. This would soon change the mentality of wasting time after a goal.

7. The 'closed shop' of officialdom also must change, with lawmakers and referees more approachable and accountable.

CHAPTER 2:
1992 AND ALL THAT

Listening to *Talk Sport* or watching either *Sky Sports* or *Match of the Day*, you would be forgiven for thinking that English football was invented in 1992, the year when the top division clubs began a revolution by breaking away from the Football League, which had been the home of every professional league club since 1888. Despite the argument that this new, financially independent top tier would allow clubs to invest in stadium redevelopment and be more competitive in Europe, the move was, naturally, motivated by money, with the deal allowing those twenty-two 'elite' clubs to access a treasure trove on offer from the newly formed, merged company *British Sky Broadcasting*. While the actual competition format of four full-time professional divisions would remain unchanged, it was immediately clear that this was a pivotal moment in the English game. In this chapter I want to explore what has been gained, what has been lost, and how we might move forward in order for the game to be genuinely competitive, from the summit of the Premier League down to the grassroots level.

It is easy to forget what a poor state the professional game had deteriorated into by the time I retired from playing full-time in 1988. When I left Wrexham, English clubs were in the middle of a five-year European ban following the Heysel Stadium disaster, while top clubs and players were casting envious eyes on European leagues such as Serie A and La Liga. Both the Valley Parade fire in 1985 and the tragic human crush at Hillsborough four years later highlighted how 'unfit for purpose' many football grounds were, both in terms of infrastructure and organisation. It was clear to everyone that English football needed to modernise and clean its act up, from the hooliganism which was giving genuine fans a bad reputation or even putting them off attending matches, to the shocking state of the stadia themselves.

Fast forward thirty years and what positives have emerged from the Premier League? Instead of remaining in the shadows of the Spanish and Italian leagues, the PL is now the most-watched sports league in the entire world, with matches beamed into a staggering 212 countries. Despite the initial fear that the broadcasting of so many live games would result in overkill or over-exposure and half-empty grounds, this has not happened. As for the stadia themselves, eight of the current twenty PL clubs play in grounds which did not exist in 1992, while most of the others have been renovated beyond recognition. This stadium revolution is mirrored in the EFL, with thirty 'new' grounds and traditional ones such as Deepdale entirely rebuilt. Today it is far easier to pick out the grounds which are *not* fit for purpose. On the pitch, the PL has attracted some of the greatest players in world football, something which was unimaginable back in the 1980s. Instead of being seen by other footballing nations as being stuck in the Stone Age, those countries now view the PL with envious eyes. It is where many top players want to be. In addition, we have also seen an influx of top foreign coaches, bringing with them new, innovative ways of thinking. For me, Arsène Wenger is someone who single-handedly revolutionised English football culture during his twenty-two years at Arsenal. It wasn't solely a case of introducing new training methods and tactics. He brought with him an awareness of how outdated we were in terms of the 'culture' of the game: casual drinking, junk food etc. The success of his methods and mentality resulted in Arsenal winning the PL in the 2003-2004 season without losing a single match, the first time this had been achieved in 115 years. [1] Drawing on his footballing and cultural experiences in both France and Japan, Wenger broke down the insular, closed mindset of English football. His team of international stars – a combination of the British 'bulldog' spirit and continental technical flair – arguably heralded a new era in which the PL has become *the* global football league. Wenger has been followed by others, such as Guardiola and Klopp. The record of English clubs in the Champions League – rebranded in that same year, 1992 – reflects a growing dominance in European competition, culminating in two all-English finals in the past four years.

If this all sounds too good to be true, like an American Dream, there is, in my opinion, a downside to the Premier League. Like a lot of people involved in the game, when the PL was formed, I was extremely wary that this was going to be all about the elite, and that it would squeeze a lot of the so-called lesser clubs who were the foundation stones or bedrock of English football. I was also worried in the build-up to the new league that it would be a closed shop, with no promotion/relegation. Thankfully, that did not transpire. However, the multi-national PL has, arguably, seen home-grown talent – players and coaches – overlooked. (You could, of course, argue that it has allowed British players and coaches to learn from the different skill sets brought from overseas.) In addition, it has created an imbalance, a growing chasm both within the PL itself and between the elite and the pyramid. A financial gap had always been there, of course, but now it is far, far greater.

There are, arguably, separate mini leagues within the PL itself, with a glass ceiling operating below the top six, unless a billionaire comes on board. It is harder than ever before for a promoted club to seriously compete – rather than simply survive – in the top-tier. Will we ever see a PL 'newbie' match the feats of Liverpool (1905-06), Everton (1931-32), Tottenham Hotspur (1951-52), Ipswich Town (1961-62) or Nottingham Forest (1977-78) crowned English champions in their initial season in the top-flight following promotion? OK, those first three are undisputedly 'big clubs' but, putting them to one side, it is hard to see how a talented manager at a moderate-sized club, such as Alf Ramsey at Ipswich, or Brian Clough at Forest, could achieve this incredible feat in today's game. Leicester City's wonderful fairy tale '5,000 to 1' title (2015-16) demonstrates that the dream is still alive, but it is, arguably, the exception which proves the rule. The financial gap and divide is most damaging in the second tier. The Championship, because of the PL 'parachute payments', has become a division where a club can find itself competing against teams relegated from the PL armed with a £40 million + pay off. Rewarding failure seems a baffling business and sporting model to me, and any notion of a level playing field is clearly nonsense. Those parachute payments have, inevitably, increased the trend of so-called yoyo clubs. Some might argue that, given the fact that fifty clubs have already experienced life in the PL, the top tier is not an impossible dream, but we could easily make the race to reach it fairer and more competitive by ridding ourselves of these financial payoffs or 'rewards'. As a player, I loved that opening day of a new season when you genuinely believed that it might be your club's time to shine. That hope can be dashed before the campaign kicks off if money is the all-important, decisive factor. For the pyramid to work, everyone must be able to genuinely believe that their club could gain promotion. A more even distribution of central payment revenues would surely help.

The Premier League, partly driven by *Sky*, has become an almost cinematic spectacle, 'blockbuster entertainment', a media-driven circus. It is fed by £ billions where image and hype have, arguably, come to dominate. For someone like me who grew up with a sense of football being a grounded, working-class sport, that spirit of the game feels largely absent in this *Sky Football* version of Hollywood. For me, the PL is somewhat akin to a glossy brochure, attractive looking but lacking soul. It is a well-known fact that top-flight football no longer needs fans in the grounds to generate income. In addition, we have to ask ourselves what type of fans clubs want to attract. Have the 'prawn sandwich brigade' corporate hospitality clients become more important than the traditional fan? Have supporters simply become customers? Has the PL created a surreal monster feeding off a global audience of armchair viewers and where many clubs are owned by 'remote' owners pulling the strings from the US, the Middle East or Asia? I'm not sure that there is a definitive answer to any of these questions which I have thrown out here, some of which will be explored later in the book. What I do know is that I am not alone in feeling a disconnect with some aspects of our post-1992 football world, a worrying sense that there is something not quite real about it all.

While many in the media would have us believe that the PL is all that matters, there has – ironically – been a positive by-product of this new, almost surreal elite. An increasing number of people have felt alienated by the business-orientated nature of the modern game, be it the inability to attend matches because of availability or cost of tickets, the sense of not being valued any longer etc. This has encouraged many to seek their football 'fix' lower down the pyramid. Some of my former clubs, such as Stockport and Northampton, are attracting far bigger gates than the regular 2,000 attendances they had in my playing days. Crowds in the National League have never been higher. [2] There is a growing sense that lower-division and non-league football is somehow more 'real', the genuine heartbeat of the game. I guess that the formation in 2005 of fan-owned FC United of Manchester is a radical example of how some supporters have reacted to the direction many PL clubs have gone in, with their overseas owners and privileging of corporate hospitality boxes and suites. [3] You could argue that the (scandalous) relocation and rebranding of Wimbledon as the Milton Keynes Dons represents the dark side of the modern game; while the founding, dramatic rise up the pyramid and 'return' to a new Plough Lane of AFC Wimbledon demonstrates the true spirit of the sport. Do fan-owned clubs such as Wimbledon and Exeter City offer a wonderful polar opposite of the way many PL and EFL clubs are remotely run? Once again, this is a topic I will return to in a future chapter…

The PL is not about to disappear. Nor is it without its merits. However, several recent events have highlighted that, even post-1992, the football 'family' still matters. The Covid era demonstrated that empty 'theatres' do not work. Without the crowd, the chemistry simply isn't there, the recipe lacks a key ingredient and its distinct flavour. Even if top-flight clubs no longer rely *financially* on putting bums on seats, the spectacle needs the supporters as much as it needs the players. The way in which football fans reacted in 2021 to the news that secret talks had taken place about a proposed European Super League demonstrated a solidarity which I believe shocked and surprised the clubs themselves, particularly those remote club owners who have no affinity to the community and simply do not understand the history, tradition and 'fabric' of the game. Putting aside bitter rivalries and tribalism, there was a collective disgust and fury. At a time when I was doubting whether the 'spirit of the game' still existed in top-flight professional football, people came together to demonstrate – in every sense of the word – that certain fundamental things were more important to them than the gloss and the glamour. Among these is a sense of belonging, of being part of a unique football brotherhood and pyramid stretching from the lofty heights of the PL to the humble grassroots. I was immensely proud of that swell of fan power. It was a reminder that not everything changed in 1992, that for many people what matters most is being part of something traditional and historic, which was created more than a century earlier. I have no doubt that the topic of a jet-setting Super League will rear its head again. It is up to the genuine football fans to maintain that 'collective' spirit. Out of that sense of betrayal, and the backlash which ensued, something touchingly positive emerged. It moved me and restored some of my faith in the sport which has been my passion for so long. [4]

1992 was not the year in which English football was invented, yet clearly it revolutionised and changed the professional game. Some of those changes, which I have highlighted, needed to happen. Nevertheless, whether you are a football fan at a PL giant or, like me, attached to a Western League 'minnow', we must sustain that collective sense of all belonging to something which connects. We need to maintain that pyramid pathway, of keeping the dream alive for any club – however modest in size – that they can progress up the football ladder, be it automatically or through the play-offs system. [5] That upward journey requires passion, energy, vision, time, patience...and, of course, money, but the dream must never be allowed to die or be dashed. Take that ladder away, and we will all end up sliding down snakes.

1. In 1888-89, Preston North End completed the League and FA Cup double without losing a single match and their team was dubbed 'The Invincibles'.

2. Personally, given the fact that the majority of the National League clubs are full-time professional organisations, I would bring them into the EFL and have a EFL 2 North and South, increasing the number of local derbies and lowering the travel costs for clubs and fans alike.

3. My dad used to say, "How can you experience a match day atmosphere behind a glass window?" and I would wholeheartedly agree with his sentiment of this diluted experience.

4. The 'closed shop' nature of the proposed ESL is what, for me, was the worst aspect of all. A hermetically-sealed league – with no promotion or relegation – is unacceptable, in my opinion.

5. The arrival in 1987 of automatic promotion/relegation from the Football League – rather than the previous re-election system which was almost a closed shop – has highlighted how important it is to maintain a competitive pyramid. I would argue that the arrival of the play-offs at the same time has been a great innovation, something that has increased that exciting sense of 'competition' and 'hope', helping to keep a season alive for more and more clubs. Rodney passionately disagrees with me, arguing that a league campaign is "a season for a reason", "a marathon, not a sprint", and that the teams finishing highest should always be rewarded. Our contrasting beliefs are part of the fascinating debates which football's evolution sparks. Opinions, eh?!

CHAPTER 3:
THE 'MAGIC' OF THE FA CUP

Here in England, we are justifiably proud of our 'football firsts'. Sheffield FC, founded in 1857 and recognised by FIFA as the world's oldest club still playing; Notts County, founded in 1862, pre-dating the FA itself, the oldest professional football club in the world; finally, the Football Association Challenge Cup – the FA Cup for short – first played in the 1871-72 season and the oldest national football competition on the planet. When Notts County were in grave danger of going out of business in July 2019, questions were raised in the House of Commons and the Prime Minister, Theresa May, acknowledged the "great importance" that clubs like County have "to their local communities". While no one is suggesting that the FA Cup is in danger of disappearing, there is a growing sense that it has lost some of its sparkle or appeal, for players, managers and supporters, particularly in the lofty world of the Premier League. In this chapter I want to explore what has made the competition special, why some of that 'magic' has arguably been lost, and how we might restore the prestige or polish.

In order to do so, I will draw upon my own experiences: the unparalleled fascination and charm which the FA Cup Final held for me and my family when I was a child; the memories which I cherish of playing in the competition as a professional footballer; and, finally, my more recent relationship with the competition as both a manager and then a director of football at a non-league club.

When I was a child, FA Cup Final weekend felt like a football version of Christmas. The Semi-Finals – played in neutral stadiums in those days – were special matches, but Cup Final day took the excitement to new levels, regardless of which teams had made it to Wembley. As a family, we would draw lots. Dad would write down all the names of the outfield players and carefully cut every individual one out onto strips of paper. Each of us would pull out strips, in turn, even Mum who normally took no interest in the game. Twenty players between the five of us, so four strips each. Whoever had the player who scored the first goal won the prize, which if memory serves me correctly was usually a packet of wine gums. Like Christmas Eve, the Friday night before the final was part of our build-up or anticipation. On the day itself, we would be glued to the television from whenever the coverage began. Over the years this developed to include the teams leaving their hotels and making their way to Wembley. Back in the early 1970s, it was the first time that you had the opportunity to peek behind the curtain, to see players laughing and joking on their team coach, dressed in Cup Final Moss Bros suits rather than in their tracksuits or kit. Today, that sort of behind-the-scenes coverage is commonplace, but back then it was, for want of a better word, 'magical'. Even going into my teenage years, I felt that Cup Final weekend was sacrosanct: you didn't go anywhere. Shopping trips, weddings...not on Cup Final weekend! For many of us, the world outside stopped on that day every year. This was the weekend which drew the curtain on the domestic season and nothing else mattered. Even if you were not a football fan, you got involved, you bought into the magic. When we ate lunch, when we had tea...everything revolved around the game itself. Later in the evening, *Match of the Day* would focus on the winners' dressing room and post-match celebrations. All of this fascinated me; I wanted to see inside the world of the professional footballer, particularly on the one day of the year that every player dreams about being involved in.

Fast forward a few years to my professional career, and I was now experiencing that magic first-hand, rather than through a television screen. Instead of being in the audience, I was now an actor on the stage. Not the Cup Final stage, unfortunately, but as a lower-division footballer, there was the annual challenge of reaching that New Year appointment with the Third Round of the FA Cup, when the top two divisions enter the competition. As you get older and begin to realise that you probably are not destined to reach the top tier of the game, you start to fully appreciate that a cup run – and favourable draw – is your sole opportunity to test yourself against the top players. Part of that FA Cup magic is understanding that this works both ways. I was part of a struggling Cambridge United side that, having been in the second tier just two years earlier, suffered the humiliation of being knocked out of the cup by part-time Dagenham, who must have felt that the victory was their equivalent of winning a cup final. If this represented an all-time FA Cup low, for me personally, the ultimate high came three seasons earlier, at Fourth Division Northampton Town...

Any FA Cup draw is like a lucky dip. As a fourth-tier side, being drawn away against a Third Division club in the Second Round is not the tie anyone wants. However, having held Gillingham 1-1 at their ground, this was where the magic sparkle was sprinkled on the two clubs. The Third-Round draw offered up the mouth-watering prospect of a home tie with Aston Villa who, at that time, were the reigning European champions. The atmosphere at the replay – three days later, under the lights – was one which I have never forgotten, nor have my brothers who were watching with my late father in a packed main stand. The roar and subsequent celebrations which greeted our late winner – *my* late winner – in a seesaw 3-2 victory – were ones you simply cannot get in a league fixture. It was a heady mix of the thrill of winning an exciting cup tie in the final minutes and the realisation of what the victory meant to everybody. For the chairman, an unexpected financial windfall for the club, for the fans a rare opportunity to see their heroes take on a footballing giant, and for us as players the chance to test ourselves against a team full of international stars. For the next few weeks there was a genuine buzz of anticipation around the town which only a cup run and 'prize draw' can bring. Unprecedented demand for tickets, special pull-out features in the local newspaper, national media coverage, and, in the build-up to the game itself, BBC *Match of the Day* cameras being set up, top-flight players arriving to inspect the type of humble surroundings they are not used to, the hope that an upset might, just *might* happen, even though, in the days before massive squads and 'rotation' this might seem like mission highly improbable. Part of that magic is knowing that these so-called cup upsets do occur, as fans of Yeovil, Hereford, Harlow, Sutton will tell you. [1]

As I sit here recording these memories – by sheer coincidence on the day when half the FA Cup Fifth Round matches are taking place – it is clear that some of that magic has been lost. Nor is it a case of me wearing rose-tinted glasses. In my opinion, the Football Association is partly responsible.

First, there was the decision to have the 'new' Wembley host the semi-finals each season. For me, this takes away or diminishes the prestige of Wembley being an 'exclusive' cup final venue. Nor am I alone in thinking this. Whenever polls have been taken amongst fans, the overwhelming majority want Wembley to be reserved for Cup Final day. Ten years ago, a poll in the *Guardian* found that 86% were opposed to Wembley semi-finals. [2] For players and fans alike, Wembley is a sacred place which is the stuff of dreams. By hosting semi-finals, its unique status as the venue of the final is lost. As supporters and teams arrive on Cup Final day, they are now returning to somewhere they experienced just weeks earlier. The magic of the competition has already been diluted by that one key decision.

Secondly, the Cup Final fixture itself has been messed around with on several occasions. Instead of always bringing the curtain down on the domestic season, it has occasionally been played before the end of the league campaign, and even on the same day as other fixtures. If Wembley semi-finals take away some of the appeal of the stadium, then shifting the date of the fixture itself takes away the sense I had as a child of a sacred occasion at the end of the season, a day when nothing else mattered.

I mentioned earlier that I am writing this chapter on FA Cup Fifth Round day. What I didn't add is that this is a weekday! Today, Manchester City fans faced a long trip down to Ashton Gate, Bristol, for an evening match, while tomorrow night Grimsby supporters will embark on a 460-mile round trip to Southampton. Given this scheduling, it is little wonder that, despite reaching the last sixteen stage of the competition, some of these games were played out in half-empty stadia, such as a mere 12,949 at Stoke for a match against a top PL team. Expecting supporters to be able to afford to take time off work during the week to travel vast distances for a cup match suggests to me that neither the fans themselves nor the competition is being properly valued by the FA. [3]

In addition to the current 'cost of living' crisis, a further reason for low attendances may well be that, as Rodney has suggested to me, many fans are losing some of their passion for the competition. Supporters feed emotively off the clubs themselves. When they see the manager rotating his squad, giving 'fringe' players game time in cup fixtures, it is little wonder if football fans sense that the FA Cup has lost some of its sparkle. You hear more and more of those managers talking about 'prioritising' the league, in terms of titles, European qualification, relegation, or – in the EFL – promotion. Part of their argument centres on the fear of 'fixture congestion'. Foreign coaches have often arrived in England only to be dismayed by the sheer volume of matches and British managers have followed suit. I'm convinced that it is the pressure from elite clubs which led to the FA dropping cup replays from the latter stages of the competition. Nor is it a question of pointing the finger of blame solely at top-tier clubs. When you even have some EFL 2 clubs putting out 'weakened' teams for FA Cup fixtures, this will inevitably send out negative messages to the supporters.

Speaking of replays, the decision to get rid of semi-final and final replays was probably a good one. If anything, it adds to the sense of occasion and atmosphere for those massive games, knowing that you will see a definitive result on the day. Nevertheless, if replays were scrapped from earlier rounds it would be a financial blow to lower division clubs and you would be ensuring that magical nights such as the one I experienced at Northampton all those years ago could never happen again. [4] In addition, a bumper-sized replay crowd for a lower-division or non-league club can bring a vital financial reward.

Talk of financial reward brings me on to where the FA Cup cash prizes highlight the vast chasm separating the PL from the minnows which enter the competition. The monetary reward for winning the cup final this season is £2 million, a mere drop in the ocean if you compare it to the £100 million which the bottom side in the PL will receive. By contrast, for a part-time non-league club, the cash prizes are more than welcome. If, hypothetically, a club progresses from the Extra Preliminary Round to the Third Round Proper, we are talking about a prize bonus of more than £140,000, even before the gate money, bar takings etc have been added in.

I would suggest that it is grassroots football which continues to carry the torch for the FA Cup competition. In many ways the non-league fraternity has championed the cause more than their professional counterparts. Maybe this is helped by the fact that – rather than arriving as a mid-season 'distraction' – the competition is there in black-and-white near the top of our fixture lists. While for PL fans and players, the cup begins in January, for 416 clubs across the country the adventure commences in the August summer heat. That Extra Preliminary Round is where the dreams of cup glory begin. For those of us operating at Level 9/Step 5, what I still think of as the greatest cup competition in the world starts while the cricket season is still in full swing. When I arrived at Helston Athletic, a key part of my vision for the club was for it to enter the FA Cup. While the FA Trophy or FA Vase is, arguably, the only realistic route to a Wembley final for non-league teams, the FA Cup is unique in connecting 732 clubs, from Helston to Hull, and beyond. Whether the aim is the dizzy heights of the First Qualifying Round or the First Round Proper, there is a sense of anticipation which greets each draw. Every club from Step 1 down knows that a decent cup run not only excites players and fans alike, but can fund a wide range of future projects, including ground redevelopments, and squad strengthening, in addition to the unique opportunity to raise the club's profile. Players at every level of non-league football dream about causing a cup upset, playing against a professional team, making an appearance in front of 'live' television cameras. It was a dream that I maintained and held dear throughout my professional career, and which still means a great deal to me in my role at a progressive non-league club.

I have frequently used words like 'magic' and 'dreams' in this chapter, and – although these are qualities of the 'beautiful game' which cannot be measured – they are vitally important ingredients for any player or supporter. What is a football pitch, after all, if it isn't a 'field of dreams'? Nevertheless, we also need to map out the future in more concrete ways. What can we do in practical terms to restore a sense of pride and passion in the FA Cup amongst the professional hierarchy? It needs to begin with the FA itself. It is surely no coincidence that the moment the Football Association created the Premier League, as its new flagship, a breakaway from the Football League, their interest in maintaining the prestige of the FA Cup started to wane. The FA needs to move semi-finals to neutral venues and hold Wembley back for Cup Final day. The latter rounds of the competition need to take place in their traditional weekend slots. While I would be tempted to apply pressure on top clubs to put out full-strength sides for these cup matches, it is probably unrealistic in practice. Ironically, what I would do is put some of the onus on the fans. If we made it obligatory for PL and EFL season ticket holders to purchase cup tickets as part of their package, this would ensure bigger gates. Instead of the current trend to market cut-price admission to cup games – which in itself devalues the competition – making the FA Cup fixtures part of the season ticket would ensure that those matches felt as if they were equally important, rather than simply an option which can be ignored or discarded. A full house of supporters who have paid 'top dollar' to attend would, in itself, place pressure on the clubs to field a team worthy of the occasion. As an extra financial incentive to the clubs themselves, perhaps the FA could divert the funds from its ludicrous 'parachute payment' and 'reward for failure' policy, instead offering prize money in the cup to match that which is on offer in the PL. It makes no sense to offer far greater financial reward for league mediocrity than for cup success.

When the first wave of foreign players arrived in the English game in the late-1970s, many of them commented on how their first taste of the British game had been watching FA Cup finals, which were beamed across the world, from Amsterdam to Buenos Aires. They reflected on the powerful effect that these matches had on them, how these finals had inspired them. They referred to the unique atmosphere and a sense of tradition or occasion utterly different from their own country's cup finals. Perhaps it has become a popular trend to knock tradition; yet part of what makes English football appealing, on a global scale, is that rich cultural heritage.

If you had told me back in my own playing days that we would be sat here now discussing the FA Cup being disrespected or devalued, I would have laughed in disbelief. Nevertheless, there is more than an element of truth when we talk about the competition's freefall and potential demise, sadly. My own experience of the FA Cup over sixty years, as armchair fan, player, manager and director of football, has allowed me to see that the competition offers the only tangible connection between the hundreds of clubs which comprise the football pyramid, from the tiniest Step 5 club to the PL giants. [5] It is a magical adventure which starts in August and ends in the following May, which spans the four seasons, which marks out key dates in the footballing calendar, covers a minimum of 731 matches and provides the type of upsets and drama which are simply not possible in the bread-and-butter of league football. It is up to everyone who loves the game to do their bit to cherish the FA Cup, from the administrators of the sport, the coaches, to the fans. For me, it is also a question of restoring certain principles and values. [6] The 'magic of the cup' has, let's be honest, become an overused cliché, often used by commentators desperate to reassure listeners, viewers and maybe even themselves that the competition still matters. However, actions will always speak louder than words. Instead of employing another well-worn cliché favoured by so many modern managers after limp cup exits − "Now we can concentrate on the league" − let's hear more people enthusiastically talking about concentrating on the cup, whether that journey begins in the height of summer or in the bleak mid-winter. [7]

Ibis Hotel, Bridgwater 28/02/2023

1. For the record, Aston Villa won that game 1-0, with a teenage Mark Walters striking what would be crowned the 'goal of the season' by the BBC. Despite the disappointment of losing, the experience of playing against top players in front of a packed crowd and the television cameras is the stuff of dreams for any lower division footballer. In terms of non-league giant-killers, Yeovil lead the way with 20 wins against league opposition, with Altrincham achieving 17 such victories.
2. Paul Campbell's *Guardian* article and poll result appeared on 11/04/2013 at a time when the FA were predicting 15,000 empty seats for the forthcoming Wigan v Millwall cup semi-final.
3. The poor gate at Stoke almost certainly reflects two things: the midweek trek for Brighton fans; and a more general

disconnect between supporters and the competition. As a further observation, back in the 70s and 80s, as a player involved in a run-of-the-mill midtable league match, I was acutely aware of the 'more important' 5th or 6th round FA Cup matches taking place that same Saturday afternoon. Those were the fixtures, I sensed, that really mattered.

4. Part of the 'magic' of that Northampton v Gillingham replay – which coloured the occasion – was the shared knowledge amongst players and fans alike of the prize on offer for the winners, a tie against the champions of Europe, something which only a replay can offer.

5. It was a genuine incentive when I arrived at Helston to elevate our league position to the point where we could apply to participate in the FA Cup. Indeed, it felt like a crucial step in putting the club firmly on the footballing map. Our unprecedented 2022-23 FA Cup run not only provided the players with a 'buzz' they still talk about; in addition, it inspired one fan attending an exciting cup replay at Helston in front of a bumper crowd to come forward and offer to invest financially in the club, literally buying into the dream. (Wimbledon's rise from non-league to FA Cup winners is the perfect example of the sort of fairy tale adventure which can inspire all of us.)

6. Money has, in my opinion, been the driving force behind many of the detrimental changes to the FA Cup. Unfashionable though this opinion may be, I believe that certain things are more important than money.

7. As a final thought, returning to my own memories of Cup Final day as a child, the irony is that never before have we had the scale of football media 'circus' which exists today, tailor-made, you could argue, to provide armchair viewers with the ultimate FA Cup Final day TV feast or bonanza.

CHAPTER 4:
ARTIFICIAL INTELLIGENCE:
THE 3G FORCE

It is the first day of March 2023, bitterly cold, and Rodney and I are recording this chapter in the cosy front parlour of the elegant Georgian Grosvenor Arms in the centre of Shaftesbury in Dorset. We built up an appetite for a light 'working lunch' by climbing the steep cobbled street of Gold Hill, made famous by Ridley Scott's iconic 1970s Hovis advert in which a delivery boy pushes his bicycle uphill, before freewheeling back down again. However, before you start to think that this book has turned into some form of travel guide, I should point out that we didn't choose Shaftesbury for its picture-postcard cottages or scenic views. We were here to visit Cockrams, Coppice Street, the home of Shaftesbury FC. The reason for the trip was to take a close look at their state-of-the-art 3G pitch, a surface which – on my previous visit – had played a significant role in changing my mindset about artificial 'turf'...

As a teenager, on schoolboy forms with a professional club, I grew up with gluepot pitches, where the general mentality was that the dirtier you and your kit were by the end of a match, the more you had contributed to the game. Nor were these muddy terrains limited to youth football or lower-division clubs. One of the first things you notice if you look at *YouTube* clips from almost any mid-season English league match from the distant past – alongside the dated hairstyles, sponsor-free shirts, and vast banks of terracing – is the terrible state of the pitches themselves. Most of those games were played out on quagmire mid-winter mud-baths devoid of grass. Far worse, I can vividly recall playing professional matches on surfaces which were downright dangerous. I remember arriving at Oakwell, Barnsley, where the ground staff were shovelling snow from the marked touchlines, and then repainting the lines in a vibrant colour, while the playing surface itself – under a decorative covering of icing-sugar snow – was rock hard. The match itself became a farce, a lottery. On another occasion we travelled from Hull to Bournemouth, forewarned that Dean Court would resemble an ice-skating rink. We came armed with Astroturf-type boots with little pimples on the soles. I cannot recall whether these helped us to combat the treacherous conditions. What I do know is that the pitch was unplayable, and that there is no chance that the match would have passed a modern-day inspection. You could argue that the dodgy terrains of yesteryear were a test to see how robust a player you were, both mentally and physically; that the challenging surfaces forced players to be resilient. On the other hand, not only did the poor state of the pitches sometimes undermine the spectacle for the fans, but it also left players at far greater risk of injury. There was no interest, it seemed, in 'safeguarding' either the footballers or the pitches. To illustrate the lack of respect many clubs had for their playing surfaces, when I was an apprentice at Stockport County in the mid-1970s, *we* were responsible for maintaining and repairing the Edgeley Park pitch; I'm sure that County were not unique in not employing an expert groundsman. Autumnal mud-baths, mid-winter ice rinks, springtime bald, bobbly pitches...it is no surprise that some visionaries in the game were beginning to dream about viable alternatives more conducive to playing football.

Across the 'pond', Astroturf pitches had been in use in the USA since the mid-1960s, a growing phenomenon across a range of sports which split opinion. The advantages of Astroturf were obvious ones: it was far more weather-proof, you could train on it without the wear-and-tear of a traditional grass pitch, and it was 'low maintenance'. Others mistrusted it for a variety of reasons, from the 'unnatural' bounce of a ball, to fears about injuries, to the mere fact that it was artificial. As baseball star Dick Allen put it: "If a horse won't eat it, I don't want to play on it." That used to be my opinion too. My first experience of an artificial pitch came in the summer of 1979 when I headed out to the US to train with the NASL club Seattle Sounders who had an indoor dome with an Astroturf pitch. I was, in effect, on a working holiday, and it was a novelty to play on the surface. I was aware that there were many similar pitches in the States, but I do remember thinking that these would never catch on, though, in a football-mad country such as England.

My theory would soon be put to the test. Between 1981 and 1994 the English Football League saw a pitch experiment. QPR started this mini revolution when they installed an Omniturf playing surface at Loftus Road, which remained in place until 1988. It was a sand in-filled 'second generation' artificial turf. Essentially, a carpet laid on a concrete base with a layer of sand supposedly acting as a cushion. [1] Three clubs followed suit: Luton (1985-91) installed a Sporturf International multi-layered artificial surface and other so-called 'plastic pitches' were laid at Oldham (1986-91) and Preston (1986-94). A debate raged among players, coaches, fans, and journalists, ranging from the 'plastic fantastic' brigade through to Jim Smith's "fake football" opinion. Some argued that these synthetic surfaces rewarded 'footballing' sides; others countered that it took the character and soul out of the game.

People tend to distrust change in general, and traditionalists are never going to approve of any revolution. However, part of the fierce debate revolved around whether these pitches gave the home side an unfair advantage. Understandably, critics felt that there was no longer a level playing field, no pun intended! Preston's artificial surface was the longest-lasting one, and therefore offers us the most accurate gauge. 182 league games were played on it over the course of eight seasons. Of these, PNE won 94 of those matches, but 88 were either drawn or lost, which equates to a 48% no-win ratio. It was hardly an impressive record and certainly not one which backs up the theory of an unfair home advantage. [2] As for the quality of the surface, I can offer my own views, having experienced it first hand during my time at Wrexham. My recollections of playing at Deepdale are that you had to consciously think about your footing and how you ran; whereas on grass you wouldn't hesitate about making a block tackle, you tended to pull up short on their pitch. There was, therefore, far less physical contact in the encounter. The bounce of the ball was an exaggerated one, while firm passes simply flew on; you found yourself over-compensating for this by under-hitting the ball. After the match, we compared it to playing football on a car park. There was no cushion or 'give'. You couldn't place your foot under the ball to lob or chip it. It felt rock-hard and utterly alien, a world away from grass. I certainly did not leave Deepdale that day as a convert.

Those early artificial pitches were crude, green-coloured thick carpets, rather than synthetic turf. The bounce was as unnatural as the surface, sliding tackles were only for the foolhardy and it was clear that non-contact injuries were increased on these unforgiving hard pitches. [3] It was no surprise when they were initially banned from the top-flight in 1991 and then from the professional game itself in 1994. Few fans or players shed tears as the carpets were rolled up and replaced by 'the real thing'. The experiment, it seemed, had failed...

Except, of course, that it was not simply an experiment. With the benefit of hindsight, we can laugh at images of the earliest mobile phones or computers; today they look ridiculously clunky. However, they were the first stages of a technological evolution. Similarly, the development of artificial pitches continued. Like many other football fans, I was blissfully unaware of how far they had evolved, until I took my Truro City side on a pre-season training weekend to Exeter University back in 2005. I knew that we would be on their artificial pitch and – while I thought it would be a novelty for the squad – had pre-warned my players to be careful on the surface. I remember walking on to it for the first time and thinking that it not only looked like grass but that it almost felt like it too. I think my mindset had been stuck in the 1980s, with a fixed image of what a 'plastic pitch' resembled. I was impressed, but I still wasn't 'converted'. The traditionalist in me felt that it was part of the skill set of any footballer to adapt to the changing seasons of a grass pitch. Nevertheless, that weekend had opened my mind to the potential which these new generation pitches provided.

The evolution or development has, of course, continued. 3G surfaces today combine three elements: synthetic turf, sand infill and rubber infill. Ever more advanced pitches are in the 'development' stage. In addition, the boundaries between natural/ unnatural have become blurred. Many so-called 'natural' grass pitches are now hybrid ones, with 95% natural turf reinforced with 5% synthetic fibres. This in itself makes the debate about artificial pitches far more nuanced, no longer a simple case of black-and-white, of yes or no.

Professional football clubs — the elite, if you like — might point to the fact that, nowadays, almost every pitch in the PL and EFL is lovingly looked after by expert groundsmen who maintain surfaces which resemble bowling greens, even in mid-season. Just a fortnight ago, Rodney and I were watching a fourth-tier match at Sixfields, and the pitch was almost in pre-season condition. The technology and know-how have radically evolved, as has the clubs' respect for creating a surface befitting a professional sport which people pay good money to watch. You could argue that there is no need for 'the 92' to look for artificial alternatives.

The picture is very different in the non-league game, where there simply is not the money required to employ full-time ground staff and invest in expensive equipment. In recent years at Helston, we have had periods where we have lost a succession of games to the weather, leading to a backlog of fixtures. In addition, it becomes a vicious circle if you are a progressive club which fields a number of teams which play their matches on the same pitch, inevitably leading to wear-and-tear. The installation of a modern, artificial pitch is a game changer for a non-league club. You can eliminate the cost of hiring pitches for training, which at a club such as ours — running thirty or so teams — is a considerable financial burden. It would enable us to keep everything 'in house'. In addition, it would provide a revenue source, allowing us to hire the pitch out to local schools or clubs. This 'open door' policy would then permit the football club to become a genuine hub in the community, somewhere which local people could proudly identify with.

Shaftesbury FC's new pitch is a perfect example of how the entire perception or feel of a 3G surface changes once it is located in a stadium. I had always had an image of artificial pitches as being somewhat cold and clinical, fenced-off training grounds with an entrance gate, lacking any sense of atmosphere. As soon as you instal one in a proper football ground it completely alters the picture or ambience. Surrounded by covered stands, terraces, a clubhouse...the so-called 'plastic pitch' comes alive, however surreal that might sound. The cover photograph for this book perfectly illustrates this.

We know that, like any form of technology, artificial pitches will continue to develop, getting better and better until they reach the point where it will probably be impossible to distinguish them from the genuine, natural surfaces. [4] In addition, the game of football itself is evolving. The latest generation of young players has grown up training on 3G, honing their skills on it, playing a faster and more technical pass-and-move game on these reliable surfaces. It makes perfect sense to provide them with a match day pitch which, in a sense, they were 'born' on. 3G is second nature to the new breed of footballer. Ironically, it is the uneven grass pitches which they find themselves having to adapt to.

The cost of laying a 3G pitch is somewhere in the region of £400,000 to £500,000. While revenue incomes from hiring the surface out might conceivably see that initial outlay covered over a relatively short period of time, something arguably needs to be done by the FA to fund any progressive non-league club looking to join the evolutionary revolution, in terms of grants (or, at the very least, interest-free loans). The Football Foundation has helped fund more than a thousand 3G pitches over the past decades, but their current criteria exclude clubs within the National League system (Steps 1-6). I would suggest that there could be a pecking order for these grants, based on several factors or criteria: is the club situated in an economically deprived area; how many teams does it operate, including youth, women, disability, veterans, walking football etc; how many people in the wider community will be positively affected by the installation of a 3G pitch? [5] This would ensure that the football clubs which benefit from the grants are ones which already make a conscious effort to have a genuine impact in their region. This ties in with how football clubs were perceived when they were founded back in the Victorian period, as focal points in their towns or cities. A 3G pitch would help to make a club like Helston Athletic more visible in its community and more useful to it. Central or local funding would enable us to become a genuine hub.

There are dystopian science fiction books and films where AI has taken over from humans. In the world of sport, a different type of Artificial Intelligence is having an increasing impact, but in this case a positive one. I am convinced that a 3G pitch helps players, technically, and provides a better spectacle for the supporters. However, the 3G revolution is about far more than laying down a practical, artificial surface for a first team to play on. It can change, even transform, the entire dynamic of a club and what it can deliver. It makes no sense – commercially and for the community – for a stadium to lie dormant and empty all week. Far better that it becomes a vibrant place of activity, morning, afternoon and evening. I am convinced that 3G (and beyond) is the future of the game. Possibly not in the professional leagues, but certainly at – no pun intended again – 'grassroots' level.

The Grosvenor Arms, Shaftesbury 01/03/2023

1. With thanks to Steven Scragg for his article, 'They used to play football on plastic', *These Football Times* online, 19/10/2015.
2. As historian Ian Rigby's 1994 article – reproduced in the *Lancashire Post* on 03/09/2019 – observed, PNE's record contradicts the theory that the surface gave them "a great advantage".
3. Dr James Voos, 'Artificial Turf versus Natural Grass', University Hospitals online, 26/08/2019. Part of the continuing artificial turf versus natural grass debate revolves around injuries. In 2019, Dr James Voos reported the findings of the University Hospitals Sports Medicine Institute. The data collected and analysed led to the discovery that injury rates were 'significantly higher' on artificial surfaces. 58% higher, in fact. However, before any cynics start knowingly nodding their heads in a "Told you!" manner, the research findings observed that many of these injuries might be related either to incorrect footwear/cleats, or to inadequate maintenance of the surface.
4. Or even, dare I suggest, a far better option.
5. This can even include, for example, the use of the pitch by the local NHS for the rehabilitation of patients, including both physiotherapy and people with mental health issues.

CHAPTER 5:
ONE CAREFUL OWNER?

In the beginning – as it were – before the professional era, football clubs did not need owners. There was nothing to own: footballers were not 'assets'; they were simply playing for the love of the game. In addition, most matches took place in public parks or hired grounds used for other sports: athletics, cricket and even baseball. Clubs were run by committees made up of volunteers. The rise of professionalism saw clubs become limited liability companies run by a chairman and board of directors, joint stock ventures with shareholders, co-owners. In the late-Victorian and Edwardian eras, when the main task was the construction of football-specific stadiums, those 'new era' club chairmen and directors tended to be local businessmen. This was still very much the case when I started playing at Stockport County. My first chairman owned a chain of hotels in the Manchester area; the second was a local scrap metal merchant. Why did they want to own a fourth-tier football club? There were very few assets at County in those days to either invest in, or strip; the club did not even have its own training ground. Nevertheless, there was – and still is – undoubtedly a sense of status attached to owning one of 'the 92' clubs. Being a chairman of your local football club is a position which gives you a certain prestige in the community, one which a normal business or commercial deal – however profitable – can never provide. We should be wary of making dangerous generalisations, but my experience both in the professional game and grassroots football leads me to believe that many are simply on an ego-trip, looking for adulation from the fanbase, reflected glory, hoping that if the team does well, supporters might even chant their name. Football provides some of these owners with a unique stage, an elevating pedestal. For every low-key chairman I have come across, I can think of an owner who fits that egotistical profile.

The history of English football is littered with both 'nightmare owner' stories and 'fairy godfather' ones. These are the two extremes which we need to take a brief look at, before examining the more general picture...

In an ideal world, a football chairman or owner would be emotionally invested in a club. He would see himself as a steward or custodian. He would use his financial clout and knowledge to run a club properly, while leaving his manager free to run the footballing side. In an ideal world...

East Yorkshire factory owner Ken Richardson already had a criminal record before he became the majority shareholder of Doncaster Rovers. As the Sheffield *Star* observed, "In 1984 he was fined £20,000 for his part in a racing scandal in which horses were swapped in a scam to sting the bookies." [1] Richardson arrived at Belle Vue promoting himself as the saviour of a financially stricken club, but player-manager Kerry Dixon revealed that Richardson insisted on meddling in on-field affairs and that the former England international had no say in team selection. Sadly, as I know from both my own playing days and subsequent managerial career, this is not uncommon. Many club owners fancy themselves as football experts and feel that their investment gives them the right to interfere. A little knowledge, as they say, is a dangerous thing. However, in Richardson's case it was far worse than this. When it became clear that a stadium relocation would not happen, he hired men to set fire to the main stand at Belle Vue, hoping to pay off debts through the insurance money. The arson attack was bungled, and Richardson was tried and convicted of 'conspiracy to commit arson'. He was described by a detective as "the type who would trample a two-year-old child to pick up a 2p bit". [2]

Richardson is clearly an extreme example. Nevertheless, there are several 'businessmen' who have been allowed to take charge of professional football clubs despite previous criminal convictions. George Reynolds – who would later take Darlington into administration – had already served time in prison on four occasions, for various offences from smuggling, safe-cracking, and handling explosives to theft and burglary. You might ask yourself why the Football League and the FA allowed convicted criminals such as Richardson and Reynolds to become involved in the sport. Or – albeit within the letter of the law – how others have been permitted to buy into a club with loans secured against the club's assets, as was the case at Brighton, where DIY tycoons Bill Archer and Greg Stanley arrived at the club armed with £800,000 as Albion faced a winding-up order, only for it to later emerge that the money was a bank loan, secured using the stadium as collateral. In the cases of Doncaster, Darlington and Brighton, the long-term damage to each club was immense. Doncaster dropped into non-league football, Brighton fans ended up facing a three-hour round-trip to Gillingham for *home* matches, while Darlington's phoenix club has never returned to the Football League.

The common factor in each of these nightmare scenarios is that these men took advantage of clubs which were already in financial turmoil, with fans desperate to see a white knight arrive on the scene. When people are (emotionally) drowning, they will clutch at anybody offering to help. Ultimately, players and managers can move on; it is the loyal supporters who end up suffering. In the worst-case scenarios, they face losing the club they have emotionally invested in. [3]

The fairy tale opposite is the lifelong fan, the almost mythical 'local lad made good' who, having accumulated a personal fortune, chooses to 'invest' in his boyhood club. Jack Walker (Blackburn), Jack Hayward (Wolverhampton) and Steve Gibson (Middlesbrough) would doubtless count among these wealthy benefactors who involved themselves in clubs they genuinely loved. No doubt all three had their club's best interests at heart and understood the significance and responsibility of becoming the 'custodian' of a precious hub in the community, rather than seeing themselves as the 'owner' of an acquired 'property'. However, there are clearly not enough of these fairy godfathers to go around the 92, never mind drip-feeding into non-league football. We need a more realistic blueprint for club ownership.

We might argue that the PL is a world apart. Attracting a global following of viewers and sponsors, its teams packed with foreign international stars, many coached by overseas managers...it is unsurprising – given the global reach and riches on offer – that the ownership of the clubs themselves reflects this. A 2021 UEFA club benchmarking report indicated that 40% of the clubs were 'majority owned' by foreign investors, while a further 35% had foreign investors as 'minority stakeholders'. The wording reflects what I discussed in an earlier chapter, that the PL has become a global entertainment business or brand. Online research suggests that most PL clubs are owned by groups: holding companies, private equity firms, sports investment corporations, travel retail groups ...Viewed as a collective body, those clubs have links across the globe: China, UAE, Saudi Arabia, Iran, Egypt, Pakistan, Thailand, Greece, Italy, and the United States. Rodney asked me during our conversation for this chapter whether I felt that the nationality of a football club owner matters. My answer was 'no', *if* they pass a 'fit and proper' investigation of their finances, businesses and background. [4] Part of the problem, unfortunately, is that a watertight system does not appear to be in place. Do the football authorities genuinely care about the morality of club ownership? Or does that only become an issue when political conflicts intervene, as in the case of the situation in the Ukraine? It is undoubtedly an issue which divides fans, highlighted by the response following takeovers such as the recent one at Newcastle. For every fan unhappy at the ethical source of that investment, there are probably a dozen simply happy at the thought of vast sums of money being pumped into their club.

In all honesty, the PL does not operate in a community-based, knowable world that a traditional football fan like me can relate to. Nor am I alone in feeling alienated by the ownership model of treating a club as a multi-national business with transferable assets. For me, it undermines the foundation stones which the sport was built on. That was clearly the thinking or philosophy of those fans who founded FC United of Manchester. The fan-owned club revolution is also underway in the EFL, with Exeter City leading the way. The Devon club has demonstrated that the model can work …on two conditions. First, that there are business-savvy people at the heart of the operation. Second, that there is a thriving youth academy which can provide a conveyor belt of local talent, both helping to strengthen the first-team squad and providing significant transfer windfalls when bigger clubs come calling. The fact that City are holding their own in EFL 1, and investing in both the stadium and training ground are healthy signs. [5] It will be interesting to see whether this fan ownership model catches on. In theory, it makes more sense than simply hoping to attract one wealthy and 'careful owner'.

Between global ownership, individual ownership and local fan-ownership, there is an alternative blueprint for clubs in the lower-reaches of the EFL and at grassroots level, one which is rarely discussed. Rodney asked me for my opinion about multi-club ownership, a topic in the news recently, with a study suggesting that at least fifteen English clubs are part of a multi-club ownership system. It is a growing trend which is worrying UEFA in terms of European club competitions and transfer fees, and some fan groups in terms of previously independent clubs potentially becoming 'feeder' ones. Is it a depressing case of larger clubs snapping up fiscally weaker ones? Or financially strong ones keeping smaller ones afloat, almost protecting them? My interest, though, lies in the possible ties which could be created between – for the sake of argument – a mid-size EFL club such as Plymouth Argyle and a Step 5 non-league club such as Helston Athletic. People tend to react negatively when you talk about parent and feeder clubs, partly because of the emotive language involved. What I have in mind is working partnerships, rather than EFL clubs buying up non-league neighbours and stripping or exploiting their assets. Instead of scouting and cherry-picking young players who are playing for their local non-league club, the League club could share resources – coaching, training facilities, even loaning inexperienced professional players in need of meaningful, competitive "men's football" [6] – and invest money in the grassroots game, such as helping to fund a 3G pitch at Helston, for example. In return, not only would a club such as Argyle be having a positive impact in the surrounding area –

and with it garnering plenty of goodwill – but also a genuine player pathway would be created, one where the senior club would have built up a proper knowledge of our Cornish youngsters. Instead of having to pay out inflated transfer fees and agent commissions, the EFL club would be able to tap into local talent where – contrary to popular myth – the high standard of grassroots coaching is developing potential gems. A future Argyle striker could be currently playing in Helston, rather than Helsinki. [7]

Whichever model of ownership you prefer – be it a powerful global business, local entrepreneur, fan-run club, or club partnerships [8] – it is clear that far more thought needs to go into the appointment of head coaches/managers and far more patience is required once the new boss is installed in the proverbial hotseat. Today, so many club owners – and fans – demand instant success from the managers they hire and fire at an increasingly rapid rate. The following chapter is dedicated to that hotseat, but as we prepared to move on to that conversation, Rodney shared with me the story of brewery owners and landed Suffolk gentry, the Cobbold family. For generations they ran Ipswich Town with eccentric charm and unflappable patience. They were on the board of directors which hired an untried Alf Ramsey, who delivered two promotions and then the league title in the club's first ever season in the top tier. Later, when fans were calling for the young, inexperienced Bobby Robson to be sacked, John Cavendish Cobbold called him in, apologised for the fans' behaviour and rewarded his manager with a pay rise. Robson subsequently delivered nine top-six league finishes, an FA Cup, a UEFA Cup and regular European football. You might argue that the Cobbold family played a significant role in preparing two of England's most successful international managers. With the Cobbolds at the helm, there was never a trigger-happy approach to football managers; instead, they offered unwavering support. Indeed, John Cavendish Cobbold once famously said, "There will never be a crisis at Ipswich Town unless the white wine runs out in the board room." It is, naturally, a story from a now vanished age. Nevertheless, it demonstrates how a left-field vision or approach to managerial appointments, and patience thereafter, can reap dividends, both for club and country. The Cobbolds were not billionaire owners, nor were they even football fanatics, but – more importantly – they were careful custodians.

28/03/2023, Mannings Hotel, Truro

1. ON THIS DAY: 'The Downfall of Doncaster Rovers supremo Ken Richardson', 03/03/2016, *The Star*.
2. Quoted by Georgina Turner, 'The fall and rise of Doncaster Rovers, *Guardian*, 30/11/2005.
3. There are, sadly, a host of other examples we could have explored, including Sam Hammam's sale of Plough Lane, or the more recent example of mis-ownership at Bury.
4. I'm not even convinced that a club owner needs to love football, as long as s/he runs the club properly and puts people in place who have both knowledge of and passion for the game. And lets them get on with it. In addition, I feel that it is vital that a club's stadium is protected from falling into a private individual's ownership, to prevent the worst possible case of asset stripping.
5. Nick Hawker, leader of The Trust: "Listening to what fans want could solve a lot of football's problems. Who owns the club? Nobody really. Most clubs in the United Kingdom were born in the late 1800s or early 1900s often through churches or working men's clubs and they are so deeply rooted in the community. We don't own Exeter City, it's in our safe keeping. That's what some Premier League owners

have to understand." Cited by Alistair Magowan, BBC online, 05/05/2021. What we must bear in mind with fan-ownership clubs is the fact that there will, almost inevitably, be a glass ceiling.

6. In the absence of proper reserve team football at EFL level, and the almost no-contact nature of Under 18 and Under 21 leagues, Football League clubs would, arguably, benefit as much as non-league ones from this arrangement.

7. During the week we put this chapter together, the FA announced that PL clubs spent almost £320m in agents' fees over the past year. My old club Stockport spent a staggering £236,944.

8. I guess that one of my former clubs – Wrexham – has discovered another type of ownership, the celebrity one, with the global, or at least US, heightened interest which the arrival of actors Ryan Reynolds and Rob McElhenney has created. On a recent visit to the Racecourse, I could almost touch the excitement and buzz which the new ownership has generated. I guess that – as a fan – you have to enjoy the ride, and hope that their interest is sustained.

CHAPTER 6:
SURVIVING THE HOTSEAT

In my fourteen years in the Football League, in the 1970s and 80s, I played under sixteen different managers, a reminder to myself that the crazy managerial merry-go-round is not a modern invention. Nevertheless, the fact that only one of those campaigns ended in promotion suggests that hiring and firing managers at will is normally a recipe for mediocrity, at best. As discussed in the previous chapter about club owners, patience – that rare commodity – is more likely to be rewarded, in the long-term. I highlighted the example of a young Bobby Robson at Ipswich Town – retained when fans were calling for him to be sacked – where the refusal of the club chairman to press the panic button led to an unprecedented decade of success at the Suffolk club.

Looking back through the post-war history of English football at the highest level, the managers who have brought the greatest achievements at their respective clubs tend to have been ones allowed time – a decade or more – to create and build a 'culture': Matt Busby at Manchester United (1945-69); Bill Shankly at Liverpool (1959-74); Bobby Robson at Ipswich (1969-82); Brian Clough at Nottingham Forest (1975-93); Graham Taylor at Watford (1977-87); Alex Ferguson at Manchester United (1986-2013); Arsène Wenger at Arsenal (1996-2018)...

Perhaps, though, we should briefly delve back further in time. In 2004, The Sunday Times named Herbert Chapman as the greatest British manager of all time in a poll, and a brief look at his unique career backs up this 'award'. Chapman had been a journeyman footballer, often playing as an amateur for a club near where he could find employment, usually in engineering. When he became player-manager at Northampton Town in 1907, his third spell at the club, he was taking charge of a team which had finished bottom of the Southern League in successive seasons. Within two years he had won the title, having become one of the first managers to instil a tactical system: a highly organised defence and a counter-attacking formation based on short passes and two pacy wingers. Always open to picking up ideas from other countries, he even took the Cobblers on tour to Germany. With no automatic promotion into the Football League in those days, he moved on and, post WW1, at Huddersfield he was given full control of footballing matters and insisted that the reserve and third teams adopted the same tactics as the first team. He introduced an unheard-of wide-ranging scouting network and brought Huddersfield their first trophies: two league titles and an FA Cup. In 1925, moving on again, at Arsenal his revolutionary ideas went even further, signing foreign players, employing physiotherapists and masseurs, installing floodlights for training, introducing brighter modern kits, helping to redesign Highbury stadium, and advocating several things which would later become reality: numbered shirts, white footballs, European club competitions. On the pitch, Chapman's reign brought the Gunners their first ever title successes in addition to an FA Cup.

Clearly, Chapman was a revolutionary, a one-off. He somehow had the ability to foresee the future. Fast forward to 2015 and one of his successors at Arsenal, Wenger, set out his own blueprint for the successful manager. Despite his observation that modern football throws up challenges which are "consistently evolving", he suggested that "the fundamentals of a successful manager remain the same":

"There are many factors in measuring that success, but the key ingredients will always be the passion an individual has for the sport; man management; the ability to evolve and adapt; and, of course, an eye for talent." [1]

I am a huge admirer of Wenger and how he – like Chapman before him – revolutionised the English game. As someone who has managed for thirty years myself – albeit at non-league level – I would add a fifth key element: the willingness to surround yourself with a coaching team which compliments your own skills. Knowledgeable, trustworthy people, but not 'yes' men who will simply reinforce your own views in front of the playing squad or provide an 'echo-chamber' when discussing formations, tactics or team selection. I believe that as a football manager you need to be brave enough to assemble a coaching team willing to question your own decisions and provide alternative ideas and voices. The cliché about there being no 'I' in 'team' refers to the management team almost as much as it does the playing squad.

As for the other qualities Wenger lists, having a mind open to change is so important – whether that be diet, training methods, or even the use of data, which we employ even at non-league level. In terms of man-management, that works in a number of different ways. On the one hand, it might be taking a player aside who you are not going to be selecting for a forthcoming match and explaining your decision. Equally, it could be the need to take a hard-line approach with a player who is a toxic influence in the dressing room or who is under-performing because his attitude in training is not spot-on. You learn very early on in football management that you cannot please or appease everyone. Nor should you try to, I would add. Perhaps a further 'quality' we need to add to our managerial blueprint is the ability to develop a 'thick skin', a mental 'armour'. Faced by the 'noise' from the stands or social media, you need to retain a belief in yourself and shut out all those dissenting voices. A self-confidence, without allowing it to trip over into arrogance.

The managerial success of the likes of Chapman, Wenger and Mourinho is a reminder that the ingredients needed to become a top manager are not the same, necessarily, as those required to play at the highest level. All three had played most of their football at amateur or reserve team level. Conversely, the two biggest stars of the 1966 World Cup, Bobby Moore and Bobby Charlton, both failed to transfer their playing talents to the hotseat. Appointing a 'legend' such as Frank Lampard or Steven Gerrard might, initially, fire the imagination of fans, but there is no guarantee that their iconic playing qualities will transfer from pitch to bench. It could end up being a gimmick rather than a gimme, perhaps. Another unknown factor, of course, is whether top PL managers like Jurgen Klopp or Pep Guardiola would be able to work their magic at the likes of Accrington Stanley, or even Helston Athletic! In theory, the qualities required of a head coach or manager are the same whether it is in the top-flight or at grassroots level. In practice, it would be fascinating to see how they coped...[2]

Having agreed on a manager blueprint, there remains the elephant in the room: the merry-go-round I referred to at the beginning of this chapter. With trigger-happy owners and keyboard-warrior fans demanding instant success, the current record of managerial longevity – or lack of – makes painful reading. Rodney and I were putting this chapter together at the end of March 2023 and the statistics at the time of writing were genuinely appalling. Of the current 92 PL and EFL managers, only twelve had been in their position for three years or more; only twenty-one had occupied their current post for two years. Graham Taylor managed Watford for ten years, taking them from the fourth tier to the first, even bringing European football to Vicarage Road. His club chairman, Elton John, allowed him the time to build something never seen there before. Yet in the same ten-year time frame, Vicarage Road has more recently seen almost twenty bosses come and go. Watford is a radical example, but with little sign of owners or fans in general showing more patience – the hope rather than expectation talked about in the previous chapter – what can we do to change this self-defeating 'instant success' culture?

Part of the problem is that in this age of social media and the 24/7 rolling 'news' offered by the likes of *Sky* and *Talk Sport*, people are always looking for a story, including undermining managers whose teams are going through a barren spell. With club owners often looking to appease unhappy fans, all-too-often they end up reacting to all the 'noise', rather than sticking with the man they themselves hired in the first place. In addition, the sacking of a manager often has a snowball effect. The owner of club 'A' sacks his manager and approaches club 'B' for theirs...The fallout can disrupt any number of clubs mid-season, clubs who have maybe been doing well on the field and where the owner has allowed the man in the hotseat to 'invest' in his own coaching staff, players, etc. I do have a solution to this chaos, albeit a radical one.

We have transfer windows for players, but not for managers. This makes no sense in terms of the stability of any club, or football in general. Imagine that we 'ring fence' the football season in terms of managers. Once the campaign kicks off, the man in the hotseat is in place for the duration of the following nine months. Instead of the current culture of owners pressing the panic button at the first sign of trouble, they would be forced to work with the manager to find solutions. Rather than raiding and unsettling another club, it would then become a question of solving problems internally. Club owners even might think more carefully in the future before making managerial appointments – employing more due diligence, as it were – rather than either seeking the adulation of supporters by hiring a marquee name, or else playing safe with one of those tired old club-hopping firefighters. [3]

We need to take some of the heat out of the hotseat, as it were. My proposal would also put a stop to the current trend of a manager being 'tapped up' by another club and resigning mid-season. Obviously, this would not prevent a club from taking action against a manager for a serious breach of discipline. However, in purely footballing terms, it would counteract what Wenger referred to as "a growing trend" of clubs frequently changing managers amidst the constant "pressure for short-term results". [4] We need to encourage clubs and their owners to look at the longer-term picture, creating stability, allowing a manager "the time to create a culture at the club, which is so important." [5] This applies at any level of the game and, indeed, in any business. We need forward thinking approaches to football management, rather than the current hotseat version of musical chairs. This includes putting measures in place to reduce the stress levels on managers which are considerable, even at non-league level. In today's culture, that stress includes dealing with – and placating – individual players who are unhappy about being left out the side. In the modern game, one sometimes gets the impression that it is players and agents who hold all the aces, rather than the manager. The managerial stability which my proposed rule change would bring to the game could help to counteract this shift of power. We need balance, in football as in life. A manager needs to respect and nurture his players; however, we also need players, clubs and their owners to do the same with their managers. In essence, we need to cool the temperature in the hotseat, dampening the fire, making it a more positive environment to work in. We must be mindful of managerial burn-out, and the mental well-being of those head coaches. As I know from bitter experience, the hotseat can be a lonely place, despite the coaching team you have around you.

The stark reality is that nothing can totally prepare you for the stresses and strains of football management. What we can do, though, is provide the sport with a reality check, one which irons out some of the bumps in the rocky road ahead, offering future generations of would-be bosses a measure of stability and support. In a world where club owners and fans are increasingly impatient, it is up to the rule-makers to take the first steps towards changing that unhealthy hire-and-fire culture. [6]

The Arts Café, Truro, 29/03/2023.

1. Arsène Wenger, Foreword to *Living on the Volcano: The Secrets of Surviving as a Football Manager*, Century, 2015, p. xiii.
2. Even at EFL level, you do not necessarily have to go down the route of appointing a manager who has played at the professional level. Lennie Lawrence never kicked a ball in the Football League yet managed more than 1,000 games and took nomadic Charlton into the top-flight.

3. The world of football management is unique in the sense that a manager can seemingly fail at numerous clubs and yet bounce back each time to secure a position in charge of another team, or even – in some cases – at the very same club. I cannot imagine many professions where this would apply, apart from politics perhaps!
4. Wenger, *Living on the Volcano*, p. xiv.
5. Wenger, *Living on the Volcano*, p. xiv.
6. As a postscript to this chapter, at the beginning of May 2023, the number of both PL and EFL managers sacked this season had reached record numbers, with many dismissed late on in the campaign. Roy Hodgson – who himself had benefited from this musical chairs 'game' by re-joining Crystal Palace – commented: "I don't quite know what the new manager is really expected to do...I do find it a little bit strange to see that there are so many changes so very, very late in the season. There is no magic, there is no dust you can sprinkle over the team, you can only work with the players who are there. It will be if the players can react to the new manager and find something they haven't found before. If I was the owner of the club, I'd be asking the question if they find something that hasn't been there before, what's stopped them up to this point?" BBC online, 04/05/2023. It is clear that the managerial merry-go-round is out of control.

CHAPTER 7:
THEATRES OF DREAMS

My earliest and fondest childhood memories of football are intrinsically connected to the trips my dad and I took to both Old Trafford and Edgeley Park in the 1960s. They genuinely felt like pilgrimages to special places, particularly if we took a 'football special' train from Manchester Piccadilly to Old Trafford. We would arrive early so that we could secure Dad's favourite spot, a crush barrier near the corner flag in the Stretford End paddock. Dad carried a heavy, folded-up wooden stool (painted red, of course!) for me to stand on, to enable me to see the action on the pitch. Any floodlit game, particularly European Cup nights, with the four illuminated pylons drawing you in from the iconic forecourt, added to the magic. I have never lost that indescribable buzz of excitement as you make your way to a match. [1] Those memories of massed ranks of supporters on vast terraces are from a now vanished age, but we need to venture even further back in time before I describe my own experiences of football grounds as a professional player...

The opening chapters of Simon Inglis' fascinating 1983 book about English football grounds explore the history behind stadium development, from the late-Victorian era to post-WW2. Re-reading those pages is a reminder that several Football League clubs played at already established cricket grounds: Derby County (the Racecourse), Notts Forest and Notts County (Trent Bridge), and Northampton Town (County Ground) among many others. The Oval was the original venue for FA Cup Finals and England international matches. Inglis observes:

"Cricket grounds were not in use during winter, often had a pavilion of sorts, and certainly had the best pitches, so they were perfect for staging football." [2]

The last observation makes me smile; it carries a certain irony for me as, by the time I signed for Northampton in 1982, the County Ground was the only cricket ground left hosting professional football. The two pitches only overlapped by about twenty yards, but the Cobblers' pitch was used as a car park and picnic area during the summers, leading to a bumpy, uneven surface. It certainly wasn't 'perfect for staging football'.

As I mentioned in a previous chapter, some clubs moved into grounds which were already being used for sports such as athletics, horse racing, or even baseball. The 1890s saw the first purpose-built football grounds constructed, with Goodison Park leading the way. [3] Some of the sites chosen had previously been used as amusement parks, duck ponds, meadows, or farms, as some of their names indicate: The Old Show Ground, Gay Meadow... Others had been quarries, chalk pits, or even rubbish dumps. Indeed, talking of tips, Inglis notes that early banks of terracing were often constructed from ash, cinders and people's rubbish. Wooden stands for seated spectators soon followed. Most football grounds were constructed in an ad hoc, piecemeal fashion, a work in progress. This partly explains why there tended to be a unique, higgledy-piggledy charm about most of them.

In truth, once these grounds had been established, maintenance was often minimal. To give you an example, one of our roles as apprentices at Stockport County in the early 1970s was ground 'improvements' at Edgeley Park: anything from touching up the paintwork on the turnstiles to repairing parts of the terraces between the sleepers which had worn away. We had to dig out soil and stones, filling in the gaps and stabilising the steps. I doubt that I did a great job; as my far more practical brother, Trevor, would tell you, I have never been any good at DIY. However, the fact that we were left to fulfil these tasks probably indicates that cash-strapped clubs did not prioritise ground maintenance and improvements, a topic which – tragically – we will need to return to later in this chapter.

I do remember, quite early in my playing career, arriving for an away match at Scunthorpe United and looking around The Old Show Ground, taking in the surroundings, and thinking what a neat and tidy ground it was. Equally, I never liked either Somerton Park (Newport) or The Shay (Halifax) simply because the speedway track distanced the pitch from the stands. [4] However, my memories of specific grounds tend to be formed by one specific feature – such as a scoreboard or clock – or a quirky stand or paddock: anything from the dangerous-looking muddy grass bank of open terracing at Wigan's old Springfield Park ground, to the covered Hotel End at Northampton or the vast Kop at Wrexham where a couple of thousand fans could create an impressive atmosphere. Rodney asked me if any particular grounds stand out from my fourteen years playing in the Football League. In terms of noise, both Bramall Lane and Fratton Park were venues which made me momentarily stand there on the pitch, drinking in the atmosphere as a football fan, rather than as a player. However, in terms of the structures themselves, there are two well worth mentioning.

As a raw teenager, just a few weeks after my seventeenth birthday, I played at Griffin Park, Brentford. It was a fourth-tier match, but the 37,000-capacity ground had the imposing feel of a top-flight club. Like so many at the time, it was surrounded by small, terraced houses, but once inside you were in awe of the spaciousness, including the vast, covered Brook Road terrace with a capacity similar to the entirety of the Bees' new state-of-the-art stadium.

My vivid memories of Charlton's aptly-named Valley are undoubtedly influenced by the fact that I was playing there in a reserve fixture, in a near empty stadium. The site itself – a natural bowl – is impressive in itself, but what dominated it in those days was a vast bank of terracing, the largest side in English football, created when volunteers dug a derelict chalk pit in 1919 and formed the sloping shape of The East Terrace, opposite the Main Stand. The tall bank of open terracing, which I believe had once accommodated more than 40,000 fans, has stuck in my mind ever since. Its sheer scale – on a day where its countless crush barriers were unpopulated – was mightily impressive. [5]

Purely as a fan – unfortunately I never played there – Newcastle's St James' Park takes some beating. Situated in the heart of the city, you climb out of the metro station and bang...it rises in front of you like a cathedral. It is something far more than a stadium; a genuine landmark in a football-mad city. A magical theatre of dreams, on a giant scale.

With the tragic benefit of hindsight, Valley Parade, Bradford, is another ground which has stayed in my memory banks. I had travelled there with Hull, as an unused squad player, and sat in the wooden main stand watching the match. There was no doubt that it had character; however, I did notice the gaps beneath the seats where you could see the accumulated litter beneath. This would have been just a year before the tragic fire which cost so many lives. Naturally I wasn't anticipating the potential disaster which could occur, but as a player one was acutely aware in the mid-80s that many football grounds were not fit for purpose, be that the changing rooms or the facilities on offer for spectators. The football authorities, the clubs themselves and the police seemed more interested in fencing in potential hooligans, rather than updating their facilities to provide welcoming, modern venues for spectators. In addition, perhaps we were all guilty of nostalgia, looking (for example) at that old wooden stand at Bradford and equating its creakiness with 'charm', or 'character', rather than wondering whether it was safe and fit for purpose. [6] I was playing for Hull City on that final day of the 1984-85 season but — even in those pre-internet days — news of the fire filtered through. While watching the horrific scenes later, on the news bulletins, my thoughts for the people who had died, or were seriously injured, were mixed with more selfish ones: that could easily have been us playing there, my dad could have been sat in that stand...A large crowd had turned up that day at Bradford to celebrate their team's promotion. Fifty-six would never return home and many more were both physically and emotionally scarred. Both the fire at Valley Parade and the crush at Hillsborough four years later ended up providing (horrific) wake-up calls for everyone that English football clubs needed a stadium revolution in terms of both safety procedures and infrastructure. I recall my dad frequently complaining about the state of the toilets at football grounds, open urinals which in some cases probably dated back to Victorian times. It was symbolic of the way many grounds had been allowed to deteriorate to the point where some were falling apart. Looking back now, it is little wonder that football was failing to attract women or families, in an era where you were herded into fenced enclosures. However, it should not have needed human tragedies to provide the catalyst for change. The year after

Hillsborough, a further reminder of how outdated most English professional grounds had become came in the form of the World Cup in Italy. Rebuilt stadiums such as Genoa's eye-catching Stadio Luigi Ferraris were like structures from another planet, never mind another country. Arguably, the ultra-modern stadia we saw at Italia 90 should have provided the models and inspiration for how we needed to rebuild and look forward. As a side note, it was a tournament which made football sexy again; where fans and journalists were talking about the matches, shiny stadiums and the generally positive atmosphere, rather than English hooligans abroad. From that perspective, it felt like a watershed moment.

A huge amount has changed since Inglis wrote his book, since I retired from professional football and since that World Cup which restored many people's faith in 'the beautiful game'. Of the current 92 PL and EFL clubs, almost half have relocated to new purpose-built grounds, with yet more stadiums either under construction or in the planning stages. There is no doubt that the 'relocation revolution' has seen fans – and corporate hospitality 'customers' – offered far better facilities: from decent toilets and catering, to safer, more comfortable environments which you would be happy to take your children or grandchildren to for a match. In addition, the vast majority of those clubs which have stayed put have either rebuilt or at least renovated their grounds.

Renovate or relocate? It sounds like the title for a property-based reality television show. In the world of football, it isn't always a simple matter of choice. Sometimes, as is the case at Luton Town, the football ground has become hemmed in by housing and there simply isn't room to rebuild, never mind expand. [7] Equally, for poorer clubs, the only viable option has often been to sell off what was a prime town centre site – to a supermarket chain, property developer etc. – and relocate to an out-of-town location where there is space for things which the Victorian football player or fan didn't need, such as car parks. In addition, there are other obvious advantages, such as the opportunity to design a purpose-built modern stadium which also fulfils requirements such as access for the emergency services and – in today's new football world – conference and other commercial facilities. Inevitably, though, you instantly lose that powerful sense of history. For older supporters who have been making that 'pilgrimage' for maybe half a century or more, there are decades of precious memories held in that place and it can be heart-breaking to see it demolished in the blink of an eye. If a club does relocate to an out-of-town site or – in the case of Bolton – to another town – you are taking a genuine hub or heartbeat of the community out of its natural setting. Most new grounds are, of course, all-seater stadia. I would argue that the loss of terracing at most football stadiums has been huge, both in terms of atmosphere and aesthetic appeal. They created the bulk of the atmosphere, the sounds and sights which first attracted many of us, and they still do at lower-league and non-league clubs such as Exeter with its imposing Big Bank. [8] Equally disappointing are many of the soulless settings and unimaginative stadium designs which we now find at the likes of Southampton, Derby, Scunthorpe, Colchester...Characterless industrial or retail sites cannot replicate the terraced streets and chimney pots of yesteryear, the type brought to life on canvas by LS Lowry in both *The Football Match* and *Going to the Match*. [9]. Whereas most of those old grounds had unique characteristics and even eccentricities – such as the Cottage at Fulham or the Dolls House at Bradford Park Avenue – many of the post-1990 stadiums which have been constructed tend to be Subbuteo or Lego-like identikit designs, which lack any identifying features or architectural details. Far too many look as if they have come off a conveyor belt and have been dropped into place, like a new McDonalds outlet. In a sense, for me the lack of atmosphere in many modern grounds and their drab settings are connected. By creating these out-of-town, park-the-car and walk-in grounds, you arguably lose that sense of occasion; of joining a seething mass, a crowd walking from the town centre or railway station, through the back streets, towards a ground situated in the heart of its community. That collective walk – which you still get at a traditional venue such as Portman Road – helps to create the carnival atmosphere which Lowry evokes, in *Going to the Match*; the anticipation building as everyone makes their way towards a special event. I felt it as a small child, and still do today.

In an ideal world, clubs rebuild an existing ground or, if this is not possible, relocate in the same neighbourhood, as has been the case at the likes of Tottenham and Arsenal. Unsurprisingly, it is usually the PL clubs who can afford the luxury of these prime site relocations. However, Rodney had asked me to find him a blueprint for the lower-league and non-league clubs which don't have either vast income streams or a wealthy owner. What would be on my shopping list or blueprint for a relocation? Somewhere you can easily access by foot and public transport, rather than solely relying on cars. An attractive setting. A ground which provides a choice in terms of terraces or seating, where you can stand at an end or on the side. Somewhere with character, where there are interesting architectural features to feast your eyes on. A stadium which has been imaginatively designed so that it is modern yet manages to evoke the rich history which – after all – is what makes English football unique and special. With my manager's hat on, I would want it to be the sort of place which would have potential new players wanting to sign, on the spot!...It sounds like a mission improbable or pipe dream. However, I was feeling quietly confident when I picked Rodney up from a railway station in Dorset that he would agree that I had managed to go one better than a mere blueprint or wish list. We were heading off to something a little different, in Thomas Hardy's Casterbridge, in reality the pretty, historic market town of Dorchester.

I had been to Dorchester Town FC's new Avenue Stadium a few years before and instantly fell in love with it. For me, it demonstrates what can be achieved in either the lower divisions or non-league by a football club relocating, if someone is willing to take the time and use his or her imagination to create something 'outside the box'. Care and creativity do not have to cost extra money. Perhaps it is telling that The Avenue was not designed by a 'football architect', under pressure from a developer, local council or a football club to deliver a 'no-thrills' stadium for the cheapest price possible. That is not to say that The Avenue was more expensive than the featureless new grounds which were constructed around the same time. As a point of comparison, Scunthorpe's Glanford Park – which opened in 1988 – cost £2.5 million to build; the Magpie's Avenue, completed in 1990, cost £3 million. While Scunthorpe deserve credit for leading the way in the stadium revolution – it was the first new purpose-built FL ground since the 1950s – it is a soulless affair both inside and out. You could almost mistake it for a warehouse or retail outlet. In stark contrast, The Avenue puts many of the grounds which have been built since to shame. It is an easy ten-minute walk from the town centre and two train stations. Despite being located on a retail park, the approach has been tastefully landscaped, and the stadium is surrounded by trees. The main entrance evokes the Edwardian era with its (mostly) brick façade. There are twin staircases topped with ornate, pillared roofs and a traditional clock on a central gable. The use of brickwork – rather than raw concrete – means that the characterful main building now looks weathered rather than tired. That gabled clock on the outside is matched by one in the centre of the main stand. Each corner of the ground has a quaint turret-like cottage housing practical things from a snack bar to groundsman's equipment. Everywhere you look there are balancing features such as a pair of covered side terraces separated by matching towers decorated with attractive porthole windows, similar sized covered home end and open away terraces, two open terraces either side of the main stand. That beautiful main stand towers over the other spectator areas yet manages to bring them all together. Somehow the architects have designed four very different sides but also created a sense of unity. The Duchy of Cornwall has delivered a quite brilliant stadium, immediately identifiable and unique. Admittedly, if your idea of new stadium design is cutting-edge modernity, curving smoked glass and steel, then the Magpies' home will disappoint. [10] It is unapologetically traditional, in that sense. Nor would it provide a template for top division clubs. What it does have, though, is plenty of soul, character and warmth, features lacking in many smaller new grounds. My advice to any lower league or non-league club looking to relocate would be to visit The Avenue before committing to yet another identikit design.

I must thank the Magpies' coach Brian Churchill who was kind enough to give us a guided tour. He told us that the setting unfortunately seems to inspire visiting players, and I imagine it is also a favourite for visiting away fans too. Talking of inspiration, The Avenue is a wonderful reminder that football stadium design should never be solely about practicalities such as capacity and car parks.

[11] As I have already suggested, imaginative design and attention to architectural detail do not have to cost more money. They simply require more careful thought. Dorchester Town FC have a home which would be the envy of many EFL 2 clubs; it wasn't even a match day when Rodney and I visited, but there was still that thrill for both of us of going through one of the turnstiles and surveying our surroundings. I can think of modern out-of-town grounds, such as Colchester, where I haven't felt a similar buzz, even though I was watching an FA Cup tie; the sterile setting and the stadium left me cold. The Magpies, by contrast, have a genuine (treelined) Theatre of Dreams, in a great location, a perfect footballing stage. [12]

Casterbridge House, Dorchester, 20/04/2023.

1. I even had first-hand experience of the sensation of being in a crush. It was a 1968 European Cup quarter-final against Polish champions Gornik Zabrze. We were in the uncovered scoreboard end as Dad had trouble securing tickets. As always, I positioned my stool against a barrier. That evening, lots of fans came in late and, in the surge, I found myself pinned against the barrier. In future, Dad would always place my stool behind a barrier.
2. Simon Inglis, *The Football Grounds of England and Wales*, p. 12.
3. Inglis' book offers a reminder that Everton had played at Anfield (1894-92), before Liverpool FC were even formed.
4. Inglis' book notes that "the Halifax manager liked to sign new players in the nearby railway station, before they had the chance to see the ground." I'm not surprised!
5. Just four years after my visit, the Valley was abandoned by Charlton (1985-1992) and the photographs taken during this period tend to focus on the mountainous East Terrace as it was rapidly overtaken by a jungle of weeds: eerie, haunting, yet still mightily impressive in its sheer size.

6. Simon Inglis probably spoke for many of us 'traditional football ground fans' when he wrote the following about Bradford's old wooden stand, back in 1983: "So many apparent disadvantages, yet this is one of my favourite stands; quaint, run-down and uncomfortable certainly, but homely, and I think fully deserving preservation." That now cruelly ironic description stands as a reminder to all of us of the dangers of nostalgia. In addition, despite the fact that I still yearn for some of those echoing, atmospheric terraces of yesteryear, I would suggest that no one in their right mind who visited the Old Wembley in its latter years would swap it for the New one.

7. In reference to Luton's hemmed-in ground, Inglis observes that when the club moved in, "there was little to indicate how cramped the site would become in future years. A picture taken soon after 1905 shows an open field surrounded by white railings", p. 205. Even if a ground might not change, its surroundings can.

8. We have chosen not to enter the debate about whether traditional terracing is safe or not; or whether rail seating offers 'safe standing'. This is solely because it requires expertise about health and safety which are beyond our knowledge. What I do know is that the current situation of people continually standing in areas designed for sitting is far from ideal, both in terms of safety and the tension between fans that it can create, as I experienced first-hand at the FA Cup Final last year.

9. Lowry's *The Football Match* (1949) sold for £5.6 million in 2011, while *Going to the Match* (1953) – painted for a Football Association competition – was bought by the PFA for £1.9 million in 1999.

10. In case this description of The Avenue gives the impression that Dorchester Town FC is an old-school, traditional club, I should point out that they are now a fan-owned club, something we have already briefly explored in *Life's A Pitch*. Their website sets out the club ethos: "We believe that

football belongs to the people. Not to the property developers, the oligarchs or the oil-rich nations ...but to the fans. To the people who turn up each week, come rain or shine. As we all know, most football clubs up and down the country are privately owned organisations with wealthy investors plugging large funding holes with their own cash. As Dorchester Town FC found out under the previous ownership of a property developer, and what many clubs are discovering today, no matter how big they are this is a rather unsustainable business model that has seen some clubs cease to exist. In 2015, Dorchester Town FC transformed the club into a Community Benefit Society, thereby allowing fans of the club to become owners themselves. We believe that thousands of fans owning an equal share is a more sustainable, not to mention appropriate, way of doing things. No one can own more than one share in Dorchester Town FC, no matter how much money they put in. Our system is, 'one owner, one share, one vote'. This is to protect the club from being bought by one unscrupulous owner. There are quite a few doing the rounds in non-league we feel." While this may have created something of a glass ceiling for the club's on-field ambitions, it clearly is something which fans can feel proud of and part of. In addition, five years ago they installed a 3G pitch, another topic we have already discussed in this book, which has allowed the ground to be used all week, for school football, youth training, walking and disability football, making The Avenue a genuine hub in the community.

11. The Avenue does have both: plentiful car parking and a decent spectator capacity in excess of 5,200.

12. The Avenue feels to me like a venue designed for 'normal' fans, rather than somewhere driven by what Roy Keane contemptuously referred to as the 'prawn sandwich brigade'. Call me old-fashioned, if you like, but for me a football ground should centre on the loyal supporters,

rather than be driven by corporate hospitality or designed as a general entertainments' venue which just happens to hold football matches. For me, watching football is not about sitting behind glass in a private box, or even watching replays on a giant screen. I genuinely believe that an increasing number of people are getting their footballing fix from non-league football because they can still get that 'real' experience and connection at a ground, something which is, arguably, absent now at many top division stadiums.

CHAPTER 8:
MEDIA MOUNTAIN

On the final day of the 'regular' 2022-23 EFL season, Rodney shared the images with me – from *Sky Sports* on *YouTube* – of Sam Hoskins's glorious winner which sealed promotion for one of my former clubs, Northampton Town. Three different angles, perfectly capturing his exquisite chest and volley winner. I messaged back: "What a strike! He can look back on that footage with great pride. Memories made for ever!" It reminded me of the revolution which has taken place over the past decades both in terms of technology and coverage. Even in the lower divisions, the in-depth content on television and online is a visual feast: every game filmed, every goal captured for posterity. Every club with its own media department, putting together in-house content: interviews, behind-the-scenes match-day footage, social media goal celebration gifs...As a player, I would have relished and embraced this 'media frenzy'. Back in the 1970s – when I was establishing my playing career and Rodney was falling in love with the game as a young fan – we were mainly limited to newspaper articles, programmes and photographs, all lovingly collected in scrapbooks. As the contents yellow and curl up with age, I'm tempted to make a simple comparison: yesteryear's famine versus today's feast, but it is all relative. After all, we had our weekly dates with *Match of the Day* and *The Big Match*, while my dad's generation grew up in a vanished age before television coverage, when the print media journalists were kings...

Having been born in 1958, I was part of the first proper television generation. Yes, the BBC had been broadcasting twenty years earlier, but only to 10,000 homes in London. At the beginning of the

50s, when England first entered the World Cup, most people in Britain had never set eyes on a television set, never mind rented or owned one. Yet by the time I came along, the popularity of the Coronation coverage (1953) and the arrival of ITV (1955) saw the number of households with a set rise from 764,000 (1951), 4 million (1955), 10 million (1960), to 13 million by the mid-1960s, in time for the '66 World Cup Final which I vividly remember watching from our sofa. That World Cup fever saw the BBC transfer its *Match of the Day* weekly highlights – one game only, as the title suggests – from BBC 2 to BBC 1, which, I guess, was a statement in itself: football had genuinely arrived as an important element of television broadcasting. [1]

It makes me feel extremely old to recall that my early televised football watching was in black-and-white, and without the 'luxury' of slow-motion action replays. With *Match of the Day* already a firm favourite in our house, Granada Television [2] now offering Sunday afternoon highlights shows from 1968, and with colour arriving, it felt as if we were spoilt. In terms of domestic football, this state of affairs remained much the same throughout my early playing career. Yes, those highlight shows began to cover three matches as opposed to one, but that was about it. As a young professional at Stockport, in the shadows of the two Manchester and Liverpool clubs, you were unlikely to feature as the Granada match of the week. For fans, particularly in the lower reaches of the Football League, you either went to the match or missed out on the action and goals. There was no 'catch up' option. Up until the mid-1980s, most Football League matches – including top-tier games – simply disappeared, fading images in players and supporters' memory banks. [3] Much the same applied to radio coverage. There was the Saturday *Sports Report* at 5pm, with its iconic musical introduction and classified results. However, many local BBC stations only arrived in the 1980s and the idea of them offering live commentary of matches was a mere pipe dream. Generally speaking, you had to rely on your local newspaper keeping you updated, including the now vanished Saturday early evening football editions which carried hastily assembled match reports, hot off the printing press. [4] I have fond memories of being sent to the local newsagent by my dad. There was a genuine sense of anticipation, waiting for the Manchester Evening News van to screech to a halt, the side door slid open, and a huge bundle of Pink 'Uns flung out. Rather than bring the paper straight home, I would spend time on the street corner, scanning the results, scorers, attendances, the latest league tables...before heading inside and passing it on to Dad. [5]

All these nostalgic memories emphasise how rapid the more recent changes and developments have been in terms of radio, television and newspaper coverage of football. Arguably the two biggest televisual landmarks were 1983, when both BBC and ITV began broadcasting league matches live, and 1992 with the dawn of the PL/Sky revolution. The biggest fear in terms of live coverage had always been that it would affect the attendances. Would fans still pay for travel and tickets if they could watch the same match in the comfort of their own home or in the local pub? Would it take the edge or magic away from going to a match? As for the world wide web, it has created an ever-changing 'brave new world' and football is part of that...

Today's mass communication coverage of football is a microcosm of the more general evolution and revolution which is taking place in our increasingly technology-driven society. New platforms have emerged – such as social networking services and podcasts – while the way we view traditional media has also changed, such as people now reading newspapers online. Once upon a time we relied almost exclusively on local and national reporters to offer us insights into the sport. Today, we have a multitude of competing voices: professional journalists/ex-players, the clubs themselves, and fellow football fans. For this chapter, we have broken the current media mountain into those three 'voices'. We will begin by exploring the coverage offered by 'objective' broadcasters and journalists, both local and national. We can then examine football clubs' in-house media. Finally, we can turn to the increasing amount of coverage offered up by football fans themselves. [6] As a generalisation, there are, inevitably, advantages and disadvantages to all three and it is probably only by consuming a mixture of them that a genuine overview of the real picture emerges, be it the fortunes of an individual club or the state of the sport in general. By exploring these avenues, we can then discuss the key question: has football coverage reached saturation point? Is there a surfeit of 'news' – speculation, gossip etc. – on radio, television and online? Is today's football-related media a genuine feast, or is it possibly a case that less was more?

The night before we put this chapter together, ITV offered a re-run of the dramatic title decider at Anfield, in 1989, when Arsenal scored a second goal in stoppage time to overhaul Liverpool on goal difference and be crowned champions. Re-watching the game was a genuine eye-opener: the far more physical nature of the contest, the lack of alternative camera angles, even the crude-looking table which was brought on to the pitch for the post-match presentation of the trophy. It was reminiscent of a camping table or a school sports day! In some respects, revisiting the relatively low-key nature of the broadcast was refreshing, yet it was also a stark reminder of how Sky Sports has revolutionised both football coverage and the game's image. English football in the 70s and 80s – in the twin shadows of hooliganism and crumbling stadia – had such a seedy reputation but, in the wake of the positivity of Italia 90, Sky brought a genuine razzmatazz to the sport. Huge credit must go to charismatic 'anchor man' Jeff Stelling who, from 1994, hosted their Saturday afternoon marathon of discussion, rolling scores and live reports, animating his panel of ex-professional pundits. [7] It was a world away from terrestrial television's more sober coverage: BBC's *Grandstand* (1958-2007) and ITV's *World of Sport* (1965-85). In addition, Sky's coverage of live matches upped the tempo: the pre-match build-up, multiple camera angles, cinematic sound effects, post-match analysis...Many football fans view the dual emergence of the Premier League and Sky Sports as an 'elite' modern marriage, but it is easy to forget that Sky has also offered inclusive, extensive coverage of the previously neglected EFL divisions, while BT Sports has helped to raise the profile of the top-tier of non-league football. The breaking-up of the BBC/ITV monopoly has led to a far wider reach in terms of television coverage of the football pyramid. Those satellite channels have, arguably, democratised the game's image, making the lower leagues both more visible and attractive. Sky's revolutionary approach has also forced terrestrial channels to up their own game, as it were. You could argue that Sky overhypes football. As one journalist wrote: "If every Sunday is 'Super Sunday', then there's no such thing as Super Sunday." Nevertheless, for those of us old enough to recall how negative English football's image was back in the 70s and 80s, it is great to see the sport talked up again.

I think it is also great that radio still has a major role to play. In many respects, nothing compares to listening to a live commentary on the radio. Dad and I shared many a happy evening listening to a midweek match while Mum was next door watching the television. There is a unique set of skills required by a radio commentator, painting the pictures for his audience: the patterns of play, goals, the reactions of the bench and the crowd. In addition, stations such as *Talk Sport* offer listeners endless debate – amidst the 'hot air' – about clubs' fortunes, the managerial merry-go-rounds etc. Yes, often the pundits are there to be deliberately provocative or controversial, in order to spark interaction with and reaction from fans, but that, arguably, is part of the fun. After all, football is a game of opinions. [8]

The world wide web has, to a large extent, killed off traditional print media. Why, for example, would you buy a (physical) newspaper when you can read the latest news online in a constantly updated format? It is hard to find a counterargument. However, for me, one of the drawbacks of website-based football reading is that it cannot replicate the ability to sit there with a double page spread of the paper, scanning all the results and league tables. Instead, I find myself moving between half a dozen tabs, rather than being able to take in the full picture.

Inevitably, more and more national and regional newspapers are asking us to pay for online content, to become subscribers. I'm sure I'm not alone in hesitating when I see these financial demands to access articles. The problem, I guess, is that we have become so used to being able to access online content for free. Nevertheless, as Rodney observes, we wouldn't expect to walk into a newsagents and pick up a national or local paper without paying for it, so we probably shouldn't in the virtual world either. If we want objective, traditional 'print' journalism to survive, it will be online and someone has to pay for it. Without national and local reporters offering their insights, we would be relying on the clubs themselves and fans. As we will explore, both have their own agendas, and it is vital that professional journalists continue to offer us that third 'voice'. When things are going badly wrong at a football club – both on the field and off it – the first thing an owner often does is ban the local press. This in itself should represent a reminder to us all about the vital role which the local media plays, investigating and reporting on a club's state of health.

Early in this chapter I observed that football clubs' in-house media is a relatively new phenomenon. In my playing days, the match programme might offer up a brief manager or captain's column, possibly ghost-written by the editor. That was it in terms of most clubs' output. Today, even the most modest EFL club has a department dedicated to media coverage and even non-league clubs often employ a media officer. Some clubs even have their own 'tv channel'. The benefits are, to a certain extent, obvious. A club's website and social media platforms can access all areas, offering us the opportunity to peep behind the curtain in ways we never used to: from interviews with a club owner or member of staff, to alternative footage of a match. In theory, this adds a new level of transparency. In practice, we must take some of the content with a degree of scepticism. A post-match interview with a manager or a post-season update with a CEO will, inevitably, be differently handled when it is in-house. Questions may well have been agreed upon pre-recording, or even carefully rehearsed. Club-driven media has offered us a whole new stream of football content, but – by its nature – it will never be wholly objective. It will be sugar-coated and selective. As we recorded this chapter, Rodney and I agreed that it is far healthier when clubs invite outside journalists to conduct some of those interviews, rather than keeping it all in-house. Nevertheless, I think it is safe to say that football fans are able to interact with and access their beloved club as never before.

This brings us on to fan-driven content. We have come a long way since 1986 when an independently published fanzine *When Saturday Comes* was launched. [9] While a number of printed fanzines still flourish, the alternative avenues available to supporter-writers have proliferated. WSC's own evolution illustrates this. While its print media magazine form continues, now with 'staff writers' in addition to commissioned fan articles, it also offers a twice-monthly podcast and both social media and website content. The virtual world has enabled any football fan to voice his or her own opinions, from a throwaway post-match tweet all the way through to full-on podcasts and match day blogs.

This is where – as a former player and manager – I must put my hand up and confess that I have a few issues. Freedom of speech is a fundamental right in any democratic society. Football fans spend huge sums of money passionately following their teams. They are entitled to offer their opinions, whether it is venting their frustrations during a poor performance or questioning the running of their club on a podcast. Obviously, it is questionable whether they can front a show with the polished charisma of a professional broadcaster like Stelling, and the online fan content is variable in terms of quality. Understandably. What I would question is the fan's ability to analyse a match or a manager's tactics with a similar level of knowledge as that of an ex-professional. This ties in, I guess, with my argument about the need to bring ex-pros into refereeing. The insights you gain from a long career in the game cannot be matched, in my opinion, by the layman. I don't want this to sound condescending. However, it is far too easy for a football supporter to assume that s/he is an expert, or to downplay ex-players' expertise. You wouldn't visit a doctor, dentist, plumber, electrician, or solicitor and argue that your knowledge was greater than theirs. Yet as football fans there is a tendency to believe that it is a level playing field in terms of understanding the game. Some fans feel that they are as qualified to analyse a football game as ex-players are. In addition – and here I am as guilty as anyone – when we watch a game, we sometimes think that we could have selected a better side or come up with better tactics. We haven't attended the week's training or possess an insider's knowledge of a knock a player might be carrying, or his current state of mind. The football supporter may be well placed to comment on the way a club is being run, or how it communicates with its fan base. However, the virtual world has enabled anyone who so desires to share their opinions in areas of the game where, arguably, they lack the in-depth knowledge to do so with any level of expertise. [10] I hope that readers take this in the spirit it is intended, rather than find my comments disrespectful or offensive!

Unsurprisingly, Rodney takes a somewhat different view on fan-driven content. He observes that top class players have often proved to be both uninspiring managers and poor pundits, while both professional broadcasters and 'amateur' fans can offer insightful observations on a match. I cannot argue with the first comment, and I do feel that many player-pundits have their own agendas, but I still feel that the best in-depth analysis of a game will come from people who have played the sport.

We are faced today with a melting pot of football content, made up of professional journalists and broadcasters, ex-players, club in-house content, and fan-created material. As part of his research for this chapter, Rodney spoke to podcaster Benjamin Bloom, who offered up the analogy that it is like a long restaurant menu which, as consumers, we can scan and then select from, choosing both the type of content we want and where it comes from. [11] Some may seek out the immediate, 'fast food' raw explosion of a video of a fan reacting from the stands, others might prefer a delayed, more considered, 'fine dining' post-match analysis. Some will want both. In a not dissimilar way, while some viewers enjoy the hour-long build-up to a live televised game, I prefer to switch on as the game is about to start. We could fill an entire book with a debate about the variable quality of the media mountain but, ultimately, it is also a question of personal taste.

Despite my earlier rose-tinted memories of the magic of waiting for the Saturday Pink 'Un to arrive at my local newsagent, or the comforting sound of that old-fashioned music heralding BBC radio's *Sports Report*, there is little point in wallowing in nostalgia. Like society, football coverage has evolved. Certain things have been eroded, including local BBC radio and the traditional print media. Others will no doubt disappear, such as match day programmes, possibly. [12]

One thing which I feel must remain sacrosanct or ringfenced is the tradition of 'Saturday 3pm'. Televised matches must never encroach on that. If the timeless charm of 'going to the match' on a Saturday afternoon has to compete with a live TV game, then the fallout could be a serious one. Not at PL level, possibly, but lower down the football pyramid. Particularly on a wet and windy day in February.

In terms of sheer quantity, we have never had it so good – to paraphrase a former Prime Minister – and, as the number of options on that media menu continues to grow, it is up to us, surely, to be increasingly choosy and discerning about our selections. There is, inevitably, plenty of 'clickbait' shoddy content out there, but part of the pleasure is seeking out either our comfort food – the ritual of watching *Match of the Day* might be an example – or being adventurous and sampling something new. Given the speed with which technology is evolving, coupled with the media mountain of football-related content already out there, producers in the future will have to be increasingly inventive to grab our attention. That, surely, can only be a good thing for all of us consumers.

The Lowry Hotel, Chapel Wharf, Salford, 30/05/2023

1. *Match of the Day* had originally been created by the BBC as a one-off series, a trial run to prepare the cameramen for England's 1966 World Cup.
2. Other ITV regions either offered their own local match or picked up LWT's *The Big Match*.
3. It was only halfway through my playing days that clubs themselves began to take advantage of the VCR revolution, taping games and putting together season highlights videos.
4. Daniel Gray's *Black Boots & Football Pinks: 50 Lost Wonders of the Beautiful Game* explores the magic of these Saturday football specials: "It was an astonishing accomplishment: a detailed, printed record of a match starting at 3pm could be read in the windy streets by teatime."

5. I knew, after all, that once Dad got his hands on the paper it would be hours before I got a look in!

6. We have chosen not to explore one particular area of the football media mountain in this chapter: printed books. You could publish an entire volume on this subject. It is another arena where fans increasingly rival professional journalists and ex-players in a highly competitive marketplace. Nick Hornby's *Fever Pitch*, published in 1992, can arguably be seen as a landmark in football print media history. It has inspired a library full of fan-focused books.

7. Stelling's impact is a reminder that, while there is a tendency today for television broadcasts to be dominated by ex-players, the impact of a trained journalist as the 'anchor' can be instrumental to the show's appeal. As a sidenote, there is clearly a downside to Sky's impact, with fans forced to travel to matches at inconvenient times, be it a Saturday teatime, or a Sunday in a country where trains have a tendency to turn into bus replacement services. Television today dictates the football calendar. As Alex Ferguson memorably put it: "When you shake hands with the devil, you have to pay the price. Television is God at the moment." In addition, we are bombarded with (often meaningless) data and statistic-driven content.

8. This is where we gain from having the insights, for example, of a mixed panel, as it were: broadcasters, pundits, or even someone like Simon Jordan who can offer an insider's knowledge of how a club is run, or how contract negotiations are conducted.

9. Within two years of being launched, *WSC* was available in newsagents nationwide. In more recent times it has branched out into book publishing too.

10. Social media and video-sharing platforms have, in addition, encouraged people to seek their fifteen minutes of fame. Critical commentary is one thing but, in the worst-case scenarios, anonymous keyboard warriors drip-feed

unacceptable personal abuse. As we all know, there is a distinctly dark side to the web.

11. Ipswich Town fan Benjamin Bloom is a podcaster who has evolved his online football content from offering informal post-match reviews and analysis from his car seat, to delivering polished coverage examining football in general, focusing specifically on The Championship. Asked about the increasing significance of fan-created media football content, Bloom feels that the growing popularity of Arsenal Fan TV (AFTV) in the *YouTube* community – created in 2012 – "destroyed the barrier to entry", demonstrating that fan-led content could rival both traditional journalism and a club's in-house material in terms of both quality and viewing figures. Bloom observes that fan-led material has the obvious benefit of being "relatable", unlike a club's in-house content which will, understandably, "toe the line". He considers the present and foreseeable future to be a case of a Darwinian survival of the fittest or most inventive and articulate. Whether the producer is a trained journalist, ex-player or fan, it is a constant challenge of "building and maintaining an audience". Bloom senses that, ultimately, media content "will all converge somewhere". This theory is backed up, for example, by the increasing number of supporters who, having built up an online presence, have either crossed over into mainstream journalism or exist in both worlds. This blurring of the boundaries, and the emergence of imaginative fan-created content, are aspects which Bloom feels have helped to provide us with a satisfying "meritocracy".

12. You have to wonder whether the recent cutbacks in local BBC radio coverage is simply a case of the corporation tightening its belt, or whether this spells the beginning of the end. Arguably where the demise of local print media is most keenly felt is in the lower reaches of non-league football. Unsurprisingly, most of these clubs cannot offer the level of in-house coverage provided by EFL clubs, nor

can non-league fans rely on national media. *The Non-League Paper* is a rare voice in this respect, but its nationwide distribution is patchy. Here in Cornwall, for example, the *Sunday Independent* was the 'bible' for football fans and its loss – after more than 200 years of publication – is a significant blow.

CHAPTER 9:
PLAYER PATHWAYS &
'DREAM ACADEMIES'

In the previous chapter I could have highlighted one of my genuine bugbears about today's media coverage: the suggestion that top-flight football only began in 1992 with the arrival of the PL. There are professional broadcasters, ex-players and supporters who are all guilty of dismissing what came before then. We are bombarded with statistics such as 'top goal scorer in PL history', or 'this club has reached the PL for the first time in its history'...In much the same way, some people refer with hushed reverence to 'football academies' as if their arrival/branding created the first ever 'player pathway'. Believe me, nothing could be further from the truth. Player pathways existed long before the Elite Player Performance Plan, the PL and so-called academies. They were there long before the term 'pathway' had been coined as one of the latest fashionable football buzzwords. [1] There never has been, nor ever will be, a single route into the professional game...

The statistics – in terms of conversion rate – from organised youth team football to becoming a professional in the top-tier of English football have always made for sober reading. The blurb on the back cover of Michael Calvin's 2017 book *No Hunger in Paradise* suggests that the success rate is 0.012%. This grim figure alone should probably have us asking what purpose is served by so-called football academies, particularly at the elite PL clubs, which process hundreds of footballers in a single age group as each individual in each crop attempts to stay on the conveyor belt from Foundation

(9-11), through Youth Development (12-16) to Professional Development (17-23).

A brief overview of my own journey – from kicking a ball about in our own backyard to making my Football League debut as a teenager – will offer you an insight into some of the issues I have with today's club-run football academies. In some respects, my pathway was a typical one back in the 1970s. From representing my primary school, I was selected for various Manchester Boys district sides. By the age of twelve, I was playing school matches, district games, and also competing in a local Sunday league. I couldn't get enough football, sometimes playing four times a week. Where I struggled was when – like many boys selected for their district squads – I was invited over to Manchester United's iconic Cliff training ground for twice weekly coaching sessions. I was, by nature, quite a shy, introverted boy. The twin sights of this vast arena and scores of young footballers overwhelmed me and I told my dad that I didn't want to go back there. I simply wasn't mature enough to cope with that type of environment.

In the end, my route into the professional game involved a couple of pieces of good fortune. First, due to a misunderstanding, I arrived late for a Stockport County trial match one Sunday morning, meaning that my preferred midfield position had already been filled. Asked to play as a striker for the first ever time, I notched a first half hattrick and inadvertently discovered my natural attacking role. Second, County's first team coach had decided to watch that game in the local park, spotted my performance, and invited me to train with the club's youth team just a couple of days later. Schoolboy forms swiftly followed and, at sixteen, I was one of four young players offered a two-year apprenticeship. A few months later, I scored on my first team debut and a fourteen-year career in the professional game had started. Many people within the game do not believe in the concept of luck, but I promise you that it is something which every young player needs, alongside natural ability, mental strength and resolve.

I often ask myself whether, with today's academies contracting players as young as nine, and scouts making value judgements about children far younger still, how I might have fared. For one thing, I simply hadn't been ready for the sheer size and scale of United's Cliff set up. I struggled to cope with the pressure of being 'on show'. I sense that life in a 'football factory' would not have been one in which I would have thrived. I would probably have felt lost. I was far better off having the freedom to play in a variety of teams, including the opportunity to still have fun with my school mates. Fun is such a key factor for any football-loving kid. It can be swiftly drained away if the sport becomes too serious, too early in life.

When I signed on as one of just four apprentices at Stockport, I still felt that I was an individual. It was a non-pressurised environment that gave me space and time to develop. In a large academy, stockpiled with young players, would I have simply become a number? Several coaches who have been involved in PL and EFL academies admit that there are plenty of young players retained each year simply to make up the numbers, to allow the few, genuine young stars to shine. One director of football told Michael Calvin:

"Football academies, and the staff that run them, are fully aware that the vast majority of the kids are not good enough and are only there to support the very best coming through. Most of the kids, and to an extent their parents, are being used. My personal view is that the whole venture is morally bankrupt". [2]

Those are strong words indeed. What we must ask ourselves is whether it matters that most academy footballers will never 'make it', not even in the higher echelons of non-league football, never mind in the PL. If clubs do not deceive those boys and their parents by offering them false hope, yet *do* offer them a safe environment in which the importance of education is placed on a par with the game itself, is any harm being done? Possibly not. In some respects, there has been progress made. Unlike in my early playing days at a professional club, when the importance of further education was not emphasised and mental health was not even a vague consideration, clubs today are obliged to look after their young players, be it ensuring that they continue their academic journey, or protecting them from pushy, abusive parents on the touchlines, or from changing room 'banter', something which I know only too well can easily cross over into mental bullying.

One of my issues with football academies is the nature of the relationship between the clubs and its very young players. If these boys were simply training under the umbrella of a PL or EFL club, I would not have a problem. However, what I do question is whether we have the moral right to legally contract pre-pubescent youngsters to a professional organisation. I have seen photographs of impressionable kids signing their contracts like seasoned pros. Inevitably, this will have a profound impact on many of them. In addition, this is an environment where, at the end of each year, they will either be re-selected or rejected. Should we be labelling any twelve-year-olds – never mind ten-year-olds – as failures?

Psychologically, that can be damaging. That would be considered immoral in almost any other setting. On a purely footballing level, I am not convinced that you can make accurate judgement calls on such young boys. You simply do not know how they are going to grow, technically, physically or mentally. Having been involved in youth football for many years now, I have seen, first hand, some young players who you initially think have outstanding talent but who then stand still, as it were. Others, who you might have been less sure about at first suddenly shoot up in size and stature, physically and mentally. There is no way that an academy coach can turn around and reliably inform a young boy — and his parents — that he is not going to make it. Equally, that coach cannot accurately predict that a youngster will go on to live the dream. The man would need a crystal ball. [3]

A second concern of mine is how money has been allowed to become a factor in youth football. This includes PL academies being allowed to cherry-pick players from smaller clubs in return for set compensation fees, including children as young as ten; financial 'incentives' offered to parents; and private 'academies' selling the dream, quite literally. It seems to me that the modern-day culture of 'football as business' has been allowed to spread like a cancer, drip-feeding down into an age range where the game should be solely about enjoyment and carefree fun.

Between 2014-18, *Mirror Football* conducted an investigation, the results of which suggested that top academies were viewed by their clubs' owners as potential sources of revenue, as opposed to player pathways. The published statistics indicated that the 'Big Six' had collectively sold £114 million worth of ex-academy talent during this four-year period, £64 million of which concerned players who had not played a single first team match for their parent club. The *Mirror* described these academies as "cash factories". The figures for Manchester City made staggering reading: more than £70.6 million for academy products who had played ten games or fewer; over £44.4 million for players who had not made a single senior appearance. [4] Does this not undermine the image of top clubs providing centres of excellence with a genuine player pathway from academy football into their PL sides? If these academies are being run as businesses, does that make the term somewhat misleading, if not hollow? [5]

A third major issue for me concerns the final stages of that journey. Back in the 1970s, at fifteen years of age I was already playing in competitive men's fixtures for Stockport County, in the Lancashire 'A' League against, for example, Everton's third team. What that meant was that, by the time I made my Football League debut, I was − to a certain extent − battle-hardened. [6] Today, FA regulations do not allow fifteen-year-olds to play against adults, presumably for safeguarding reasons. However, with competitive reserve team leagues now abandoned, what we have instead are academy Under 18 and Under 21 leagues. If you have ever watched any of these games you will have noticed that these fixtures are virtually non-contact, uncompetitive matches. [7] It is an almost surreal environment which − while the games themselves may well encourage the development of technical ability − simply does not prepare players for the rigours of PL or EFL football, where teams are fighting for every point and both league status and players' careers are on the line. Rodney picked out a recent quote from an experienced, current professional player who had grown up in the death-throes of the traditional reserve leagues. The player described the current academy matches as "pointless":

"I have to say that I think U21s football right now is pretty pointless, it doesn't mean anything...I remember playing reserve team football when I started, just before the point when they changed it...I played against really good players...The football [today] is not real, it doesn't translate to actual men's football and for a lot of these kids it isn't helping them improve...A lot of kids completely fall out of football because of that jump, because how they're taught to play in the academies at the big clubs just doesn't correlate to men's football...When you are playing in a team and the win bonus is everything because it pays somebody's mortgage or it pays for their car, it's a very different thing to playing in the '21s." [8]

These comments are not from a journalist looking for an attention-grabbing 'story', or a disgruntled ex-footballer who ended up on the scrapheap. Janoi Donacien is an established EFL player with over 300 competitive games under his belt. He has experienced life in an elite academy, at Villa, but also a succession of loan moves, and then the rigours of lower-division football at Accrington Stanley. I would echo many of his sentiments. In theory, a seemingly obvious solution to this chasm – what Donacien calls "the jump" – is to loan these young and inexperienced players out to lower division clubs. Rodney cited the example of two current England internationals who were 'blooded' by parent club Sheffield United on loan at Northampton: Kyle Walker (in 2008) and Dominic Calvert-Lewin (in 2015). In both of their cases, the temporary switches clearly worked. However, for each of those success stories, there are countless others where an academy product simply could not adapt to competitive men's football. As a director of football at a non-league club, I know several managers at grassroots level who simply are not willing to take that calculated risk, unconvinced that a young loanee, or ex-professional who has been released by an EFL club, will be physically and mentally ready for the fire-and-brimstone which awaits them. This predicament seriously calls into question the academy 'pathway'. Modern football is often dismissive of anything which went before it, labelling it as 'old school'. However, in an ideal world, we would return to the old-style competitive reserve leagues, where raw talent rubbed shoulders with seasoned pros. That about-turn seems unlikely, though. Unless an alternative solution is found, as Donacien observes more and more kids will become 'lost boys'. [9]

Of course, rejection is – and always has been – part of the harsh world of football. Most academy players will get rejected at some point on the journey, while many more young footballers will not have been selected for one of these elite establishments in the first place. With my glass half full, I would point out that there are plenty of examples of players who have been let go as teenagers by professional clubs but who have eventually bounced back. Equally, players who have matured later than some, in their early twenties, and have risen through the football pyramid. As I said at the beginning of this chapter, the much vaunted 'academy' system is only one possible route. As someone who has spent the past three decades involved in non-league football, I would throw that out as an alternative pathway, illustrated here by just three of many real-life 'fairy tale' stories...

The Jamie Vardy story is the most recent, dramatic example of how a player's pathway can be a rollercoaster one: released by his local professional club (Sheffield Wednesday) at sixteen; combining non-league football with factory work until he was twenty-four; arriving on the PL stage at twenty-seven; making his England debut at twenty-eight; winning a PL champions' medal at twenty-nine...it is the sort of unlikely tale you might expect from a *Roy of the Rovers* comic.

While the timeline of Vardy's journey is an unusual one, the route he took is far from unique. Many players have made the rise from the non-league pyramid into professional football. Having failed a trial at QPR and rejected an offer from Hull City as a teenager, Stuart Pearce spent five years combining non-league football with his day job as an electrician, before enjoying a long professional career which included 78 England caps and a Championship winners' medal in his final season, four days before his fortieth birthday. Interestingly, he put his success down to two factors:

"I had five-and-a-half seasons there [Wealdstone] which is a hell of a long time in non-league. But I stuck at it and when I was given a chance by Bobby Gould I didn't look back after that. You've got to be lucky – and I was." [10]

That final comment is an important one. Pearce's journey is an inspirational story of a dogged, determined individual, but, as he acknowledges, he also needed the good fortune of a top-flight manager taking a gamble on him. As I remarked earlier in this chapter, while talent allied with grit will, hopefully, be recognised and rewarded at some point, every player also needs that slice of good fortune.

My third and final non-league tale comes from down here in Cornwall where I now live. It concerns Britain's first £1 million goalkeeper, Nigel Martyn. His incredible, and equally unlikely, journey – from Heavy Transport FC to England international – was kickstarted by a bizarre connection between a Cornish shop owner and a tea lady:

"My story of getting recognised was playing for a local team and there was a guy there who owned a carpet shop in St Blaise, who knew the tea lady at Bristol Rovers. He rang her and said, 'We've got a really good young goalkeeper down here.' The tea lady then went in and saw Gerry Francis." [11]

Just as Pearce refers to his good fortune, so does Martyn, adding that it was "a very lucky break". Obviously, luck is only one factor in these three players' stories. Talent and talent spotting are other key ingredients. In a BBC 5 Live interview, Martyn referred to his belief that Cornish football has always been full of "plenty of talent, it's just the opportunity doesn't exist." That, sadly, is probably still the case in the remotest corner of the South-West. However, today the vast scouting system in place in the top divisions of non-league football is such that talented players will, eventually, be spotted. Grassroots football continues to be a genuine potential bouncing board for young, discarded players to relaunch their careers. Sometimes making a detour – branching off the main pathway – is what is required to get back on course.

It would, of course, be churlish to ignore the success stories of English football academies. Phil Foden is a shining example of the elite academy system working; he joined Manchester City as a small child, signed an academy scholarship at sixteen, and has flourished there ever since. Exeter City is a perfect illustration of an EFL club whose academy has functioned successfully on two fronts: offering a conveyor belt of young players who have become first-team players at St James' Park *and* providing an invaluable source of revenue – for a fan-owned club – in terms of lucrative transfer fees. [12] Rather than suggest, simplistically, that academies are the modern-day equivalent of Dickensian workhouses, and that we should dismantle them, I think that the system needs some radical changes, in particular at both ends, as it were.

In summing up, I wouldn't allow club academies to contractually sign players until they are fourteen years old. I would free up younger boys to enjoy their football wherever they want – including training at an academy – rather than being tied down to a professional club. Apart from anything else, this 14+ rule would give these boys an extended opportunity to decide whether they wholeheartedly love the game or not, and whether they are genuinely fully committed to chasing that dream. Let them have fun before they enter the factory. At the other end of the production line, I would bring back traditional reserve leagues. Today's first team squads are far larger than ever before, and academy players would therefore gain invaluable experience by mixing it with seasoned professionals.

Young people – and ambitious parents – chase dreams and PL club badges are powerful beacons which attract many of them, both to the club academies themselves and the money-generating, commercially-driven, franchise style offshoots which a number of football clubs have set up. [13] Before committing to either of these, I would encourage parents to research all the other options close to home. As I have been keen to point out in this chapter, there are several potential pathways out there for young players. There is not a single 'correct' route to take. As my own football journey (as both a player and a coach) illustrates, young footballers are first and foremost individuals who are unpredictable; they develop and flourish – or flounder – at any number of different stages in their formative years. Not everyone leaves on their football journey from the same point of departure, nor arrives at the same destination. Maybe, as the American philosopher Ralph Emerson suggested, football – like life itself – is as much about that journey as it is about the destination. Young footballers, their parents, and their coaches all need to embrace both the excitement and the uncertainty of that adventure.

Bredbury Hall, Stockport, 31/05/2023

1. We might argue that 'academy' is itself a trendy football buzzword. Online definitions include: "a society of distinguished scholars" and "to protect and develop an art". Is it yet another example of football over-stating or hyping its products?
2. Phil Giles, co-director of football at Brentford, cited in 'Death of a Dream', *No Hunger in Paradise*, p. 81.
3. In much the same way, although academies rely heavily on the science of data, no one has invented any gadgets which can measure or predict the future growth of unknowable aspects such as personality, drive and mental strength, key qualities which sometimes only develop as a person matures.
4. *Mirror*, 17/10/2018. The paper does note that "these fees will include performance related bonuses, so it's possible that City will not see all of the £71 million."
5. I guess that the counterargument would be that a club such as Manchester City has sold young players to the likes of Borussia Dortmund, Southampton, Lyon, Monaco and Stuttgart, therefore City have indeed provided them with a pathway into top-flight football.
6. I would argue that we need to take a far more nuanced view on whether fifteen-year-olds should be allowed to

play in adult football. For some boys, who are still transitioning mentally and physically, placing them in the harsh environment of adult football would be the equivalent of throwing them into the lion's den. For others, who have already fully developed, we are potentially and needlessly holding them back. There needs to be a degree of common sense and flexibility, allowing experienced coaches – in conjunction with the player and parents – to make these decisions.

7. I have watched half a dozen of these matches and come away each time convinced that it was not proper football. From what I have seen, the games are more to do with the coaches than the players, in addition to providing emerging referees with gentle 'building blocks' experience.

8. Janoi Donacien, 'JD's Sport', Ipswich Town's matchday programme, 07/04/2023.

9. Rodney threw a left-field grenade to me, pointing out that in many European countries professional reserve sides play competitive football within the football pyramid itself, albeit with a glass ceiling. In France, for example, they can advance to the point of the fourth tier, but no further. Personally, I would not be in favour of that here in England. I instinctively feel that it would undermine the integrity of our pyramid system. Whatever the future solution is to the current void, it will need clubs and coaches to 'invest' in its competitive nature.

10. Cited by BBC online, 19/04/2002.

11. Nigel Martyn, from an interview with Radio Five Live's Test Match Special, cited by Bristol Live, 04/06/2018

12. Ollie Watkins, for example, earned Exeter City an initial transfer fee of £1.8 million when he joined Brentford. His subsequent move to Aston Villa entitled City to a further £3.3 million, before we even include various lucrative add-on clauses. His academy development at City has, indirectly, helped to fund both substantial stadium

redevelopments and significant improvements in terms of training ground infrastructure.

13. These offshoots also sell the dream of offering a genuine pathway. In my experience, it is an illusion, an expensive cul-de-sac. As an example, a boy I know who had trained with one of these organisations was invited to take part in a trial match, presumably sold as a steppingstone. He didn't take part, but still received a letter from the club congratulating him on successfully passing the 'trial', being selected for the next stage...oh, and please send us another cheque!

CHAPTER 10: OVERVIEW

RM: We've taken nine topics and explored each one in terms of the past, present and potential future. Rather than simply summarise those chapters, I think it would be nice to conclude our book with an overview discussion. I want to throw out a famous quote from Charles Dickens, the opening lines of *A Tale of Two Cities*:

"It was the best of times, it was the worst of times, it was the age of wisdom, it was the age of foolishness, it was the epoch of belief, it was the epoch of incredulity, it was the season of Light, it was the season of Darkness, it was the spring of hope, it was the winter of despair..."

So where are we, in terms of English football today, compared to the eras in which you started watching matches and then began playing professionally? Let's start with the areas where you feel that something has been genuinely lost from the game, aspects which are not simply rose-tinted nostalgia.

SM: When I started watching matches as a child, both at Old Trafford and at Edgeley Park, it was all about the passion, about supporting your club. At Stockport there was no demand for success; no expectation for the football club to spend money on transfers in a bid to gain promotion.

RM: But expectation, or ambition, is not necessarily a negative, is it? If it is channelled positively, I think it is good that fan bases make demands: seeking both transparency and ambitious ownership of their clubs. I sense that the main difference or sea change is that –

whether it was you as a County fan, or me as a Cobblers supporter – we had patience. Today people often expect *instant* success. We are living in a world where people demand instant gratification.

SM: Yes, that is so true. Patience is in short supply, from supporters, club owners...I also think that money talks, as never before. Of course, there was always a food chain of bigger clubs feeding off smaller ones, but there is now a chasm.

RM: It would certainly be harder for a modern-day manager to achieve the success which the likes of Alf Ramsey enjoyed at Ipswich, or Alex Ferguson at Aberdeen, without having the luxury of money to spend. Maybe Leicester's title was the exception which proved the rule that, as you say, money – rather than a manager's canny ability – is now the key factor.

SM: Leicester winning the PL was a great moment, not just for their fans, but for most football supporters. It offered the hope or belief that the dream was still alive. You need that, at any level of the game, from the top tier down to grassroots level. Money has become an ever-increasing determining factor, even in the non-league game. The concept or notion of an even playing field no longer exists at any level of the sport.

RM: It seems almost surreal now to remember the likes of Manchester City playing in the third tier as recently as 1999. You wonder if those super-rich PL clubs are now immune to finishing in the bottom half of the PL, never mind suffering relegation.

SM: Yes, it is unimaginable. We have lost that exciting sense that if a club created a vibrant youth recruitment policy, masterminded by a brilliant tactician – Bobby Robson at Ipswich or the 'Busby Babes' at United – that it would be enough to allow them to challenge for domestic and European trophies. Today you would almost certainly have to buy in that young talent.

RM: So how do we shake up the order of things?

SM: I am probably going to sound as if I am contradicting myself here, but the current 'revolution' at Wrexham, one of my former clubs, is – for me – an example of new owners inventively relaunching a football club. Yes, they are two wealthy US actors, but they identified what was a struggling but unique club – in terms of its large North Wales catchment area – and have used their sizeable, global social media presence to fire the imagination not only of the club's fan base but also engage a worldwide audience.

RM: They have also spent money to increase their chances of success! I guess that one key difference between the anonymous owners at so many big clubs and Reynolds/McElhenney is that they are visible, they do engage, they have an awareness of the community, and they seem genuinely excited to be actively involved. They behave like fans and that enthusiasm is infectious.

SM: I was there a few months ago for a book signing and they have created an incredible buzz; you could almost touch it.

RM: Returning to the elephant in the room, though, how do we prevent money from being the main determining factor in the

136

sport? Would a wage cap help to re-establish a more even playing field? Rugby Union has one, and Saracens were relegated a few years ago for breaking the rules.

SM: I cannot see that being a viable option in football. Billionaire club owners who are 'business savvy' will always find loopholes.

RM: I still think that Financial Fair Play has to be at the heart of any football revolution; though, as you say, I'm not sure how it can be policed. Maybe it needs to be an independent body, like they have in French football, one which closely monitors every professional football club's accounts each year. What about football as the people's game; its working-class roots? Have they been lost?

SM: At the top level of the game, clubs are either renovating or relocating with corporate hospitality 'customers' in mind. We are in danger of ending up with 'events arenas', rather than dedicated football stadiums. Stadiums as commercial ventures first and foremost. Function rooms rather than terraces.

RM: You say events arenas, but isn't that both a return to many grounds' original use as multi-purpose venues and a logical financial solution to these vast spaces remaining unused for days or weeks on end?

SM: That depends, I think, on whether the 'ordinary' football fan is included as an integral part of a club's vision, or if the financially lucrative corporate hospitality becomes the driving force.

RM: We explored the managerial merry-go-round in the book and this season has shattered all the records in terms of PL and EFL bosses being sacked. It's out of control.

SM: This comes back to what we've just been talking about! A lack of patience – or long-term vision – from owners, supporters. That demand for immediate results.

RM: And rich clubs being able to poach head coaches from smaller ones at any moment. It creates an instability and a house of cards effect. You will always get ambitious managers looking to climb the ladder, I get that, but that should not happen mid-season. These clubs who sack two or even three head coaches in a season...it rarely works. I do think our idea about a manager transfer window is a good solution. What about the match day experience for supporters? How has that changed?

SM: In the 70s and 80s it wasn't seen as hip or cool to go to football matches. With hooligans rampaging and so many grounds rundown, dilapidated, they weren't the sort of places where you would take the family. Clubs relied solely on that working-class family tradition of passionately supporting your local club, of fathers taking their sons to matches, the scarf being handed down to the next generation, backing your club through the bad times...The idea of family enclosures was unheard of. The game has cleaned its act up. Its image is now one where it is seen as trendy to go to a match. It's in vogue, part of the social scene. We have lots of 'football tourists'.

RM: What do you mean by that? People simply coming along for a day out, for entertainment, rather than as passionate die-hard fans? Spectators rather than supporters? I think there is room for both. There always has and always will be varying degrees of support: from the casual to the fanatic. For some, a defeat is simply disappointing, for others it can ruin their working week. Not everyone has to be obsessive! I understand the tradition of the father's scarf...but I think we are in danger here of misty-eyed nostalgia. It has to be a positive thing that we have more of a social mix in terms of fan bases; if women and small children, for example, feel welcomed rather than intimidated. If stands and toilet blocks are fit for purpose. We've said throughout the book that football is like society, it is constantly evolving. Why should the sport be the preserve of the white working-class male? We might have lost the 'edge' in terms of raucous atmospheres, but there was always a darker side to that. You described football as 'cleaning its act up'. It has left us with a more 'sanitised' match experience. There are positive and negative aspects to that. I want to test your rose-tinted glasses now. Imagine that the sixteen-year-old Steve Massey is embarking on his professional playing career. Would you choose 1975, or 2013? And why?

SM: 2023, without a shadow of a doubt. Why? The emphasis on technical ability, the ball-centred coaching, the pitches, the protection given to skilful players – even though that has gone too far in my opinion – the back pass rule, the media exposure, the awareness of mental health...I would even have relished the psychology, sports science and data. The type of footballer I was, I think the modern game would have suited me perfectly. The one thing which hasn't changed – and we saw a quote about that the other day in the National Football Museum – it is still eleven versus eleven, with a ball, and is still about scoring more goals than your opponents.

RM: I guess that the feeling when you score — in front of a crowd — is a timeless one?

SM: Yes. That split-second when you score, that elation you feel, that outpouring of emotion. Shared with thousands of others. Nothing compares to that.

RM: And it is, arguably, what makes football special. You can win a rugby match without scoring a try, but football is such a wonderfully 'simple' game. It all hinges on that one action. I still feel cheated if I come away from a goalless draw, even if it was action-packed...You didn't hesitate for a moment before choosing 2023 over the mid-70s. So are you saying then, that — overall — despite the ever-increasing role which money plays in the game, that football is in a better place now than it was fifty years ago?

SM: Undoubtedly. Whether you are a player, a coach, or a fan. I do have a 'but' to add, though. The biggest problem for me, even more than the money side, is the dark shadow hanging over the game as a spectacle: what some coaches will call 'time-management'. What we are really talking about here is not legitimate time-wasting, such as shielding the ball by the corner flag to eat up precious seconds. We are referring to gamesmanship...cheating. It has become an unofficial tactical element of most coaches' manuals. It is embarrassing. We have footballers now who are technically far better, even at non-league level, playing on bowling-green surfaces...but the sport as a spectacle is in danger of not simply being undermined but of being ruined by the dark arts. If money is the elephant in the room, then the cheating is like a cancer. Players feigning injuries, diving, goalkeepers instinctively going to ground each time they have caught a cross…It is eating up more and more game time and it kills the tempo, the momentum.

RM: You sense that it is getting worse?

SM: Absolutely. Using that cancer analogy, if we don't find ways to cut it out, if it is allowed to continue to spread, then the game will have 'gone'.

RM: We are coming around, I sense, to the subject of referees again.

SM: Why referees often don't see through those time-management antics is that they lack the instinct which you can only develop by playing the game at a reasonable level. There must be a better pathway – that word again – for ex-players to become involved, just as they are in other sports like cricket.

RM: It makes sense. In much the same way, many of the best television and film directors were originally actors. They know what it is like on the other side of the camera.

SM: You can hear in my voice how angry the subject of cheating makes me. If we can cure it, then almost everything is in place for a brighter future. We have a fabulous pyramid system, where even a tiny grassroots club such as the one I am involved with can dream of climbing the football ladder. There isn't another country in the world where the interest in football runs as deep in terms of PL, EFL, the top non-league divisions, and beyond.

RM: You are a self-confessed 'football obsessive'. You are still involved at a club, and you seem to be at a match most days of the week. Is there anything which would make you fall out of love with the game?

SM: Only one. Whenever there is talk of elite leagues with no promotion/relegation. Closed shops. If that came into football, I would walk away from the sport. It would shatter the dreams which we all have going into a new season, whether they are realistic or not. Without that dream, football dies.

Vernon Park, Stockport, 01/06/2023

BIBLIOGRAPHY

Calvin, Michael, *The Nowhere Men: The Unknown Story of Football's True Talent Spotters* (Century, 2013)

Calvin, Michael, *Living on the Volcano: The Secrets of Surviving as a Football Manager* (Century, 2015)

Calvin, Michael, *No Hunger in Paradise: The Players. The Journey. The Dream* (Century, 2017)

Conn, David, *The Football Business* (Mainstreaming Publishing, 2002)

Ferguson, Alex: *Managing My Life* (Coronet, 2000)

Gray, Daniel, *Hatters, Railwaymen and Knitters: Travels through England's football provinces* (Bloomsbury, 2013)

Gray, Daniel, *Saturday, 3PM: 50 Eternal Delights of Modern Football* (Bloomsbury, 2016)

Gray, Daniel, *Black Boots & Football Pinks: 50 Lost Wonders of the Beautiful Game* (Bloomsbury, 2018)

Gray, Daniel, *Extra Time: 50 Further Delights of Modern Football* (Bloomsbury, 2020)

Gray, Daniel, *The Silence of the Stands: Finding the Joy in Football's Lost Season* (Bloomsbury, 2022)

Hargreaves, Chris, *Where's Your Caravan?: My Life on Football's B-Roads* (Harper Collins, 2011)

Hornby, Nick, *Fever Pitch: A Fan's Life* (Gollancz, 1992)

Inglis, Simon, *The Football Grounds of England and Wales* (William Collins, 1983)

Massey, Steve, (with Rodney Marshall), *Where's My Towel? A Life in and out of Football* (Short Run Press, 2022)

Proudlove, David, *When the Circus Leaves Town: What Happens When Football Leaves Home* (Pitch, 2022)

Wignall, Steve, *"You Can Have Chips!"* (Apex, 2009)

Printed in Great Britain
by Amazon

05d54a54-31ea-42ae-8cc3-517d09b698adR01

Microsoft

Microsoft® Excel

Version 2002  ® Microsoft Office XP Application

G000135325

plain&simple

Your fast-answers, no-jargon
guide to Excel 2002!

Curtis Frye and
the epic software group, inc.

PUBLISHED BY
Microsoft Press
A Division of Microsoft Corporation
One Microsoft Way
Redmond, Washington 98052-6399

Library of Congress Cataloging-in-Publication Data
Frye, Curtis, 1968–
    Microsoft Excel Version 2002 Plain & Simple / Curtis Frye and the epic software group, inc.
        p. cm.
    Includes index.
    ISBN 0-7356-1451-2
    1. Microsoft Excel for Windows.   2. Business--Computer programs.   3. Electronic spreadsheets.   I. Title.

    HF5548.4.M523 F789   2001
    005.369--dc21   2001044398

Printed and bound in the United States of America.

1 2 3 4 5 6 7 8 9   QWT   6 5 4 3 2

Distributed in Canada by Penguin Books Canada Limited.

A CIP catalogue record for this book is available from the British Library.

Microsoft Press books are available through booksellers and distributors worldwide. For further information about international editions, contact your local Microsoft Corporation office or contact Microsoft Press International directly at fax (425) 936-7329. Visit our Web site at www.microsoft.com/mspress. Send comments to *mspinput@microsoft.com*.

Acquisitions Editor: Kong Cheung
Project Editor: Kristen Weatherby
Manuscript Editor: Judith Bloch

Body Part No. X08-24310

Contents

3 Building a Workbook — 23

4 Managing and Viewing Worksheets — 47

5 Using Formulas and Functions 59

6 Formatting the Worksheet 77

7 Printing Worksheets — 101

8 Customizing Excel to the Way You Work — 117

15 Introducing Advanced Excel Topics 219

i Index 231

Acknowledgments

It takes a great deal of time and effort to put together a book like this. Many people contributed to the content and design of this book, while others provided encouragement and support. When I founded the epic software group, inc., in 1990, I realized the most successful projects would be group efforts, in which each person would contribute his or her best work. And that was indeed the case with *Microsoft Excel Version 2002 Plain & Simple*. Without a doubt, it would have remained just another interesting idea had it not been for the combined efforts of this talented team. I would like to offer my heartfelt appreciation to the following people.

First and foremost, I would like to thank our lead author, Curtis Frye, a true "Renaissance Man," skilled in writing, acting, and public speaking. He has written extensively on Microsoft Excel, Microsoft Access, and Active Server Pages, as well as the issue of privacy law in international business. He is not only able to explain complex subjects in terms we can all understand, but also can do it on only two hours of sleep! He is a joy to work with and puts 110% into everything he sets his mind on accomplishing.

Next my thanks must go out to Rod Afshar, our developmental editor. Rod is an exceptionally bright young man who helped with virtually every aspect of this book. His knowledge of Excel 2002 is both broad and deep and his "fingerprints" are indelibly etched on every page of this book.

One of the most important aspects of any software manual is getting the details right. Our technical editor, Jodi Paul, kept us in line by checking and rechecking every example, screen capture, and word in the book. Jodi has been doing this kind of work for over 12 years and is a Certified Microsoft Office User Specialist Expert. She is also the only person I know who would wear a T-shirt that says, "Does anal retentive have a hyphen?" (Her answer? "It depends—only if it is used as a compound modifier!")

Perhaps the folks we have to thank the most are our friends at Microsoft Press. Project editor Kristen Weatherby (who I am convinced is the Patron Saint of the Chronologically Challenged) really helped us understand Microsoft style and format. The book has benefited enormously from the revisions that her suggestions prompted. Many thanks also to Kong Cheung, the acquisition editor who understands both the art and science of computer book publishing. Kong awarded the book contract to the epic software group, and for that he has our heartfelt gratitude. We also have to thank the folks from Microsoft who did such a fine job producing and perfecting the book: desktop publisher Dan Latimer, artist Jim Kramer, manuscript editor Judith Bloch, and copy editor Patty Masserman.

On the home front, we thank our support staff at epic who were instrumental in driving this book to completion. My gratitude goes to Sharon Howerton, Robert Bailey, Danny Duhon, Derek Hughes, Cliff Jones, and Victor M. Cherubini. I also have to thank Steve Rasey, who is the Leader of the Houston Area League of PC Users (HAL-PC) Excel SIG, for his ideas and work teaching Excel at all levels.

Vic Cherubini
President
epic software group, inc.

About This Book

I f you want to get the most from your computer and your software with the least amount of time and effort—and who doesn't?—this book is for you. You'll find *Microsoft Excel 2002 Plain & Simple* to be a straightforward, easy-to-read reference tool. With the premise that your computer should work for you, not you for it, this book's purpose is to help you get your work done quickly and efficiently so that you can get away from the computer and live your life.

No Computerese!

Let's face it—when there's a task you don't know how to do but you need to get it done in a hurry or when you're stuck in the middle of a task and can't figure out what to do next, there's nothing more frustrating than having to read page after page of technical background material. You want the information you need—nothing more, nothing less—and you want it now! *And* it should be easy to find and understand.

That's what this book is all about. It's written in plain English—no technical jargon and no computerese. There's no single task in the book that takes more than two pages. Just look the task up in the index or the table of contents, turn to the page, and there's the information you need, laid out in an illustrated step-by-step format. You don't get bogged down by the whys and wherefores: just follow the steps, and get your work done with a minimum of hassle.

Occasionally you might have to turn to another page if the procedure you're working on is accompanied by a "See Also." That's because there's a lot of overlap among tasks, and we didn't want to keep repeating ourselves. We've scattered some useful tips here and there, and thrown in a "Try This" or a "Caution" once in a while, but by and large we've tried to remain true to the heart and soul of the book, which is that the information you need should be available to you at a glance.

Useful Tasks...

Whether you use Excel 2002 at home or on the road, we've tried to pack this book with procedures for everything we could think of that you might want to do, from the simplest tasks to some of the more esoteric ones.

...And the Easiest Way to Do Them

Another thing we've tried to do in this book is find and document the easiest way to accomplish a task. Excel 2002 often provides a multitude of methods to accomplish a single end result—which can be daunting or delightful, depending on the way you like to work. If you tend to stick with one favorite and familiar approach, we think the methods described in this book are the way to go. If you like trying out alternative techniques, go ahead! The intuitiveness of Excel 2002 invites exploration, and you're likely to discover ways of doing things that you think are easier or that you like better than ours. If you do, that's great! It's exactly what the developers of Excel 2002 had in mind when they provided so many alternatives.

A Quick Overview

Your computer probably came with Excel 2002 preinstalled, but if you do have to install it yourself, the Setup Wizard makes installation so simple that you won't need our help anyway. So, unlike many computer books, this one doesn't start with installation instructions and a list of system requirements.

Next, you don't have to read this book in any particular order. It's designed so that you can jump in, get the information you need, and then close the book and keep it near your computer until the next time you need to know how to get something done. But

that doesn't mean we scattered the information about with wild abandon. We've organized the book so that the tasks you want to accomplish are arranged in two levels—you'll find the overall type of task you're looking for under a main section title such as "Formatting the Worksheet," "Using Charts to Display Data," "Using Excel in a Group Environment," and so on. Then, in each of those sections, the smaller tasks within the main task are arranged in a loose progression from the simplest to the more complex.

Sections 2 and 3 cover the basics: starting Excel 2002 and shutting it down, sizing and arranging program windows, navigating in a workbook, using the menu system and toolbar buttons to have Excel do what you want it to do, and working with multiple Excel documents at the same time. Section 2 also introduces task panes, which are new in Excel 2002 and make it easy to perform the most common tasks. There's also a lot of useful information about entering text and data, including shortcuts you can use to enter an entire series of numbers or dates by typing values in just one or two cells. You'll also learn about using the new Office Clipboard to manage items you cut and paste, running the spelling checker to ensure you haven't made any errors in your workbook, finding and replacing text to update changes in customer addresses or product names, and getting help from within Excel and on the Web.

Section 4 is all about managing and viewing worksheets—the "pages" of a workbook. In this section, you'll find out about selecting, renaming, moving, copying, inserting, and deleting worksheets. In Section 5, you'll get to know *formulas* and *functions*. You use formulas to calculate values, such as finding the sum of the values in a group of cells. Once you're up to speed on creating basic formulas, you'll learn how to save time by copying a formula from one cell and pasting it into as many other cells as you want. Finally, you'll extend your knowledge of formulas by creating powerful statements using the function library in Excel 2002.

Section 6 focuses on making your worksheets look great. Here's where you'll learn techniques to make your data more readable, such as changing row heights and column widths and inserting, deleting, and hiding rows and columns. You'll learn how to showcase your data by changing font sizes and font colors, adding colors and shading to cells, and color-coding your sheet tabs to make them stand out. There's also information on locking and protecting your worksheets for those times when you want to secure your information.

Section 7 is all about printing your Excel documents, whether that means printing all or just a portion of your results. Your productivity should improve after reading Section 8, where you will learn how to customize Excel 2002 for the way you work. We'll show you how to change menus and toolbars to make it easier to get at the items you choose most often, or even to create entirely new menu items and toolbars to do things that the Excel programmers didn't include. You can also save time by having Excel open multiple workbooks simultaneously and by saving documents as patterns, or *templates*, you can use to create new workbooks based on existing formats.

Section 9 is about sorting and filtering your data, techniques you can use to limit the data displayed in a worksheet and determine the order in which it is presented. Do you need to see all of the sales for a product but don't want to bother with the rest of the data for the moment? No problem. A picture is worth a thousand words, and we'll show you how to create and use charts to summarize your data visually in Section 10. In Section 11, you'll learn how to enhance your worksheets by adding graphics and pictures. You'll be surprised to learn just how easy it is to insert clip art, add a special text effect, or resize a photo you added to a worksheet.

Sections 12, 13, and 14 are all about sharing your Excel worksheets—whether it's with your colleagues, on the Internet, or sharing data with other programs. In Section 12, you'll learn how use Excel in a group environment, to add comments to your worksheets, and to accept or reject the comments made by others. Excel 2002 was designed specifically with the Web in mind, and in Section 13, you'll learn how to publish a worksheet to the Web as well as how to use smart tags to pull information from the Internet directly into your worksheet. For those times when you need to share Excel data with other applications, Section 14 will show you how to move information to and from Microsoft Word,

Microsoft PowerPoint, and Microsoft Access. One very exciting new ability in Excel 2002 is to have Excel "read a document aloud" by turning text into speech; we'll show you how to do just that.

Section 15, the final section of the book, introduces three advanced Excel topics: PivotTables, Goal Seek, and macros. PivotTables help you restructure your data dynamically so that you can look at your information in new and interesting ways. With Goal Seek, you can analyze your data from a different perspective by typing the desired result of a calculation in a cell and having Excel crunch the numbers to find the input needed to produce the result. And you'll learn how to use macros, which are programs designed to automate repetitive tasks. If you think these tasks sound complex, rest assured that they're not—Excel 2002 makes them so easy that you'll sail right through them.

A Few Assumptions

We had to make a few educated guesses about you, our audience, when we started writing this book. Perhaps you just use Excel for personal reasons, tracking your household budget, doing some financial planning, or recording your times for weekend road races. Maybe you run a small, home-based business, or you're an employee of a corporation where you use Excel to analyze and present sales or production data. Taking all these possibilities into account, we assumed you'd need to know how to create and work with Excel workbooks and worksheets, summarize your data in a variety of ways, format your documents so that they're easy to read, and then print the results, share them over the Web, or both.

Another assumption we made is that—initially, anyway—you'd use Excel 2002 just as it came, meaning that you'd be working with the standard toolbar and menu choices. If you want to change the toolbars and menus, you can certainly do so by following the instructions in "Customizing Toolbars" on page 123 and "Customizing Menus" on page 124. However, because our working style is somewhat traditional, and because Excel is set up to work in the traditional style, that's what we've described in the procedures and graphics throughout this book.

A Final Word (or Two)

We had three goals in writing this book:

- Whatever you want to do, we want the book to help you get it done.

- We want the book to help you discover how to do things you *didn't* know you wanted to do.

- And, finally, if we've achieved the first two goals, we'll be well on the way to the third, which is for our book to help you *enjoy* using Excel 2002. We think that's the best gift we could give you to thank you for buying our book.

We hope you'll have as much fun using *Microsoft Excel 2002 Plain & Simple* as we've had writing it. The best way to learn is by *doing,* and that's how we hope you'll use this book.

Jump right in!

Getting Started with Excel 2002

❋ NEW FEATURE

Microsoft Excel 2002 is designed to help you store, summarize, and present data relevant to your business or your home life. You can create spreadsheets to track products and sales for a garden supply company, or, just as easily, build spreadsheets to keep track of your personal investments or your kids' soccer scores. Regardless of the specific use you have in mind, Excel is a versatile program you can use to store and retrieve data quickly.

Working with Excel is pretty straightforward. The program has a number of preconstructed workbooks you can use for tasks such as tracking work hours for you and your colleagues or computing loan payments, but you also have the freedom to create and format workbooks from scratch, giving you the flexibility to build any workbook you need.

This section of the book covers the basics: how to start Excel and shut it down, how to open Excel documents, how to use workbooks, and—for users of other versions of Excel—there's an introduction to the new features you'll find in Excel 2002. There's also an overall view of the Excel window, with labels for the most important parts of the program, and a close-up look at the menu system and toolbars. You can use those images as touchstones for learning more about Excel.

Surveying the Excel Screen

In many ways, an Excel worksheet is like the ledger in your checkbook. The page is divided into rows and columns, and you can organize your data using those natural divisions as a guide. The box formed by the intersection of a row and a column is called a cell. You can identify individual cells by their column letter and row number—this combination, which identifies the first cell in the first column as cell A1, is called a cell reference. The following graphic shows you the important features of the Excel screen.

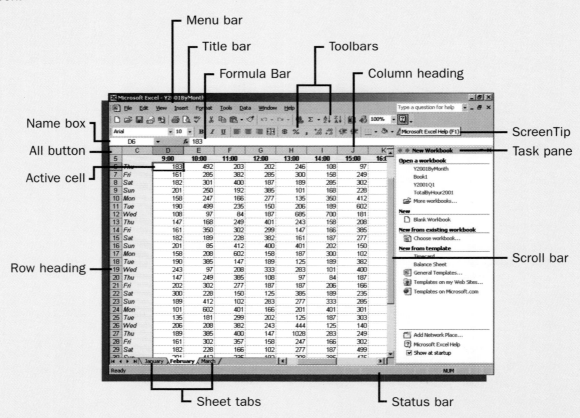

Menu bar

Title bar

Formula Bar

Toolbars

Column heading

Name box

ScreenTip

All button

Task pane

Active cell

Scroll bar

Row heading

Sheet tabs

Status bar

Touring the Excel Toolbars

Once you've entered your data into a worksheet, you can change the data's appearance, summarize it, or sort it, using Excel menus and toolbars. The menu system allows you to access every Excel command, while the Standard and Formatting toolbars (the only two toolbars that appear unless you say otherwise) let you save files, cut and paste, and format your data with one mouse click.

Standard Toolbar

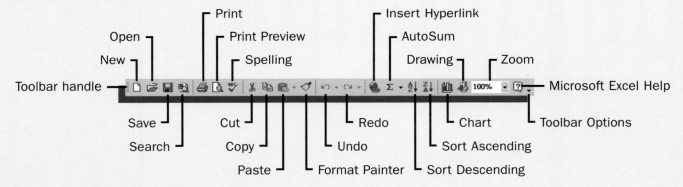

Formatting Toolbar

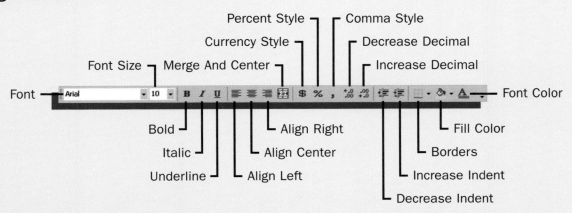

Starting Excel

Once you've installed Excel on your computer, you can start it from the Start menu, which will open the program with a new, blank workbook, or by double-clicking an already existing Excel file on your computer.

Start Excel with a Blank Workbook

(1) Click the Start button on the taskbar.

(2) Point to Programs.

(3) Click Microsoft Excel.

TIP: Pressing Ctrl+Esc will also open the Start menu.

Open an Existing Workbook

(1) Double-click My Computer.

(2) Navigate to the directory that contains the file you want to open.

(3) Double-click the file you want to open.

TIP: The Documents menu, which you can display by clicking the Start button and pointing to Documents, lists recently used files. When you click an Excel file in the Documents list, Excel will start and the file will open.

Introducing the Task Panes ⊕ NEW FEATURE

When you start Excel, the New Workbook task pane appears at the right edge of the Excel window. The task pane contains hyperlinks to a number of common tasks, such as opening a recently used file, creating a new workbook from scratch, or creating a new workbook based on an existing template. After you use the task pane, it will disappear from the screen, freeing screen space you can use to display your data.

The New Workbook task pane is actually one of five panes in Excel. The others are the Clipboard, Basic Search, Document Recovery, and Insert Clip Art task panes. The Clipboard task pane keeps track of any items you've copied or cut from your documents and makes them available to you with a single mouse click. The Office Clipboard can hold up to 24 items.

The Basic Search task pane lets you search your computer, other computers to which you're networked, or the Internet for files with specific names or content.

The Insert Clip Art task pane shows thumbnail images of available clip art, drawings, and pictures. You can search your computer for images and, after you identify the images that interest you, thumbnail versions of the images are placed on the task pane for easy access.

Document Recovery ⊕ NEW FEATURE

A final task pane you might have to use is the Document Recovery task pane. If you're running Excel and the power goes out, Excel won't have time to save your work and close the program properly. The next time you run Excel, however, the program will look for files that weren't saved correctly. Any files the program finds will be displayed in the Document Recovery task pane, at the left edge of the Excel window. You can open the file by clicking its name—Excel will recover as much of the data from the file as it can. In many cases, all of your work will be recovered. If not, you will still have all of your work from the last time you saved.

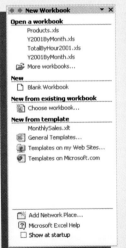

Working with Task Panes

You can use task panes to access commands that are otherwise hidden in menus to obtain information and assistance. Task panes are designed so that you can easily open and move between them, do what you need to do quickly, and then go on with your work.

Display Task Panes

1 Choose Task Pane from the View menu.

> **!** **TIP:** If you want the New Workbook task pane to appear when you start Excel, display the New Workbook task pane and select the Show At Startup check box at the bottom of the task pane.

Switch Task Panes

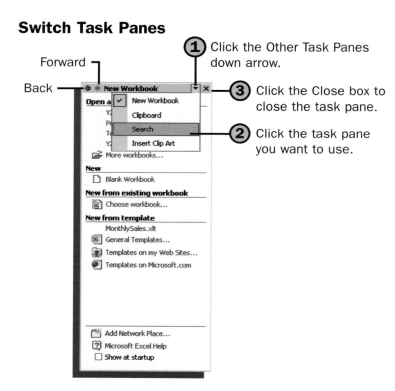

Forward

Back

1 Click the Other Task Panes down arrow.

3 Click the Close box to close the task pane.

2 Click the task pane you want to use.

> **!** **TIP:** Click the Back and Forward buttons on the task pane to move between any other task panes you have used.

Arranging Toolbars

Excel contains several toolbars with buttons that let you do things like cut and paste, print, and save your work with a single mouse click. When you start Excel, the Standard and Formatting toolbars are displayed on one row. This means that, unless you have a very wide monitor, some of the buttons will be hidden. If you prefer, you can choose to display the Standard and Formatting toolbars on separate rows so that you can see all the buttons. When you close Excel, the program remembers your changes so that you don't have to redo them.

Show the Standard and Formatting Toolbars on Two Rows

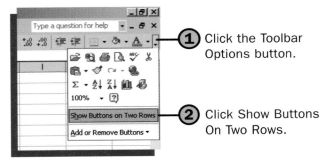

1 Click the Toolbar Options button.

2 Click Show Buttons On Two Rows.

Display Toolbars on One Row

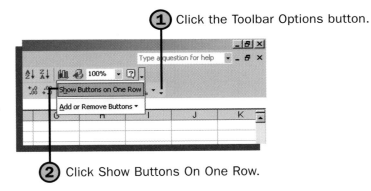

1 Click the Toolbar Options button.

2 Click Show Buttons On One Row.

> **TRY THIS:** On the View menu, point to Toolbars, and choose Formatting to hide the Formatting toolbar.
>
> To restore the Formatting toolbar, point to Toolbars on the View menu and click Formatting.

> **SEE ALSO:** For more information about how to display and create other toolbars, see "Customizing Toolbars" on page 123.

Finding and Opening Existing Workbooks

Once you've created an Excel workbook, you will probably want to open it again, whether to verify the contents, add or update data, or copy data from one workbook to another. If you don't know the exact name of the file you want to open, but do know some of the data it contains, you can search for the file and open it once you've located it.

Open a Workbook

1 Choose New from the File menu.

2 Click the workbook you want to open.

Search for a Workbook and Open It

1 Choose Search from the File menu.

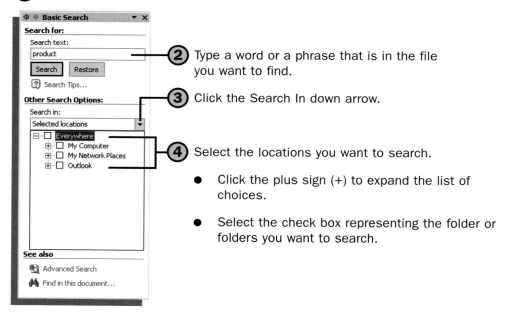

2 Type a word or a phrase that is in the file you want to find.

3 Click the Search In down arrow.

4 Select the locations you want to search.

- Click the plus sign (+) to expand the list of choices.

- Select the check box representing the folder or folders you want to search.

! TIP: If you need to search by criteria that aren't available in the Basic Search task pane, click Advanced Search at the bottom of the Basic Search task pane. In the Advanced Search task pane, you can specify many different criteria, such as subject, file creation date, owner, and keywords.

Using File Properties

Finding files can be difficult on computers you share with your colleagues, or if you've been using the same computer for a long time and have created a lot of workbooks. You can make it easier to find your files by describing them in the File Properties dialog box. You and your colleagues can then use the controls in the Advanced Search task pane to look for files using those values.

Set File Properties

TIP: In the Search In and Results Should Be drop-down lists, click the plus sign (+) to show more options.

(7) Click Search.

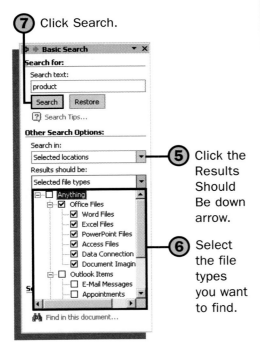

(8) Click a file name in the Search Results list to open the file.

SEE ALSO: For more information about using the Advanced Search task pane, see "Search Using File Properties" on page 14.

(1) Choose Properties from the File menu.

(2) Click the Summary tab.

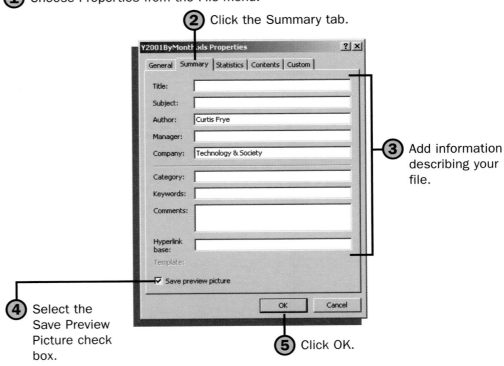

(5) Click the Results Should Be down arrow.

(6) Select the file types you want to find.

(3) Add information describing your file.

(4) Select the Save Preview Picture check box.

(5) Click OK.

Search Using File Properties

(1) Choose Search from the File menu.

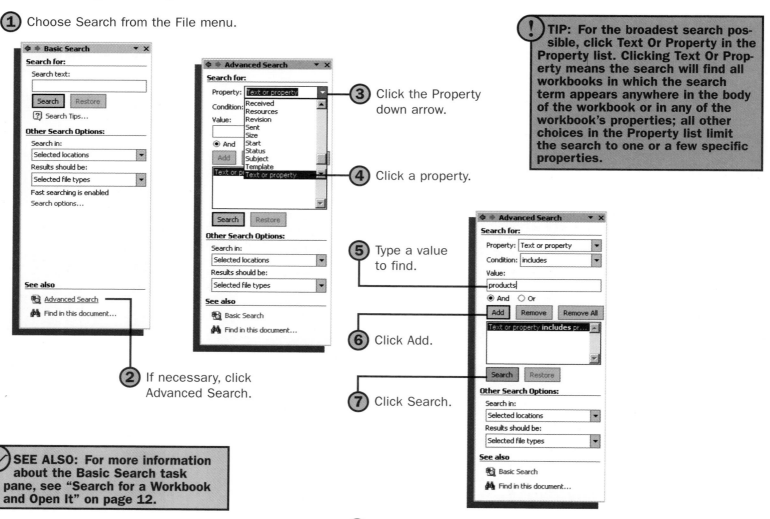

(3) Click the Property down arrow.

(4) Click a property.

(2) If necessary, click Advanced Search.

(5) Type a value to find.

(6) Click Add.

(7) Click Search.

TIP: For the broadest search possible, click Text Or Property in the Property list. Clicking Text Or Property means the search will find all workbooks in which the search term appears anywhere in the body of the workbook or in any of the workbook's properties; all other choices in the Property list limit the search to one or a few specific properties.

SEE ALSO: For more information about the Basic Search task pane, see "Search for a Workbook and Open It" on page 12.

(8) Click a file name in the Search Results list to open the file.

Creating a New Workbook

As a general rule, you should create a new workbook any time you need a place to store data on a new subject. For example, you might track your company's sales in one workbook, the products your company offers in another, and your employees' personal information and salaries in a third.

Create a New Workbook

① Click the New button on the Standard toolbar.

Opening Ready-to-Use Workbooks

Some workbooks are already built and are available to help you with some common business and personal tasks. These timesaving, prefabricated workbooks are called *templates* and can be found in your templates folder or on the Web. Templates can contain formulas, graphics, labels, and formatting. You can easily customize a premade template to your specifications.

Open a Spreadsheet Solutions Workbook

① Choose New from the File menu.

② Click General Template.

③ Click the Spreadsheet Solutions tab.

④ Double-click the solutions template that you want to open.

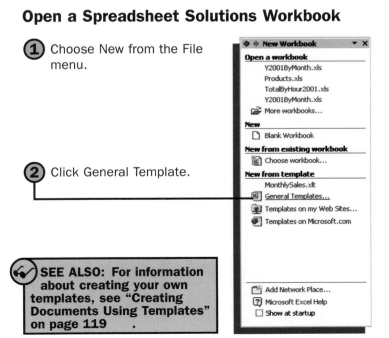

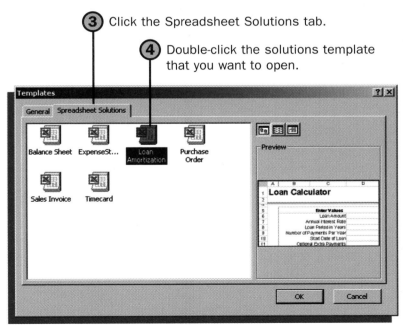

SEE ALSO: For information about creating your own templates, see "Creating Documents Using Templates" on page 119.

Working with Multiple Workbooks

When you create an Excel workbook for each subject of your business, you will sometimes need to look at data from more than one workbook to make your decisions. In cases like this, you can switch between them by choosing the workbook's name from the Window menu, or you can choose one of several arrangements so that you can work with your workbooks effectively.

Switch Between Open Workbooks

1 Choose the workbook you want to view from the Window menu.

Show More Than One Workbook

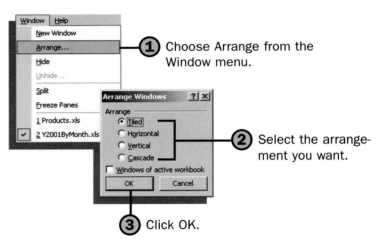

1 Choose Arrange from the Window menu.

2 Select the arrangement you want.

3 Click OK.

> **TRY THIS:** Open three workbooks, and choose Arrange from the Window menu. In the Arrange dialog box, select the Cascade option and click OK. The workbooks will be displayed with a slight overlap, with the full contents of the first workbook displayed and the title bars of the other two workbooks visible behind the first workbook.

Sizing and Arranging Windows

You work with windows in the Excel program the same way you work with windows on your desktop. You can make a workbook's window as large as the screen itself; if you have more than one workbook open at a time, you can choose from several display arrangements to order the windows most effectively.

Resize a Window

- Click the Maximize button to make the window take up the entire screen.

- Click the Minimize button to represent the window as a button on the taskbar.

- Click the Restore button to return the window to its previous size.

- Drag the left or right border of the window to resize it horizontally.

- Drag the top or bottom border of the window to resize it vertically.

- Drag a corner to resize the window both horizontally and vertically.

- Drag the window's title bar to change its position.

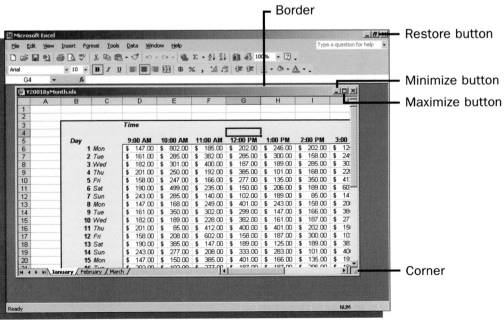

Border

Restore button

Minimize button

Maximize button

Corner

Zooming In or Out on a Worksheet

If you are not satisfied with how much of your worksheet you can see, you can make the worksheet larger or smaller without changing the window size. When you zoom out on a worksheet, you can see the overall layout, but it might be difficult to read the data in individual cells. To get a better look at the data in your cells, you can zoom in on your worksheet.

Zoom In or Out

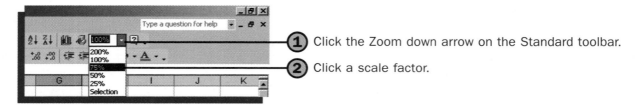

1. Click the Zoom down arrow on the Standard toolbar.

2. Click a scale factor.

Zoom In or Out to a Custom View

1. Type a scale factor in the Zoom box.

Viewing a Worksheet in Full Screen Mode

Occasionally, you'll want to see as much of a worksheet as possible. An easy way to temporarily hide any Excel toolbars is to view the workbook in Full Screen mode. Unlike the Maximize command, which only affects one worksheet, in Full Screen mode you can view multiple worksheets simultaneously. The menu bar remains at the top of the screen, though, so you can still work with the contents of your worksheets. To display the toolbars again, choose Full Screen from the View menu.

To Turn Full Screen Mode On or Off

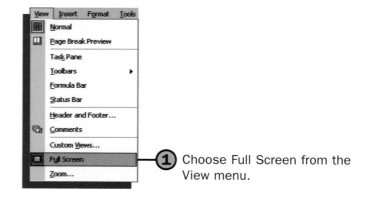

1. Choose Full Screen from the View menu.

Saving and Closing an Excel Workbook

There's nothing more frustrating than losing a few minutes or even hours of work because you forgot to save your file. When you close your workbook, Excel checks to see whether it has changed since the last time you saved it. If it hasn't been saved, you'll be asked to save your workbook before you close it. If you want to save multiple versions of the same workbook, you can also create a copy of your file by saving it with a different name.

Save a Workbook

① Click the Save button on the Standard toolbar.

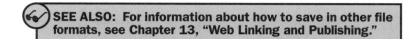

SEE ALSO: For information about how to save in other file formats, see Chapter 13, "Web Linking and Publishing."

Save a Workbook with a New Name

① Choose Save As from the File menu.

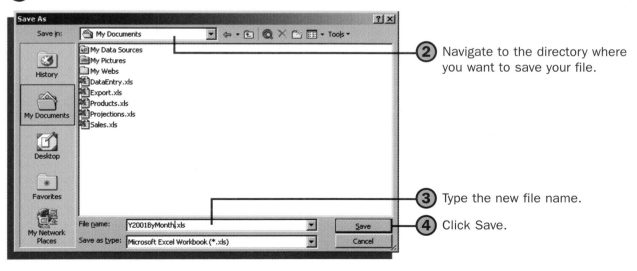

② Navigate to the directory where you want to save your file.

③ Type the new file name.

④ Click Save.

Close a Workbook

① Click the Close box at the top right corner of the workbook.

② If a dialog box appears asking if you want to save any unsaved changes, you can:

- Click Yes to save the workbook to the same name before closing.

- Click No to discard all changes since the workbook was last saved.

- Click Cancel to return to the workbook.

Exit Excel

① Click the Close box at the top right corner of the Excel window.

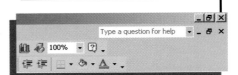

 CAUTION: Make sure you click the proper Close box. If you click the Close box at the top right of the Excel window, you'll close Excel, as well as the document you're working on.

Getting Help with the Ask A Question Box ⊗ NEW FEATURE

There are lots of ways to get help while you're using Excel. If there's something specific you want to do and you can't find it in this book, unlikely though that is, you can get help by asking a question, browsing through the range of Help files available in Excel, or by going to the Web. The Ask A Question box is new in Excel 2002 and gives you a straightforward way to get help on a specific subject. If you don't know the exact term for what you want to do, try describing it in the Ask A Question box— you'll most likely find what you want!

Ask a Question of Excel

① Type your question in the Ask A Question box, and press Enter.

② Click one of the topics in the drop-down list.

③ Click the Close box when you're done reviewing the Help file.

Using Excel Help

If you need to get help using Excel, there are quite a few places you can look. One option is to right-click an object (such as a worksheet or a graphic) to see a list of things you can do with the object. You can also open the Excel Help files and browse through them to find the answer to a specific question or just to explore.

Get Microsoft Excel Help

(1) Click the Microsoft Excel Help button on the Standard toolbar.

> **⚠ TIP: You can visit the Microsoft Office Assistance Center site directly by opening your Web browser and typing** http://office.microsoft.com/assistance/ **in the Address box.**

Get Help on the Web

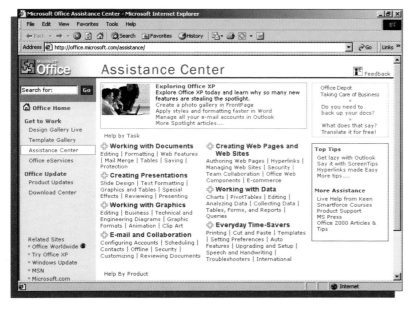

Get Suggested Commands from Shortcut Menus

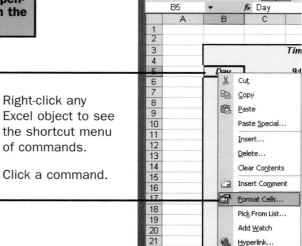

(1) Right-click any Excel object to see the shortcut menu of commands.

(2) Click a command.

(1) Choose Office On The Web from the Help menu.

(2) Browse the Assistance Center for help and resources.

Previewing a Worksheet Before Printing

Before printing a workbook, it is a good idea to view on the screen how a page will look on paper. If you do not like the way a page looks, you can return to your workbook and make some adjustments. Once you're ready to print your file, you can do it with one mouse click.

Preview a Worksheet

1 Click the Print Preview button on the Standard toolbar.

2 Click Print to print the worksheet.

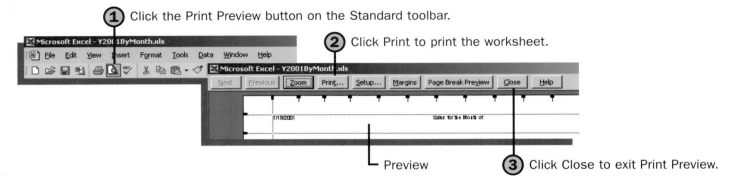

Preview

3 Click Close to exit Print Preview.

Print a Worksheet

1 Display the worksheet you want to print.

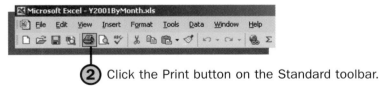

2 Click the Print button on the Standard toolbar.

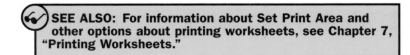

> **SEE ALSO:** For information about Set Print Area and other options about printing worksheets, see Chapter 7, "Printing Worksheets."

Building a Workbook

One of the real strengths of Microsoft Excel is that the program makes it easy for you to enter large quantities of data with ease. When you type text, Excel remembers what you've entered in previous cells in the same column and offers to complete the current entry for you. The good news is that you'll only need to type "Indianapolis" once. After the first time, typing the first three letters gives Excel enough information to guess the city name. Entering series of numbers, dates, or days is easier than ever before. If you want to enter a long series of numbers, dates, or even weekdays, you can type in one or two values and have Excel fill in the remaining values in the series! These techniques, combined with formatting and other skills you'll encounter in this section, make data entry nearly painless.

In this section, you'll learn how to:

● Navigate a worksheet.

● Select and copy contiguous (touching) and noncontiguous groups of cells.

● Enter text, numbers, and dates efficiently.

● Use shortcuts to enter series of values.

● Check the spelling of your worksheet's text.

Understanding How Excel Interprets Data Entry

Excel makes it easy for you to enter data into a worksheet by guessing the type of data you're entering and applying the appropriate formatting to that data. It's important to remember that because Excel is a computer program, it has some limitations. For example, Excel performs calculations using decimal values, such as .5, rather than using fractions, such as ½. If you do want to express some of your data as fractions and not as decimal values, you can do so by changing the cell's format to Fraction. In either case, you will be able to save the data in your preferred format.

The flip side of the bias toward decimal values is that entering dates and times is much easier than it would be if you had to type out a full date, like February 3 or February 3, 2002. For example, if you type **2/3** in a cell and press Enter,

Excel will recognize the text as an abbreviation for the third day of the month of February, and will display the data as a date using the shortest date format available. The shortest date format, which is designed to fit the value in a relatively narrow cell, would display February 3 as *3-Feb*.

You can choose the format you want for dates and times by selecting the cells that will hold dates or times and then choosing Cells from the Format menu to display the Format Cells dialog box. Inside the dialog box, click the Number tab and then click Date in the list of categories. The available date formats will appear on the right. From there, just click the format you want and click OK. If you want the data in a cell to appear as a fraction, click the Number tab and then click Fraction.

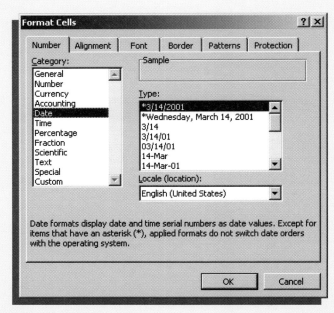

Navigating the Worksheet

Using the mouse and the keyboard, you can move from cell to cell in a worksheet, move up or down a page at a time, or move to the first or last cell in a row. The following table lists the keyboard shortcuts you can use in addition to the scroll bars and sheet tabs you use with your mouse.

Navigate Your Workbook Using the Keyboard

Key	Action
Left Arrow	Move one cell left.
Right Arrow	Move one cell right.
Up Arrow	Move one cell up.
Down Arrow	Move one cell down.
Enter	Move one cell down.
Shift + Enter	Move one cell up.
Tab	Move one cell right.
Shift + Tab	Move one cell left.
Page Up	Move one screen up.
Page Down	Move one screen down.
Ctrl + Arrow Key	Move to the next cell with data in the direction of the arrow key. If there is not another cell in that direction, you move to the last cell in the worksheet in that direction.

Selecting Cells

Whenever you make changes to the cells in a worksheet, you can save time by applying the changes to similar cells at once. You used to be limited to selecting cells that were contiguous, but in Excel 2002 you can select groups of cells that aren't even next to each other! If your worksheet stores dates in cells with other information in between, you can select all of the date cells and apply the format to them at the same time.

Select a Contiguous Group of Cells

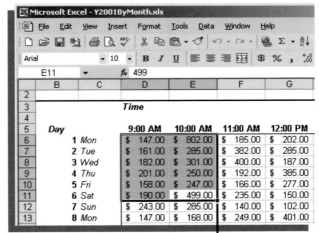

① Drag from the upper-left cell you want to select to the lower-right cell.

Select a Noncontiguous Group of Cells

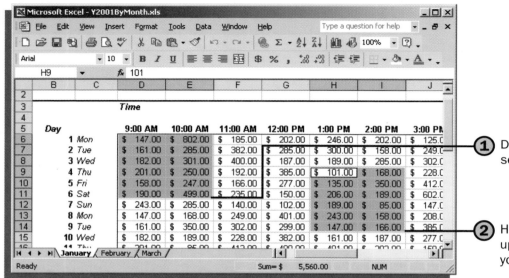

(1) Drag from the upper-left cell you want to select to the lower-right cell.

(2) Hold down the Ctrl key, and drag from the upper-left cell in another set of cells that you want to select to the lower-right cell.

Select Rows or Columns

(1) Drag from the first row or column header to the last row or column header you want to select.

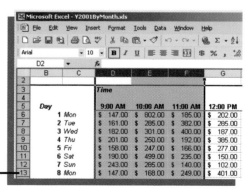

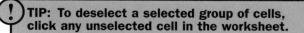

TIP: To deselect a selected group of cells, click any unselected cell in the worksheet.

Entering Text in Cells

No workbook worthy of the name stays empty for long. You can type any sort of text you want directly into a cell, whether the text is a label identifying the data in a row or a column, or an explanation reminding you and your colleagues of any limitations on the data to be entered into a cell. Most text entered into Excel workbooks is short enough to fit on one line, but if you want to have the text in a cell appear on two lines, you can easily insert a line break.

Enter Text as One Line

1 Click the cell you want to enter text into.

2 Type the text you want to appear.

3 Press Enter.

> **TRY THIS:** Type a long line of text into a cell that is on an empty row. The text in this cell will extend over the other columns. Click the cell to the right of the one you just entered text into, type some text into it, and press Enter. The overlapping text in the previous column will be hidden.

Enter Text with Forced Line Breaks

1 Click the cell you want to enter text into.

2 Type the text you want to appear on the first line. Press Alt+Enter to insert a line break.

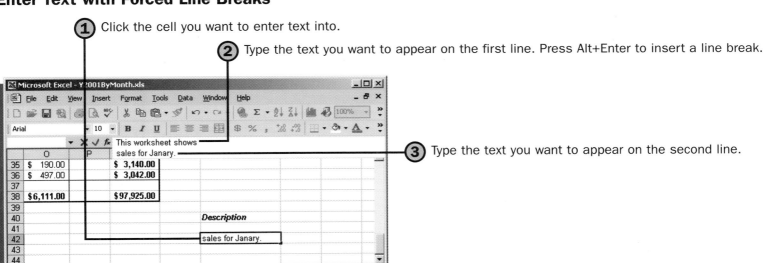

3 Type the text you want to appear on the second line.

> **SEE ALSO:** For information about how to make your columns wider to allow more text to appear within a cell, see "Resize a Column" on page 78.

Entering Numbers in Cells

The backbone of any workbook is the numerical data in its worksheets, whether that data reflects sales, employee salaries, or the quantity of a given product you have in inventory. Entering numbers in Excel is as simple as clicking the cell and typing, but you can also enter very large or very small numbers using scientific notation. In scientific notation, a number with a positive exponent is written as 1.00E+06, which is read as "one times ten to the sixth power." Numbers which are less than one can be written with negative exponents. For example, the number .001 would be written as 1.00E-03 and read as "one times ten to the negative third power."

Enter Numbers

(1) Click the cell you want to enter a number into.

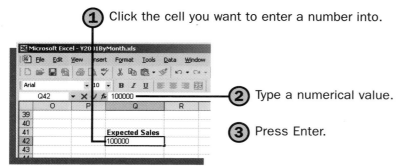

(2) Type a numerical value.

(3) Press Enter.

> **!** **TIP:** You can type a number but have it interpreted as a text value by typing ' (an apostrophe) before the number value. The apostrophe will not appear in the cell, but a smart tag will be available that provides you with some formatting options.

Enter Numbers Using Scientific Notation and Exponents

(1) Click the cell you want to enter a number into.

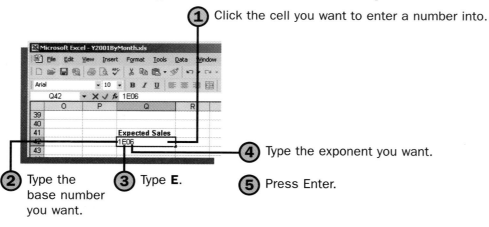

> **SEE ALSO:** For information about applying number formatting such as dollar and percent signs instead of typing them see "Formatting Cells Containing Numbers" on page 34.

(2) Type the base number you want.

(3) Type **E**.

(4) Type the exponent you want.

(5) Press Enter.

Entering Dates and Times in Cells

Dates are extremely important in any business or personal situation, so Excel takes care to get them right. Excel understands dates no matter how you type them, so feel free to type them in as needed. You can always change the formatting later.

Enter a Date

1 Click the cell you want to enter a date into.

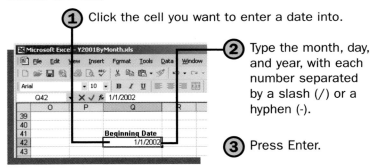

2 Type the month, day, and year, with each number separated by a slash (/) or a hyphen (-).

3 Press Enter.

> **CAUTION: Different countries have different customs for writing dates. For example, 07/04/01 could mean July 4, 2001, or April 7, 2001, depending on where you live.**

Enter a Time

1 Click the cell you want to enter a time into.

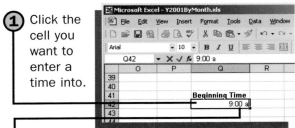

2 Type the hour, a colon (:), and the minutes. Press the Spacebar, and type **a** or **p** for A.M. or P.M.

3 Press Enter.

Enter a Date and Time

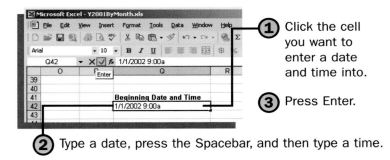

1 Click the cell you want to enter a date and time into.

3 Press Enter.

2 Type a date, press the Spacebar, and then type a time.

Enter the Current Date and Time

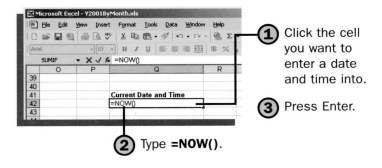

1 Click the cell you want to enter a date and time into.

3 Press Enter.

2 Type **=NOW()**.

> **SEE ALSO: For more information about formatting cells with dates, see "Formatting Cells Containing Dates" on page 35.**

Entering Data Using Fills

Entering long series of data, such as days in the month, weekdays, or a series of numbers with a definite progression, is tedious. As you type or paste those numbers, it's easy to forget which months have 31 days or what day of the week the first of a month falls on. Excel makes entering such series simple: With AutoFill, you can type a value in one cell and assign it to many other cells, type values in two cells and have Excel extend the series based on the relationship of the two numbers, or even extend dates by a day, a month, or a year.

Fill Data with AutoFill

(1) Type the value you want to appear in multiple cells.

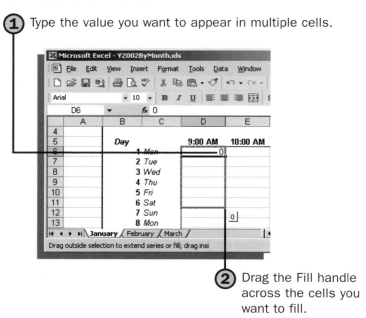

(2) Drag the Fill handle across the cells you want to fill.

Use AutoFill to Enter a Series of Values

(1) Type the first value for your list.

(2) Type the second value for the list.

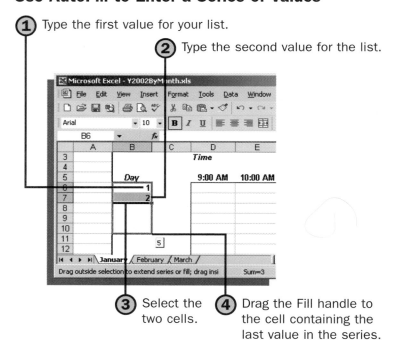

(3) Select the two cells.

(4) Drag the Fill handle to the cell containing the last value in the series.

> 🖱 **TRY THIS: Type** 1/1/2001 **in cell A1 and drag the fill handle across the cells you want to fill. Excel will fill your cells by increasing the day for every entry. Now click the AutoFill smart tag, and click Fill Years.**

Entering Data with Other Shortcuts

Excel gives you lots of ways to enter data quickly. The less time you spend typing in data, the more time you have to analyze and make decisions based on what the data tells you. One way Excel offers to help you enter data is that if it sees the first few characters of the text you're entering matches text from another cell in the same column, it will complete the rest of that text. If it's the text you want, you can accept it and move on. If not, just keep typing.

A similar way Excel simplifies data entry is by letting you pick the value for the active cell from a list of existing values in a column. That's not that important for a small worksheet, but when you're working with page after page of data, seeing a sorted list of possible values is a real help.

Enter Data with AutoComplete

① Type the beginning of an entry.

② Press Enter to accept the AutoComplete value.

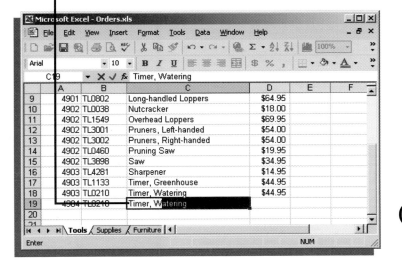

Pick Cell Data from a List

① Right-click a cell in a column with existing values, and click Pick From List from the shortcut menu.

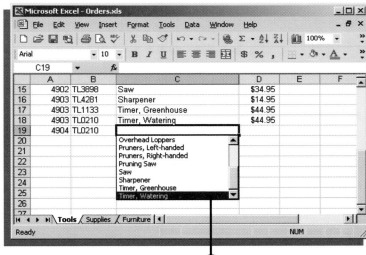

② Click the item in the list you want to enter.

> **✋ CAUTION: AutoComplete will only work if the text or data you are entering is similar to text already in the same column.**

Editing Cell Contents

You're not stuck with the first data you enter into a cell. In fact, you can change the value completely, delete it, or update it to reflect a supplier's new business name or a customer's new address. Neither are you stuck with only one way to edit the data: you can enter data either in the Formula Bar or directly in the cell.

Edit Cell Contents in the Formula Bar

1 Click the cell you want to edit.

2 Select the text you want to edit in the Formula Bar.

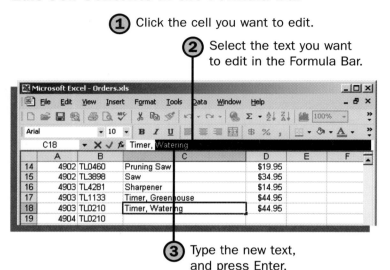

3 Type the new text, and press Enter.

Edit Cell Contents Directly in the Cell

1 Double-click the cell you want to edit.

2 Select the text you want to edit.

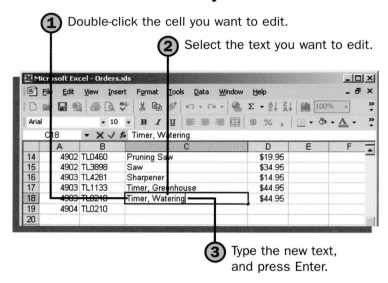

3 Type the new text, and press Enter.

CAUTION: Depending on what options you've selected, double-clicking a cell might not allow you to edit your data directly in the cell. If you find that you're unable to edit your data directly in the cell, choose Options from the Tools menu and click the Edit tab. Select the Edit Directly In Cell check box, and you will be able to edit the content in the cell.

Formatting Cell Contents

Some cells have values that need to stand out. Whether the value is a grand total for a year's sales or a label that lets your colleagues know that data entered into the worksheet must be within certain limits, you can change the font used to display the data, make the text larger or smaller, or make the text appear bold, italicized, or underlined. You can apply these settings by clicking the buttons of the same name on the Formatting toolbar, but formatting cell contents isn't an all or nothing proposition. If you want, you can choose to format a word or even a single character in a cell.

Change Font and Font Size

2 Click the Font down arrow on the Formatting toolbar.

1 Select the cells you want to format.

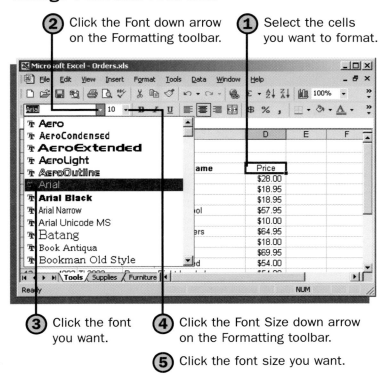

3 Click the font you want.

4 Click the Font Size down arrow on the Formatting toolbar.

5 Click the font size you want.

Change Text Appearance

1 Select the cells you want to format.

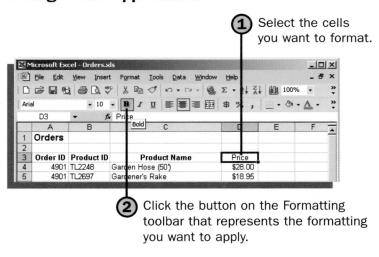

2 Click the button on the Formatting toolbar that represents the formatting you want to apply.

Format Part of a Cell's Contents

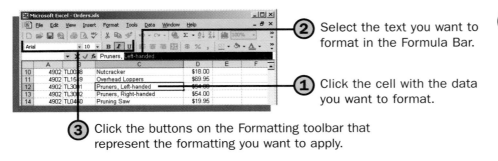

(2) Select the text you want to format in the Formula Bar.

(1) Click the cell with the data you want to format.

(3) Click the buttons on the Formatting toolbar that represent the formatting you want to apply.

CAUTION: When you select multiple cells to change their appearance, the range you select might have a combination of cells that have already had formatting applied to them and cells that do not have any formatting applied. If this is the case, you might have to click the toolbar buttons multiple times until all of the cells are formatted how you want them.

Formatting Cells Containing Numbers

Numerical data plays a central role in Excel workbooks, so it stands to reason that you have lots of options for choosing how you want your numbers to appear. Two frequently used formats are Currency, which displays a cell's contents as a monetary value; and Percent, which multiplies a value by 100 and adds a percent sign to the end. The two biggest benefits of formatting data as a percent are that you save a lot of time (and avoid mistakes) by not typing the decimal point or percent sign yourself, and that you can tell the values are percentages at a glance.

Two other options for formatting your data are to display the values in a cell with commas every third digit and to increase or decrease the number of digits to the right of the decimal point. While two decimal places is enough for most financial data, you might need to track currency exchanges to three or four decimal places.

Display Numerical Values as Currency and Percentages

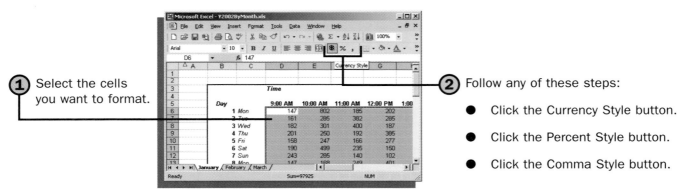

(1) Select the cells you want to format.

(2) Follow any of these steps:

● Click the Currency Style button.

● Click the Percent Style button.

● Click the Comma Style button.

Set the Number of Decimal Places

(1) Select the cells you want to format.

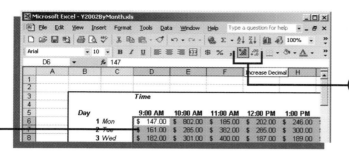

(2) Follow either or both of these steps:

- Click the Increase Decimal button.

- Click the Decrease Decimal button.

Formatting Cells Containing Dates

In many cases, knowing *when* something happened is just as important as knowing *what* happened. If you ran a garden supply store or nursery, for example, it would be useful to know that you get most of your customers on the weekends but that you make most of your large sales (most likely to landscape architects and other stores) during the week. There are lots of date formats to choose from—pick the one you like the best!

Set a Date Format

(1) Select the cells you want to format as a date.

(2) Right-click the selection, and choose Format Cells from the shortcut menu.

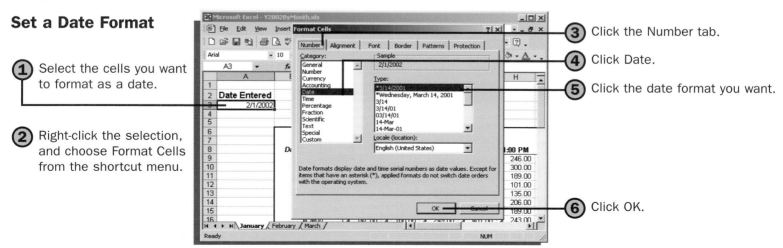

(3) Click the Number tab.

(4) Click Date.

(5) Click the date format you want.

(6) Click OK.

Aligning and Orienting Cell Contents

Most of the time you will want your text to be square with the left edge of a cell, but headings are much easier to read (and stand out better) when they're centered in a cell, and numbers are easier to read when the last digit of every number is flush with the right edge of a column. Similarly, if you want to create a tall, thin cell with text written in a vertical line, you can do so by typing your text into a cell and then changing the contents' orientation. When your data doesn't fit neatly into the width of a cell, you can choose to have the text displayed on a new line in the same cell. This setting, called *text wrapping*, treats a cell like a small word processor document with narrow margins.

Change the Text Alignment

(1) Select the cells you want to align.

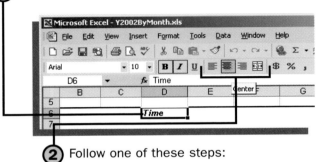

(2) Follow one of these steps:

- Click the Align Left button to align the text with the left edge of the cell.

- Click the Center button to center the text within the cell.

- Click the Align Right button to align the text with the right edge of the cell.

- Click the Merge And Center button to center the text across multiple columns.

Set Text Orientation and Wrapping

(1) Right-click the cells you want to orient, and choose Format Cells from the shortcut menu.

(2) Click the Alignment tab.

(3) Type the number of degrees you want to rotate the baseline of your text.

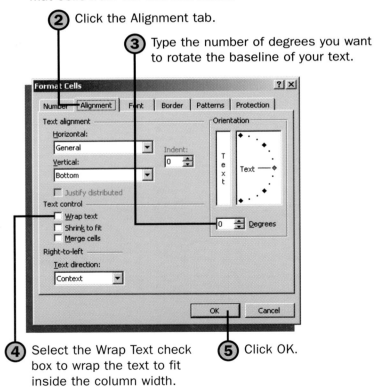

(4) Select the Wrap Text check box to wrap the text to fit inside the column width.

(5) Click OK.

Inserting a Symbol in a Cell

Not every bit of information can be communicated effectively with text. If your worksheet is meant for public consumption and you mention another company's products, you might want to include a trademark ("™") or another symbol to recognize that company's intellectual property. Excel—and the other Office programs—has lots of symbols you can use. If you use a symbol in the course of your everyday business, you can probably find it in Excel.

Add a Symbol to a Cell

1 Choose Symbol from the Insert menu.

2 If necessary, click the Symbols tab.

3 Click the Font down arrow.

4 Click the font from which you want to pick the symbol.

5 Double-click the symbol you want to insert.

6 Click the Close button.

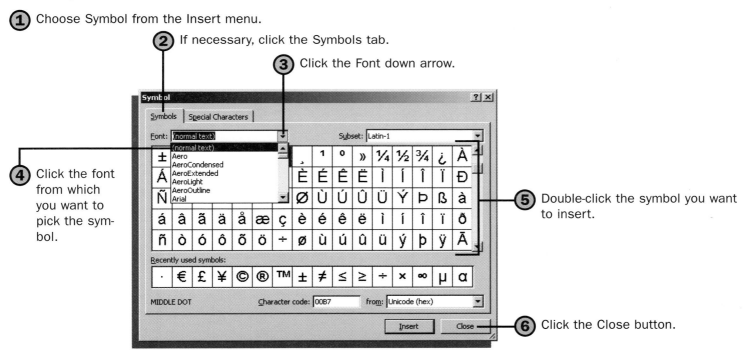

Creating Hyperlinks

One of the hallmarks of the World Wide Web is that documents published on the Web can have references, or hyperlinks, to points in the same document or to other Web documents. One great way to take advantage of this feature would be to create a workbook where you track sales by product and have a cell at the end of each product's row with a hyperlink to a Web page with in-depth product information. That information could be on another worksheet in the same workbook, in another file on your computer, or even on another computer entirely. Another type of hyperlink is the *mailto* hyperlink, which, when clicked, lets you send an e-mail message to the address referred to in the link.

Add a Hyperlink to a Place in the Same File

① Click the cell where you want to place a hyperlink.

② Click the Insert Hyperlink button on the Standard toolbar.

③ Click Place In This Document.

⑤ Type the cell reference of the cell to which you want to link.

⑥ Type a short phrase to describe the hyperlink's target.

④ Click the sheet you want to link to.

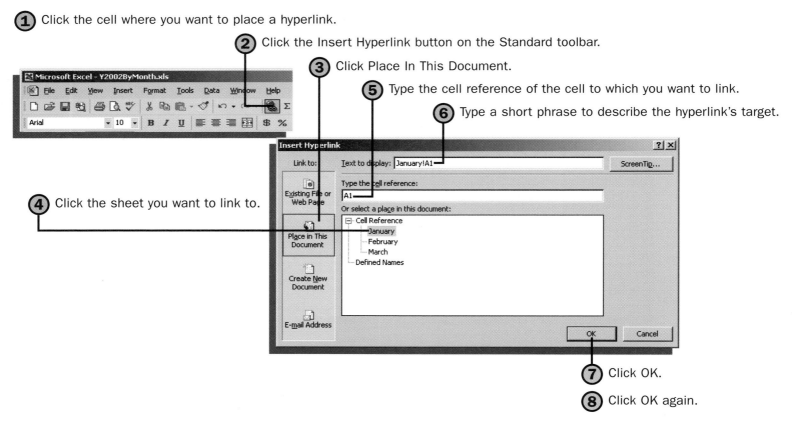

⑦ Click OK.

⑧ Click OK again.

Add a Hyperlink to Another File

① Click the cell where you want to place a hyperlink.

③ Click Existing File Or Web Page.

② Click the Insert Hyperlink button.

④ Navigate to the folder with the target file.

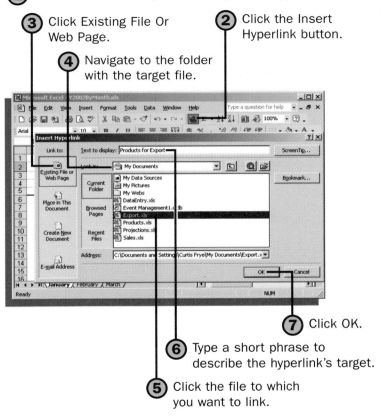

⑦ Click OK.

⑥ Type a short phrase to describe the hyperlink's target.

⑤ Click the file to which you want to link.

Add a Hyperlink to a Web Page

① Click the cell where you want to place a hyperlink.

③ Click Existing File Or Web Page.

② Click the Insert Hyperlink button.

④ Click Browsed Pages.

⑥ Type a short phrase to describe the hyperlink's target.

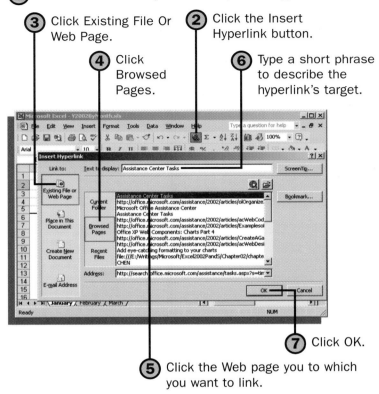

⑦ Click OK.

⑤ Click the Web page you to which you want to link.

Add a Mailto Hyperlink

1 Click the Insert Hyperlink button.

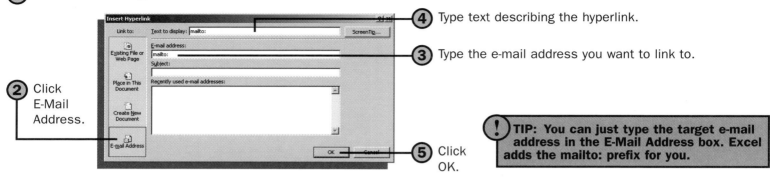

2 Click E-Mail Address.

4 Type text describing the hyperlink.

3 Type the e-mail address you want to link to.

> **! TIP: You can just type the target e-mail address in the E-Mail Address box. Excel adds the mailto: prefix for you.**

5 Click OK.

Cutting, Copying, and Pasting Cell Values

Once you've entered values into one or more cells, you can copy the values and paste them into another cell, remove the values from the cells and paste them elsewhere, or just cut the values and leave them on the clipboard. Excel 2002 gives you new abilities to control how pasted text appears in your worksheet. When you do paste data you've cut or copied from a cell, Excel displays a smart tag asking how you want to format the data you're pasting. You can choose to have the data retain its original formatting, adopt the formatting of the cell where you're pasting the data, or paste the data without formatting.

Cut a Cell Value

1 Select the cells you want to cut.

2 Click the Cut button on the Standard toolbar.

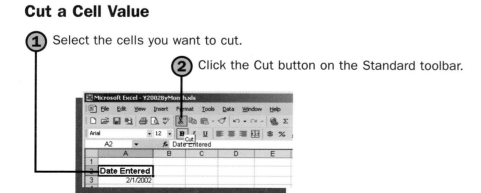

Copy a Cell Value

1 Select the cells you want to copy.

2 Click the Copy button on the Standard toolbar.

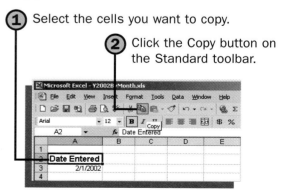

Paste a Cell Value ⊛ NEW FEATURE

(1) Click the cell where you want to paste your values.

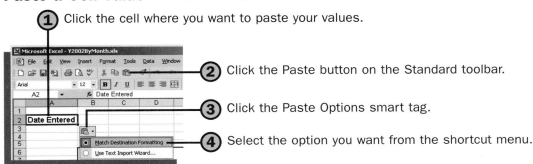

(2) Click the Paste button on the Standard toolbar.

(3) Click the Paste Options smart tag.

(4) Select the option you want from the shortcut menu.

Clearing Cell Contents

If you're lucky, you won't have to replace the data entry and formatting you've entered into a workbook; however, there might be times when you want to *clear* the data, formatting, or contents of a group of cells. Clearing is like cutting, but cutting differs because it always leaves the formatting in the cell from which you remove the data. When you clear a cell's contents, you have the option of returning the cell to its original state.

Clear a Cell

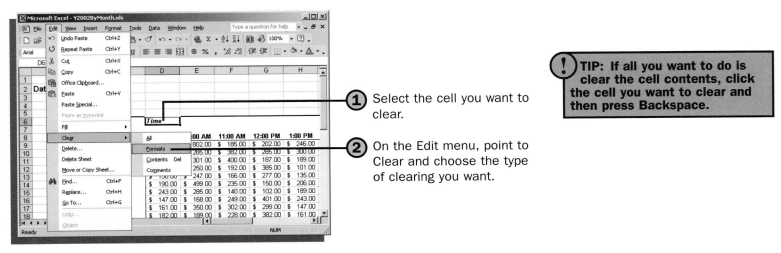

(1) Select the cell you want to clear.

(2) On the Edit menu, point to Clear and choose the type of clearing you want.

> **! TIP: If all you want to do is clear the cell contents, click the cell you want to clear and then press Backspace.**

Using the Office Clipboard

When you work in Excel, you can take advantage of the flexibility that comes with its place in the Office XP suite by using the Office Clipboard. The Office Clipboard, a task pane that's available in every Office XP application, keeps track of the last 24 items you've cut or copied from any Office document. You can open the Office Clipboard and then paste any of its contents into your workbook. If there's an item on the Office Clipboard you know you won't use again, you can always remove it.

Display the Contents of the Office Clipboard

(1) Choose Task Pane from the View menu.

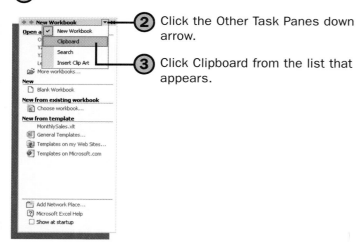

(2) Click the Other Task Panes down arrow.

(3) Click Clipboard from the list that appears.

Paste an Item from the Office Clipboard

(1) Click the cell where you want to paste a Clipboard item.

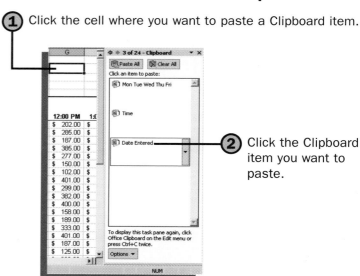

(2) Click the Clipboard item you want to paste.

Clear an Item from the Office Clipboard

(1) Point to the Clipboard item you want to delete.

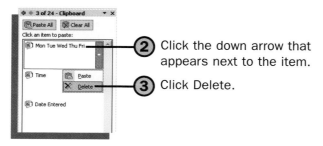

(2) Click the down arrow that appears next to the item.

(3) Click Delete.

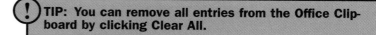

TIP: You can remove all entries from the Office Clipboard by clicking Clear All.

Undoing or Redoing an Action

One of the strengths of Excel is that it's easy to change the formatting, layout, and structure of your workbooks. The problem, of course, is that you might not have made the exact change you wanted. If that's the case, and you haven't closed the workbook since you made the change you want to get rid of, you can easily undo your changes by clicking the Undo button. Excel keeps a record of your changes, which you can see by clicking the down arrow at the right edge of the Undo button. Clicking the Redo button, as you might expect, reapplies the last change you "undid."

Undo or Redo an Action

1 Follow either of these steps:

- Click the Undo button.
- Click the Redo button.

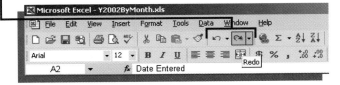

Finding and Replacing Text

After you've entered data into a workbook, you might need to search the document for a particular word or, if one of your suppliers changes the name of a product, replace some or all instances of a word or a phrase. You can do just that using Find and Replace in Excel.

Find a Word or a Value

1 Choose Find from the Edit menu.

2 Type the text you want to find.

3 Click Find All.

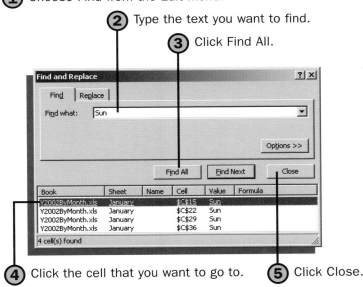

4 Click the cell that you want to go to.

5 Click Close.

> **! TIP:** The Undo and Redo buttons have down arrows at their right edge. You can click the Undo or Redo down arrow to reveal a list of recently executed and undone actions. Click an item on the list to undo or redo every action up to that point.

Replace a Word or a Value

(1) Choose Replace from the Edit menu.

(2) Type the text you want to replace.

(3) Type the text you want to take the place of the existing text.

> **CAUTION:** Clicking Replace All is a quick way to change every occurrence of one value to another value, but it can also have unintended consequences. For example, changing "ear" to "bear" would change "hearing" to "hbearing". It's much safer to use Find Next and verify each change.

Find and Replace ?| X|

Find   Replace

Find what: Sun

Replace with: Sunday

Options >>

Replace All   Replace   Find All   Find Next   Close —— **(5)** Click Close.

(4) Follow any of these steps:

- Click Replace to replace the text.

- Click Find Next to skip this instance of the text and move to the next time it occurs.

- Click Replace All to replace every instance of the text.

Checking the Spelling of Your Worksheet

After you create a workbook and fill it with data, labels, and explanatory text, you should always use the Excel spelling checker to check your text for misspellings. If Excel finds a word it doesn't recognize, the spelling checker will ask you whether it's correct and, if not, might suggest alternatives. You can have Excel ignore a word once or for the entire document, choose one of the program's suggestions, or even add new words to the dictionary. Products are often given unique names, so adding them to the dictionary Excel uses to check all documents will save you a lot of time.

Check Spelling

① Click the Spelling button on the Standard toolbar. If you are asked whether you want to save your work, do so.

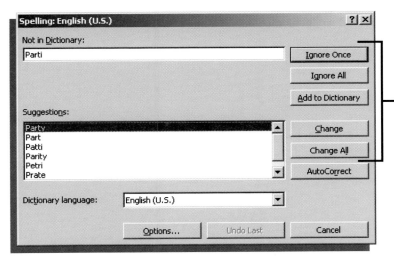

② Follow any of these steps:

- Click Ignore Once to ignore the current misspelling.

- Click Ignore All to ignore all instances of the mis-spelled word.

- Click Add To Dictionary to add the current word to the dictionary.

- Click the correct spelling, and then click Change to replace the current misspelling with the correct word.

- Click the correct spelling, and then click Change All to replace all instances of the current misspelling with the correct word.

③ Click OK to clear the dialog box that appears after spell-ing check is complete.

! TIP: Excel shares its spelling dictionary with all other Microsoft Office programs, so any words you add to your dictionary will be available in Microsoft Word, Microsoft Access, Microsoft PowerPoint, and Microsoft FrontPage.

4 Managing and Viewing Worksheets

O nce you've built your workbook, you can reorganize it as needed. If you use data in a specific worksheet often, you can move the worksheet to the front of the workbook. Similarly, if you often switch between two worksheets, you can put their sheet tabs next to each other so that you don't have to spend time moving from one worksheet to the other. Another way you can save time is to enter the same data in, or apply the same formatting to, equivalent cells in several worksheets at once.

Finally, you can change how Excel displays your data in a workbook. If you have a series of headings in the first row of a worksheet, they don't have to disappear when you scroll down. Instead, you can have Excel "freeze" the rows at the top of the screen, and then you will be able to scroll down as far as you want without losing your guides at the top.

In this chapter, you'll learn how to:

● View and select worksheets.

● Rename worksheets.

● Move and copy worksheets within a workbook or between workbooks.

● Insert and delete worksheets.

● Freeze worksheet rows and columns.

● Split a worksheet into independent areas.

Viewing and Selecting Worksheets

Every Excel workbook should hold data on a given subject, such as the products you carry, your customers, or your sales. By the same token, every page, or *worksheet*, in a workbook should store part of the workbook's data. One way to divide your data is by time. For example, if you track your sales by the hour, you could easily fit a month's worth of data in a worksheet; at most you'd need 31 rows to cover every day and, if your store were open around the clock, 24 columns to take care of the hours. You can view individual worksheets quickly, and it's simple to work with more than one worksheet at a time.

Select Multiple Worksheets

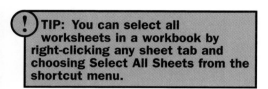

TIP: You can select all worksheets in a workbook by right-clicking any sheet tab and choosing Select All Sheets from the shortcut menu.

1 Click the sheet tab of the first worksheet you want to select.

You can select a single worksheet by clicking its sheet tab.

2 Hold down the Ctrl key, and click the sheet tabs of additional worksheets you want to select.

SEE ALSO: For information about adding worksheets to a workbook, see "Inserting or Deleting Worksheets" on page 53.

TIP: To select multiple adjacent worksheets, click the first worksheet, hold down the Shift key, and then click the last sheet tab you want to select.

Renaming Worksheets

When you create a workbook, Excel names your worksheets Sheet1, Sheet2, and Sheet3. Those names are fine when you first create a workbook, but after you've added data to several worksheets, naming the sheet tabs will help you and your colleagues find the data you're looking for. As always, if you think of a better name for your worksheets or even want to change the name of a worksheet temporarily to make it stand out, you can do so any time you want.

Change the Name of a Worksheet

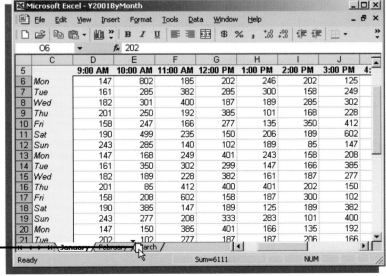

① Double-click the sheet tab of the worksheet you want to rename.

② Type the new name of the worksheet, and press Enter.

Moving Worksheets

Business needs change—the data that was so important yesterday might be of only passing significance today. In fact, if a new customer sends a big order your way, you might spend most of your time adding to and reading from a worksheet you hadn't looked at more than twice in the previous month. If that worksheet is at the back of your workbook, you can move it to the front to make it easier to find in the workbook. Or, if you keep every other worksheet relating to that customer in a separate workbook, you can move the worksheet from its current spot to its rightful place in the other workbook.

Move Worksheets Within the Workbook

① Drag the sheet tab of the worksheet you want to move to the new location you want.

Move Worksheets to Another Workbook

① Open the work-book that will receive the worksheets.

② Switch to the work-book that contains the worksheets you want to move, hold down the Ctrl key, and click the sheet tabs of the worksheets you want to move.

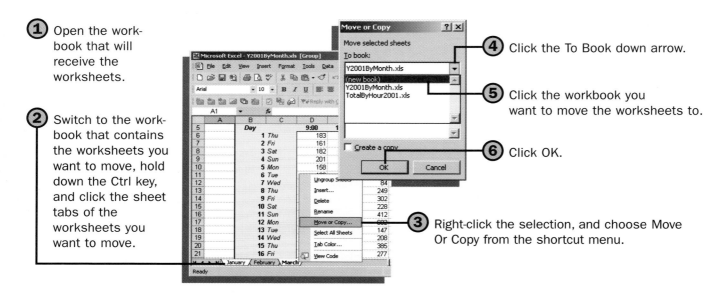

④ Click the To Book down arrow.

⑤ Click the workbook you want to move the worksheets to.

⑥ Click OK.

③ Right-click the selection, and choose Move Or Copy from the shortcut menu.

! **TIP:** If you want to position a worksheet last in a workbook, right-click the worksheet you want to move, choose Move Or Copy from the shortcut menu, click Move To End, and click OK.

Copying Worksheets

At the end of a calendar month, when you create a new worksheet to store data for the next month, you might want to include the entire worksheet as part of a monthly overview to your general manager. Rather than keep all of the worksheets in their original workbooks and flip from document to document when you create your presentation, you can copy the worksheet from the current workbook (and any other worksheets with data you want to include) to a central document. Going from worksheet to worksheet is much easier than going from work-book to workbook!

Copy Worksheets Within the Workbook

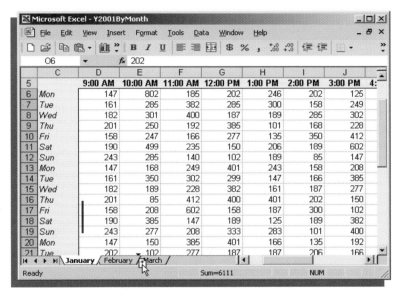

① Hold the down Ctrl key and drag the worksheet you want to copy to the new location you want.

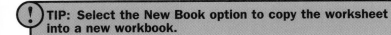
TIP: Select the New Book option to copy the worksheet into a new workbook.

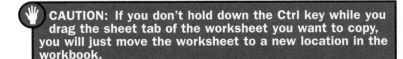
CAUTION: If you don't hold down the Ctrl key while you drag the sheet tab of the worksheet you want to copy, you will just move the worksheet to a new location in the workbook.

Copy Worksheets to Another Workbook

1 Open the workbook that will receive the new worksheets.

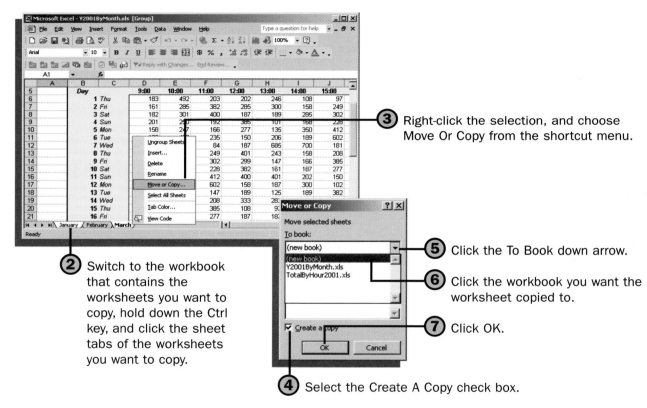

3 Right-click the selection, and choose Move Or Copy from the shortcut menu.

2 Switch to the workbook that contains the worksheets you want to copy, hold down the Ctrl key, and click the sheet tabs of the worksheets you want to copy.

5 Click the To Book down arrow.

6 Click the workbook you want the worksheet copied to.

7 Click OK.

4 Select the Create A Copy check box.

Inserting or Deleting Worksheets

If you haven't changed Excel from the way it was installed, any workbooks you create will contain three worksheets. Three worksheets are plenty of room if you're working at home and perhaps more than you'll need for small projects, but you'll run out of space quickly if you're tracking products or monthly sales. Adding or deleting a worksheet takes just a moment, but if you want to delete a worksheet, be sure you're getting rid of the right one!

Insert a Blank Worksheet

1 Right-click the sheet tab of the worksheet that follows the location where you want to insert a worksheet, and choose Insert from the shortcut menu.

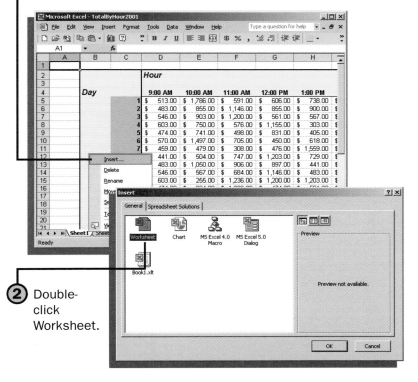

2 Double-click Worksheet.

Delete One or More Worksheets

1 Hold down the Ctrl key, and click the sheet tabs of the worksheets you want to delete.

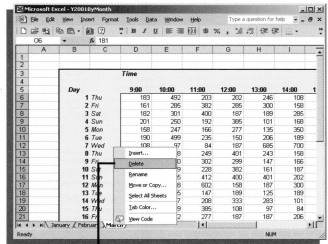

2 Right-click the selection, and choose Delete from the shortcut menu.

> ✋ **CAUTION:** If you have data in the worksheet that you want to delete, deleting the worksheet will erase all the data in that worksheet. This operation is not reversible.

Entering Data on and Formatting Many Worksheets at Once

After you've worked with Excel for a while, you'll probably develop standard worksheets you use over and over. When working with worksheets that follow a common layout, you might want to enter a set of data across multiple worksheets. For example, you might have a set of column headers that you want to appear on several worksheets, and you'd like to avoid creating them from scratch for each individual worksheet. In Excel 2002, you can save lots of time by entering data and formatting in equivalent blocks of cells on multiple worksheets. If you have existing data you want to paste into several worksheets at the same time, you can do that as well.

Enter and Format Data on Several Worksheets at One Time

1 Hold down the Ctrl key, and click the sheet tab of every worksheet on which you want to enter the same data or apply the same formatting.

2 Type the data you want to appear in the same cell on every selected worksheet.

3 Right-click the cell you want to format, and choose Format Cells from the shortcut menu.

4 Click the tab that contains the formatting you want.

5 Specify the formatting options you want.

6 Click OK.

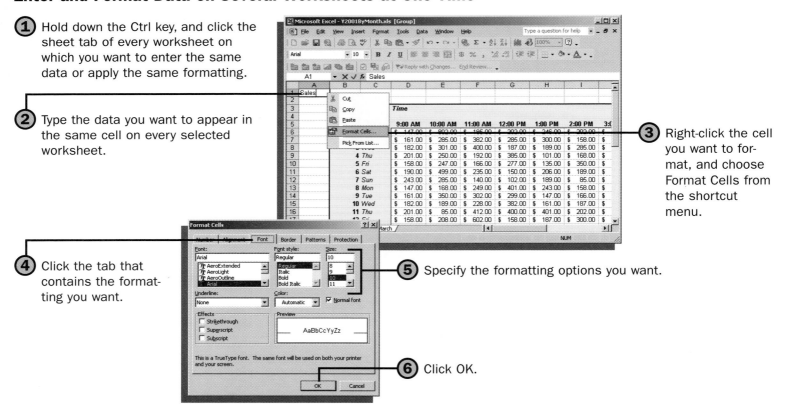

Copy Cells from One Worksheet to a Group of Worksheets

1 Select the cells you want to copy.

2 Click the Copy button on the Standard toolbar.

5 Click the Paste button on the Standard toolbar.

4 Click the cell you want to receive the data.

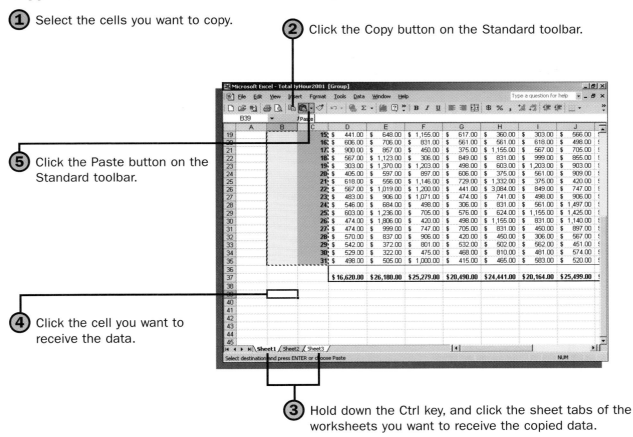

3 Hold down the Ctrl key, and click the sheet tabs of the worksheets you want to receive the copied data.

> **(!) TIP:** When you paste cells to more than one worksheet, the cells are pasted with their original formatting and the Paste Options smart tag doesn't appear. You can change the formatting of the pasted cells once they're in the new worksheet.

Changing How You Look at Excel Workbooks

When you're examining your Excel data to make a business decision, you'll probably need to look at data from more than one worksheet or even more than one workbook. Hourly sales totals can help determine when you need more staff on the floor, but if you keep track of the number of customers in the store as well, you might find that your great sales on Monday mornings come from landscape architects loading up for the week. In that case, you'd be better off having your warehouse staff and not your counter clerks show up to handle the load.

You can open more than one workbook at a time and arrange them on the screen so that you can read data from both sources at once. You can do something similar if you have relevant data in two parts of the same worksheet. If you can't see everything you need to see, you can "split" the worksheet into two or four units, all with independent scroll bars.

View Different Parts of One Worksheet at the Same Time

1 Click the cell where you want to split the worksheet.

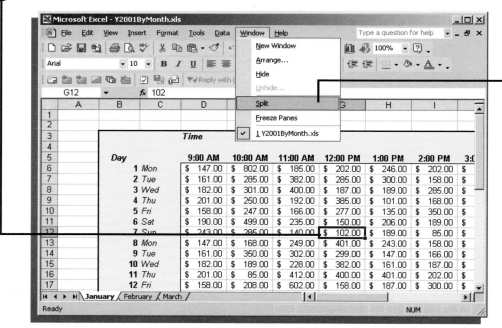

2 Choose Split from the Window menu.

> **!** TIP: To split a worksheet into two regions, click the row or column head where you want to create the split.

View Multiple Workbooks at the Same Time

(1) Open all the workbooks you want to view.

(2) Choose Arrange from the Window menu.

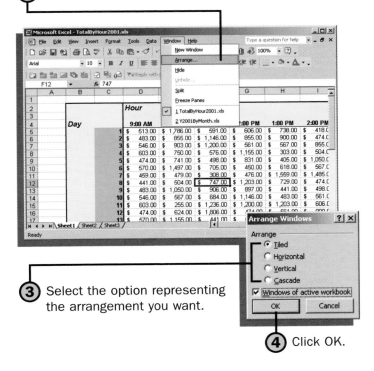

(3) Select the option representing the arrangement you want.

(4) Click OK.

> **(!) TIP:** If you want to display every worksheet in the active workbook, select the Windows Of Active Workbook check box in the Arrange Windows dialog box. You should keep in mind that if you have more than four worksheets in the active workbook, the individual worksheets will be displayed in a very small area.

View Multiple Parts of a Worksheet by Freezing Panes

(1) Click the cell below and to the right of where you want to freeze the worksheet.

(2) Choose Freeze Panes from the Window menu.

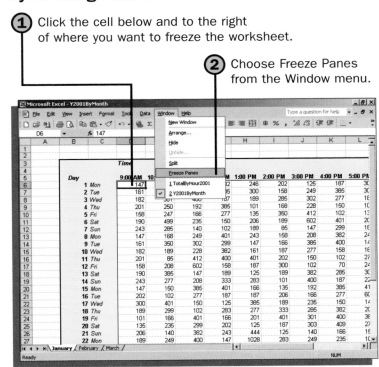

Remove the Split from a Window

(1) Choose Remove Split from the Window menu.

Unfreeze a Pane

(1) Choose Unfreeze Panes from the Window menu.

Naming and Using Worksheet Views

Once you've set up your Excel documents so that you can read them effectively, you don't need to re-create the arrangement every time you run Excel. Instead, you can record the arrangement, which includes splits, frozen rows and columns, and hidden cells, in a *view*. Views are especially handy for worksheets that will be used by different people, all of whom need different information. Different views can be created for each person, so if the data one person would view spans many columns, you can set the print settings to Landscape mode for that view.

Name the Current View of the Worksheet

(1) Arrange your Excel window as you would like it to appear.

(2) Choose Custom Views from the View menu.

Switch to Another View of the Worksheet

(1) Choose Custom Views from the View menu.

(2) Click the view you want.

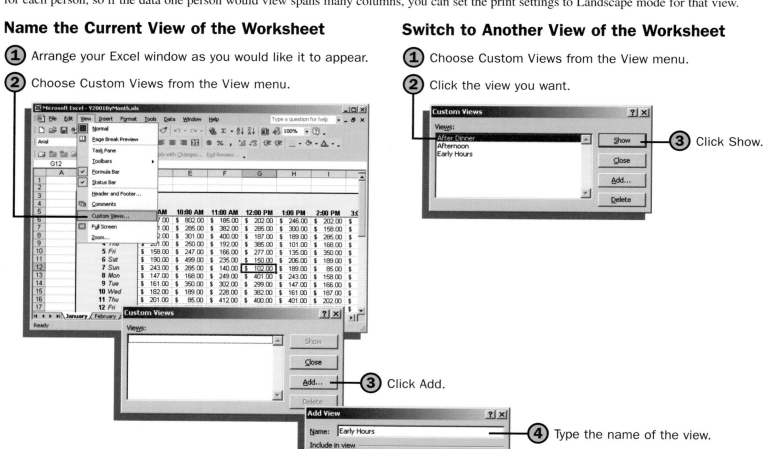

(3) Click Show.

(3) Click Add.

(4) Type the name of the view.

(5) Select what you want included in the view.

(6) Click OK.

5 Using Formulas and Functions

Microsoft Excel workbooks allow you to do much more than simply store and organize your data. One important task you can perform in Excel is to summarize the values in related cells. Whether those cells represent the sales for a day at your store, the returns from your personal investments, or your times in bicycle races, you can find the total or average of the values, identify the minimum or maximum value in a group, or perform dozens of other calculations on your data. Many times you can't access the information you want without referencing more than one cell, and it's also often true you'll use the data in the same group of cells in more than one calculation. Excel makes it easy to reference a number of cells at once, letting you build your calculations quickly.

In this section, you'll learn how to:

● Create and edit formulas.

● Create, edit, and delete named ranges.

● Use named ranges in formulas.

● Summarize the values in groups of cells.

● Explore the Excel function library.

● Create conditional functions.

● Troubleshoot your formulas.

Understanding Formulas and Cell References

Once you've added your data to a worksheet, you can summarize the data by creating *formulas*. A formula is an expression that performs calculations on your data. For example, in a worksheet that lists hourly sales for a day in a single row of cells, you can build a formula in the last cell in that row to find the total of all sales for the day. You can also build the formula to calculate the average or to find the lowest or highest hourly value.

When you build a formula, you need to identify the worksheet cells that will provide the values for the formula and the operations you want performed on those values. To identify a cell, you give its *cell reference*. The first cell in the first column is cell A1, meaning column A, row 1. If you examine a formula, you will sometimes see a cell reference written as $A$1, rather than just A1. The difference is that cell references written with the dollar signs are *absolute references*, meaning the reference won't change when the formula is copied to another cell, and

cell references written without the dollar signs are *relative references*, which will change when the formula with the references is copied to another cell.

The benefit of relative references is that you can write a formula once and copy it to as many other cells as you like. As an example, consider the following worksheet, which tracks hourly sales for a month.

The cells in column Q have formulas that find the sum of the hourly sales values in column D through column O. The formula in cell Q6, =SUM(D6:O6), finds the sum of cells in row 6, corresponding to Monday, January 1. When you copy the formula from cell Q6 to cell Q7, the formula changes to =SUM(D7:O7). Excel notices that you copied the formula to a new row and assumes you want the formula to work on that data. Had you written the formula as =SUM($D$6:$O$6), however, Excel would notice that the formula used absolute references and would copy the formula as =SUM($D$6:$O$6).

If you want to use a value from a cell in another workbook, you can do it. Excel uses *3D references,* which means that any cell in any workbook can be described by three pieces of information:

● The name of the workbook

● The name of the worksheet

● The cell reference

Here's the reference for cell Q38 on the January worksheet in the Y2001ByMonth workbook:

[Y2001ByMonth.xls]January!$Q$38

The good news is that you don't need to remember how to create these references yourself. If you want to use a cell in another workbook in a formula, all you need to do is create the formula, click the spot where you'll use the value, and click the cell in the other workbook. Excel will fill in the reference for you.

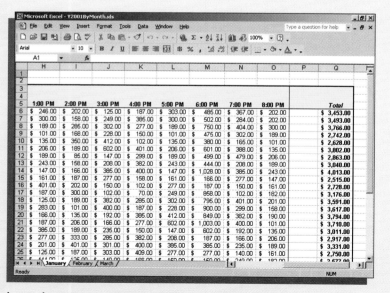

Assigning Names to Groups of Cells

When you work with large amounts of data, it's easy to lose track of which cells contain which data. In addition, it can be difficult to locate data in workbooks you didn't create. Although you might always store product prices in one worksheet column, there's no guarantee your colleagues will follow the same pattern! One way to prevent confusion is to define a *named range* for any cell group that holds specific information. For example, in a worksheet with customer order data, you can define the Totals named range to represent the cells where the total for each order is stored. Once you've defined the named range, you can display its contents, rename it, or delete it.

Create a Named Range

② Click the Name Box on the Formula Bar.

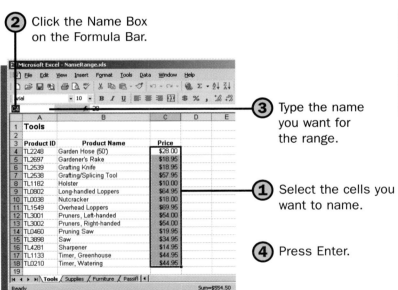

③ Type the name you want for the range.

① Select the cells you want to name.

④ Press Enter.

Go To a Named Range

① Click the Name Box down arrow.

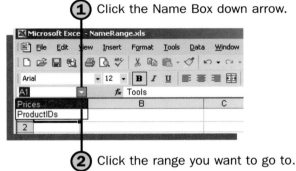

② Click the range you want to go to.

> **SEE ALSO:** For information about selecting cells from several parts of the same worksheet, see "Select a Noncontiguous Group of Cells" on page 26.

Delete a Named Range

(1) On the Insert menu, point to Name and choose Define.

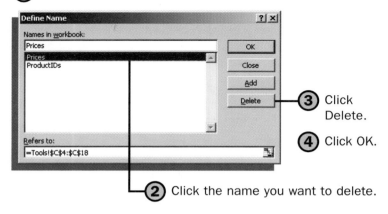

(3) Click Delete.

(4) Click OK.

(2) Click the name you want to delete.

> **TIP:** You can select more than one named range at a time by clicking the Name box's down arrow, clicking the first range you want to select, holding down the Ctrl key, and then clicking the additional ranges.

Rename a Named Range

(1) Click the Name Box down arrow.

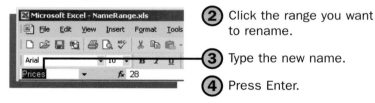

(2) Click the range you want to rename.

(3) Type the new name.

(4) Press Enter.

> **CAUTION:** When you rename a range, Excel actually creates a new range made up of the same cells without deleting the old range. If you want to use the old name for another range, you must delete the old range first.

Creating Simple Cell Formulas

Building calculations in Excel is pretty straightforward. If you want to find the sum of the values in two cells, you just type an equal sign, the reference of the first cell, a plus sign (+), and the reference of the second cell. The formula you enter will appear on the formula bar, where you can examine and edit it.

CAUTION: Be sure there's no space before the equal sign in your formula. If there is, Excel will interpret the cell's contents as text, not a formula.

Build a Formula

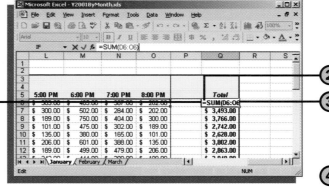

1 Click the cell you want to enter a formula in.

2 Type =.

3 Type the expression representing the calculation you want to perform. For example, **=SUM(D6:O6)**.

4 Press Enter.

Edit a Formula

1 Click the cell you want to edit.

2 Select the part of the formula you want to edit in the formula bar.

3 Make any changes that you want.

4 Press Enter.

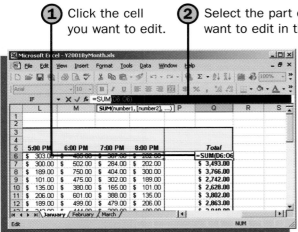

TRY THIS: Type common formulas **in the Ask A Question box, press Enter, and then click Examples Of Commonly Used Formulas from the list of available topics. The Microsoft Help file that appears has quite a few examples of formulas you might want to create.**

Using Names in Formulas

When you define a named range, you create a shortcut that you can use to refer to a group of cells. A great way to use named ranges is in formulas. Instead of entering the references of every cell you want to use in your calculation, you can type in the name of the range. When you reference named ranges in formulas, your formulas will be shorter and easier to understand. Rather than seeing a series of cell references you need to examine, you and your colleagues can rely on the named ranges to understand the goal of a calculation.

> **TIP: If you change the name of a range of cells, Excel will automatically make the name change in every one of your formulas.**

Create a Formula with a Named Range

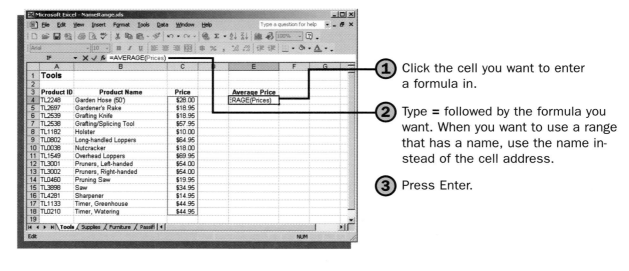

1. Click the cell you want to enter a formula in.

2. Type = followed by the formula you want. When you want to use a range that has a name, use the name instead of the cell address.

3. Press Enter.

> **CAUTION: You can only use a named range of cells inside one of Excel's built-in functions, although you can use a named cell anywhere you want. If you include a named range of cells in a normal formula that you create, you will get an error.**

Creating Formulas with Cells from Other Workbooks

One of the strengths of Excel is that you aren't limited to using cells from the current workbook in your formulas. If you want, you can use data from any other workbook in your calculations. For example, you might have a workbook where you track monthly advertising sales for your newsletter. If you want to create a new workbook to summarize all income and expenses for your publication, you can do so. By letting you create formulas with cells from more than one workbook, Excel makes it easy for you to organize your workbooks so that each workbook holds data about a specific subject. You can not only find the data easily, but also reference it anywhere else.

Once you've created links between workbooks, you can have Excel update your calculation if the data in the linked cell has changed. You can also change the cell to which you've linked or, if the workbook with the cell to which you were linking has been moved or deleted, you can delete the link and have Excel store the last value from the calculation.

Use Cells in Other Workbooks in a Formula

(1) Open the workbook containing the cell you want to reference in your formula.

(2) Choose Arrange from the Window menu.

(3) Select the Tiled option.

(4) Click OK.

(5) Click the cell in which you want to create the formula.

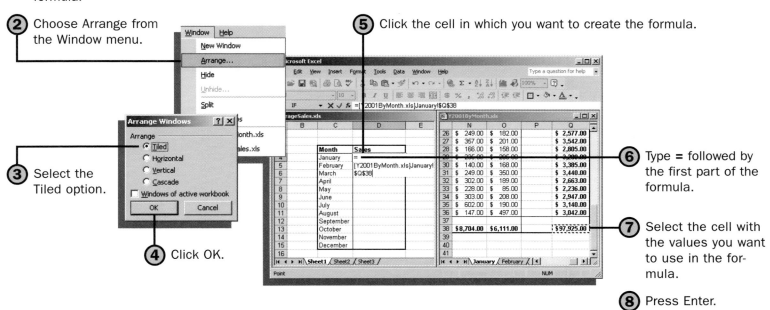

(6) Type = followed by the first part of the formula.

(7) Select the cell with the values you want to use in the formula.

(8) Press Enter.

Break Links to Other Workbooks and Convert to Values

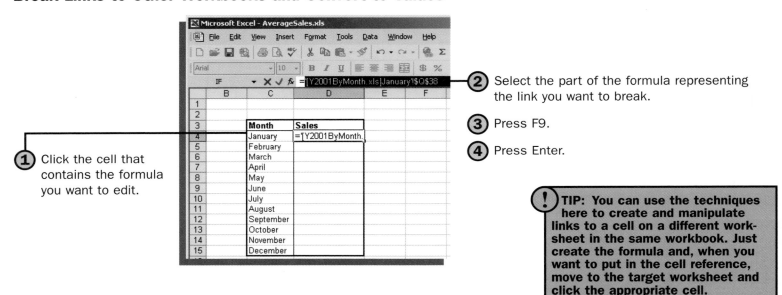

(1) Click the cell that contains the formula you want to edit.

(2) Select the part of the formula representing the link you want to break.

(3) Press F9.

(4) Press Enter.

> **(!) TIP: You can use the techniques here to create and manipulate links to a cell on a different worksheet in the same workbook. Just create the formula and, when you want to put in the cell reference, move to the target worksheet and click the appropriate cell.**

Refresh Links

(1) Choose Links from the Edit menu.

(2) Click the link you want to update.

(3) Click Update Values.

(4) Click Close.

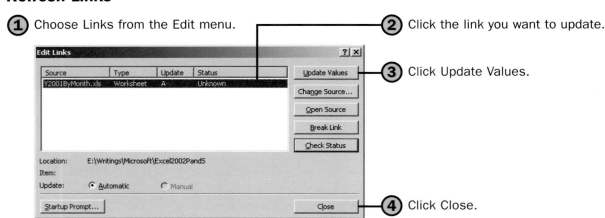

Changing Links to Different Workbooks

(1) Choose Links from the Edit menu.

(2) Click the link you want to change.

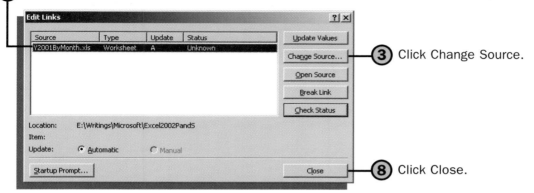

(3) Click Change Source.

(8) Click Close.

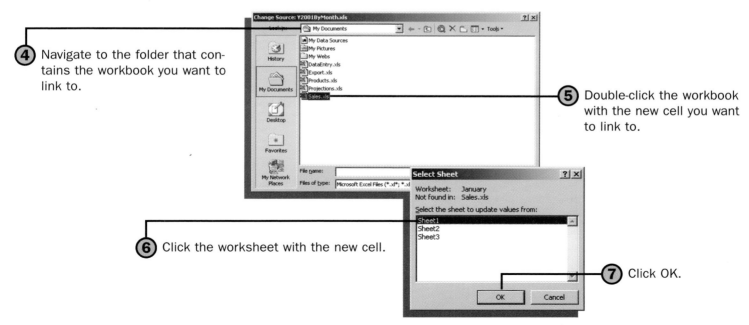

(4) Navigate to the folder that contains the workbook you want to link to.

(5) Double-click the workbook with the new cell you want to link to.

(6) Click the worksheet with the new cell.

(7) Click OK.

Summing a Group of Cells

Sometimes, such as when you're entering data into a worksheet or you're curious to find out the sum or average of the values in a few cells, it's too much work to find a blank cell and write a formula to calculate the sum or average for the cells. Rather than make you create a separate formula, Excel calculates a running total for the currently selected cells and displays the result on the status bar. Finding the sum of the values in the selected cells is the most commonly used operation, so Excel finds the sum by default. You can choose from several other operations, though, or even tell Excel not to calculate a running total for any selected cells.

Find the Sum of Data in a Group of Cells

1 Select the cells you want to sum.

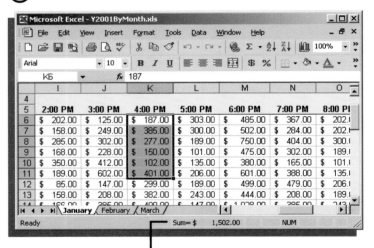

The summary operation and result of the summary appear on the status bar.

Summarize Data in a Group of Cells

1 Select the cells you want to summarize.

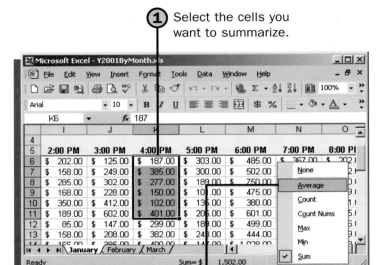

2 Right-click the status bar, and choose the summary operation you want from the shortcut menu.

> **! TIP: To turn off running totals, right-click the status bar, and choose None from the shortcut menu.**

Creating a Summary Formula

Once you've entered data into a worksheet, you can create formulas to summarize the values and display the result of the calculation. There are many ways you can summarize the values in a group of cells: You can find the total or average of the cell values, identify the maximum or minimum value in the group, or simply count the number of cells containing values. You can create these formulas by clicking the cell below or to the right of the cells you want to summarize and clicking the AutoSum button. Clicking the AutoSum button itself creates a SUM formula, which finds the arithmetic sum of the values, but you can choose other calculations by clicking the AutoSum button's down arrow. After you've created the formula you want, you can use the result in other calculations.

Create an AutoSum Function

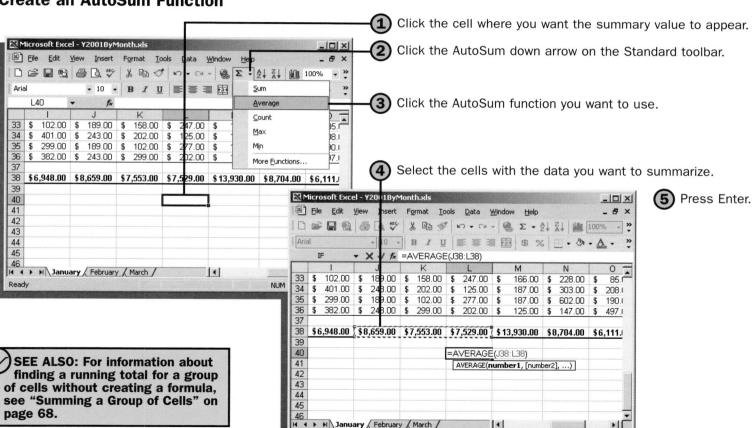

(1) Click the cell where you want the summary value to appear.

(2) Click the AutoSum down arrow on the Standard toolbar.

(3) Click the AutoSum function you want to use.

(4) Select the cells with the data you want to summarize.

(5) Press Enter.

SEE ALSO: For information about finding a running total for a group of cells without creating a formula, see "Summing a Group of Cells" on page 68.

Summing with Subtotals and Grand Totals

You will frequently need to organize the data in an Excel worksheet by one or more criteria. For example, you might have a worksheet where you list yearly sales for each product you offer, with the products broken down by category. If your data is organized this way, you can have Excel calculate a subtotal for each category of products. When you create a subtotal, you identify the cells with the values to be calculated and the cells that identify the change from one category to the next. Excel will update the subtotal and grand total for you if the value of any cell changes.

Create a Subtotal

1 Choose Subtotals from the Data menu.

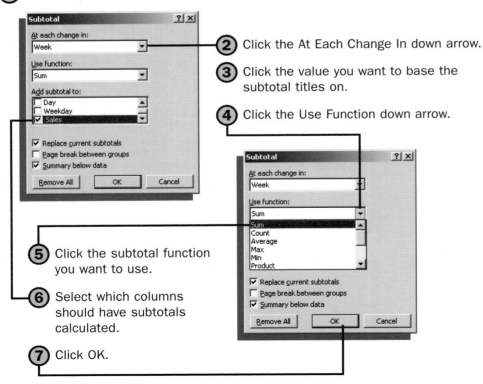

2 Click the At Each Change In down arrow.

3 Click the value you want to base the subtotal titles on.

4 Click the Use Function down arrow.

5 Click the subtotal function you want to use.

6 Select which columns should have subtotals calculated.

7 Click OK.

Remove All Subtotals

1 Select the cells that are subtotaled.

2 Choose Subtotals from the Data menu.

3 Click Remove All.

Exploring the Excel Function Library

There are dozens of different functions you can create in Excel. You can use Excel functions to determine mortgage payments, perform scientific calculations, or find the square root of a number. The best way to become familiar with the formulas available in Excel is to display the Insert Function dialog box and move through the listed functions, clicking the ones that look interesting. When you click a function, its description appears at the bottom of the dialog box.

Another way to get information about a function is to view the ScreenTip that appears next to the function. If you double-click a cell with a function, a ScreenTip with the function's structure and expected values appears below it. Clicking an element of the structure points to the cell or cells providing that value.

List Functions Available from the Excel Library

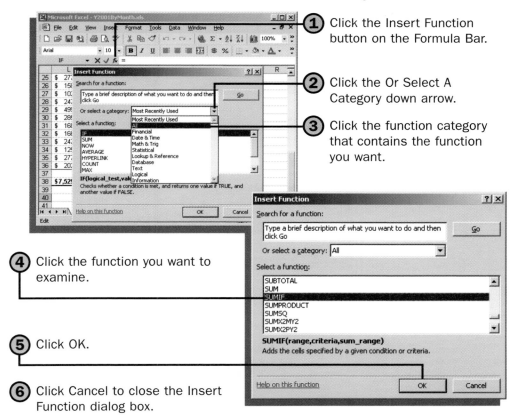

① Click the Insert Function button on the Formula Bar.

② Click the Or Select A Category down arrow.

③ Click the function category that contains the function you want.

④ Click the function you want to examine.

⑤ Click OK.

⑥ Click Cancel to close the Insert Function dialog box.

Use Function ScreenTips

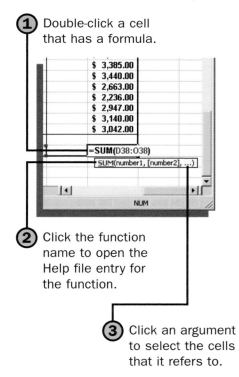

① Double-click a cell that has a formula.

② Click the function name to open the Help file entry for the function.

③ Click an argument to select the cells that it refers to.

Using the IF Function

In addition to calculating values based on the contents of other cells, you can have Excel take different actions based on the contents of those other cells by using the IF function. For example, if you create a workbook to track the times of riders in a bicycle-racing club, you can create a formula to compare each rider's time to their previous times. When someone's most recent time is the lowest time in the group, you can have Excel display "Personal Best" in the cell with the formula, alerting you to congratulate the rider in your next club newsletter.

Create an IF Function

1 Click the cell you want to enter an IF function in.

2 Click the Insert Function button on the Formula Bar.

3 Click the Or Select A Category down arrow.

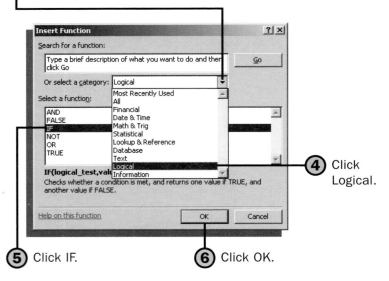

4 Click Logical.

5 Click IF.

6 Click OK.

 CAUTION: The text message must be enclosed in quotes.

7 Type a conditional statement that evaluates to true or false.

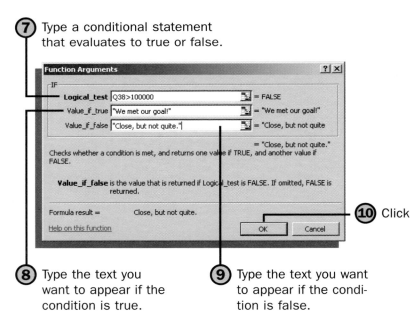

10 Click

8 Type the text you want to appear if the condition is true.

9 Type the text you want to appear if the condition is false.

TIP: You can also create an expression in the Value_if_true and Value_if_false boxes. Excel will display the result of the expression in the appropriate box.

Checking Formula References

When you create a formula that draws values from several different places in your workbook or from other workbooks, it can be difficult to see what's going wrong if your formula isn't producing the expected results. Excel helps you determine a cell's *precedents* (the cells the formula uses in its calculation) and *dependents* (the cells that depend on the current cell to calculate their own values). To help you find what you need to check your formulas, Excel groups all of the tools you need on the Formula Auditing toolbar.

Display the Formula Auditing Toolbar

1 Right-click the menu bar, and choose Formula Auditing from the shortcut menu.

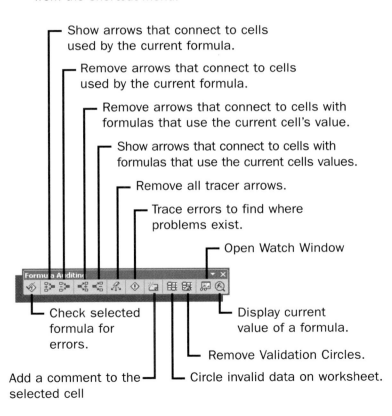

Show arrows that connect to cells used by the current formula.

Remove arrows that connect to cells used by the current formula.

Remove arrows that connect to cells with formulas that use the current cell's value.

Show arrows that connect to cells with formulas that use the current cells values.

Remove all tracer arrows.

Trace errors to find where problems exist.

Open Watch Window

Check selected formula for errors.

Display current value of a formula.

Remove Validation Circles.

Add a comment to the selected cell

Circle invalid data on worksheet.

Find Cell Precedents and Dependents

1 Click the cell you want to track.

Trace Precedents   Trace Dependents

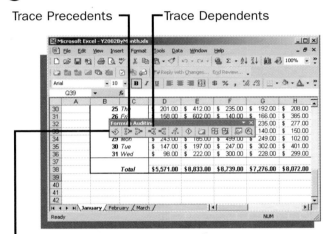

2 Follow either of these steps:

● Click the Trace Precedents button on the Formula Auditing toolbar.

● Click the Trace Dependents button on the Formula Auditing toolbar.

Remove Tracer Arrows

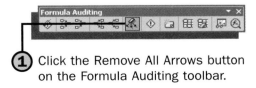

1 Click the Remove All Arrows button on the Formula Auditing toolbar.

Debugging Your Formulas ⊛ NEW FEATURE

When you share a workbook with your colleagues, some of the values in that workbook might change rapidly as new data is entered. For example, workbook data will probably change quickly if you are evaluating stock prices. Stock market values change frequently, so your data will as well. You can monitor the value in a cell even while you're using another workbook by setting a *watch*. When you set a watch, the values of the cells you're monitoring appear in the Watch Window.

Another way you can monitor your data is to check the result of part of a calculation using the Evaluate Formula button on the Formula Auditing toolbar. When you click the Evaluate Formula toolbar button, Excel displays the formula in the active cell and the subtotal for part of the calculation. You can move through the formula bit by bit, with Excel showing you the result of each piece of the formula.

Monitor a Formula for Changes

① If necessary, right-click the menu bar, and choose Formula Auditing from the shortcut menu to display the Formula Auditing toolbar.

② Click the Show Watch Window button.

③ Click Add Watch.

④ Select the cells you want to watch.

⑤ Click Add.

Delete a Watch

① Click the Show Watch Window button.

② Select the watch you want to delete.

③ Click Delete Watch.

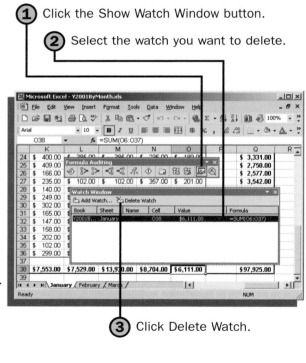

Evaluate Parts of a Formula

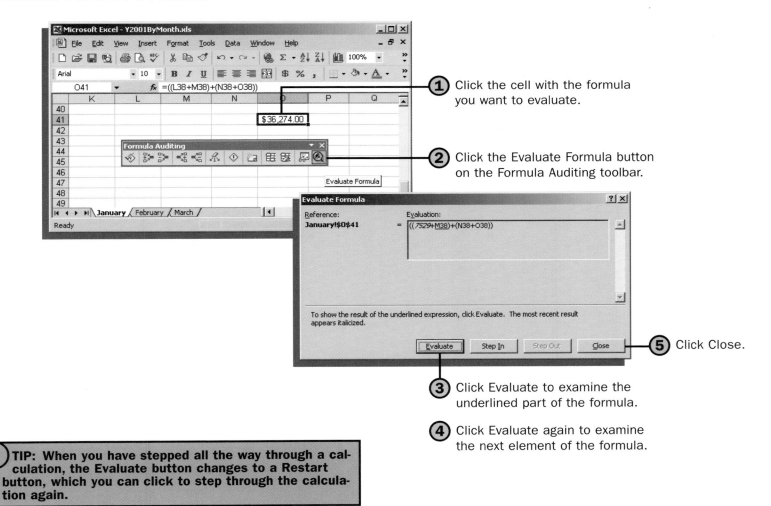

① Click the cell with the formula you want to evaluate.

② Click the Evaluate Formula button on the Formula Auditing toolbar.

⑤ Click Close.

③ Click Evaluate to examine the underlined part of the formula.

④ Click Evaluate again to examine the next element of the formula.

TIP: When you have stepped all the way through a calculation, the Evaluate button changes to a Restart button, which you can click to step through the calculation again.

6 Formatting the Worksheet

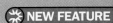

Microsoft Excel helps you manage large quantities of data with ease. One of the ways you can accomplish this is by changing how the program displays the data in your worksheet. For example, you can easily change the space between rows and columns of a worksheet, temporarily limit which data is shown on the screen, or add descriptions to your data to make it easier for you and your colleagues to understand. In this section, you'll learn how to:

- Change row height and column width.

- Insert, delete, and move rows and columns.

- Hide and unhide rows and columns.

- Add borders, background colors, and shading to cells.

- Format cell text.

- Apply conditional formats.

Changing Row Heights and Column Widths

When you create an Excel workbook, the default worksheet rows are tall enough to accommodate text and numbers entered in the standard character format (Arial, 10 point) and wide enough to display about eight characters. If your text takes up too much space to fit in the cell (because you've changed the font size for a column label, for example), you can widen the column so that the contents of every cell can be seen. You can also increase the height of rows in your worksheet to put some space between values, which will make your data easier to read. If a column is too wide or a row too high, you can make it narrower or shorter, as needed.

Resize a Row

1 Hover the mouse over the lower boundary of the row you want to resize until the mouse pointer turns into a two-headed arrow.

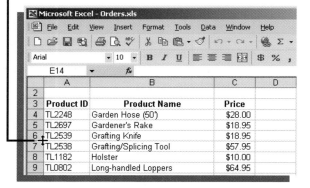

2 Drag the boundary until the row is the height you want.

Resize a Column

1 Hover the mouse over the right boundary of the column you want to resize until the mouse pointer turns into a two-headed arrow.

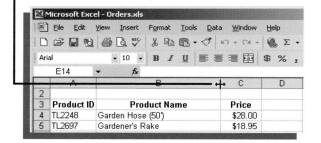

2 Drag the boundary until the column is the width you want.

> **!** **TIP:** You can resize a column to fit the text of its widest cell by double-clicking the right boundary of the column.

Resizing Multiple Rows or Columns

1 Select the rows or columns you want to resize.

2 Drag the border of any column or row to the desired width or height.

> **! TIP: If you want to set a specific row height or column width, select the rows or columns you want to format, right-click any header, and choose either Column Width or Row Height from the shortcut menu. Type the desired width or height in the dialog box that appears, and click OK.**

Inserting Rows or Columns

After you've created a worksheet and begun filling in your data, you might decide to insert a row or a column to add data you didn't think to include when you started. For example, a customer might want to add a product to an order. To accommodate this, you can insert a blank row below the last row in their existing order and add the new item there. You can do the same with columns: If you want to begin recording a new piece of information about your customers, such as a Web site or e-mail address, you can add a column to store that information. You can even use the Insert Options smart tag to format the new rows or columns.

Insert a Row in a Worksheet

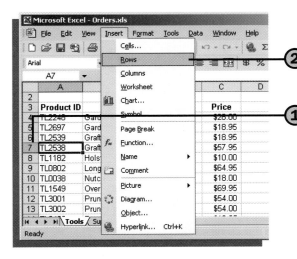

2 Choose rows from the Insert menu.

1 Click the row header below where you want the new row to appear.

Insert a Column in a Worksheet

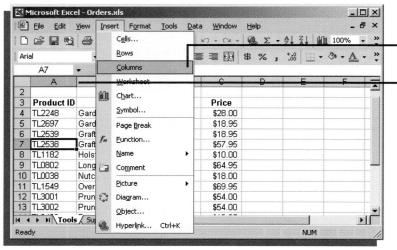

(2) Choose Columns from the Insert menu.

(1) Click the column header to the right of where you want the new column to appear.

! TIP: The Insert Options smart tag will appear only if the cells above or below the insertion point have special formatting.

Set Insert Options ⊕ NEW FEATURE

(1) After inserting rows or columns, click the Insert Options smart tag.

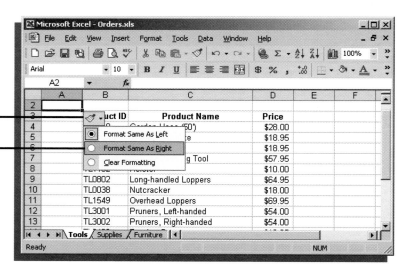

(2) Select the type of formatting you want the new cells to have.

! TIP: If you want to insert more than one row or column at a time, select a number of existing rows or columns equal to the number you want to insert, and then choose the appropriate command from the Insert menu.

Moving Rows and Columns

In many cases, the data in your worksheets will have first been recorded on paper—for example, when you record times for a race or collect customer responses on survey forms. Sometimes it's easier to type the information into your worksheet so that it looks the same way as it looked on paper. You can move rows and columns to new positions on the worksheet in order to present the information the way you want it to look.

Move One or More Columns

① Select the columns you want to move.

② Click the Cut button.

③ Click the first cell in the column where you want to move the columns.

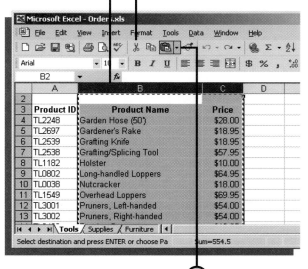

④ Click the Paste button.

Move One or More Rows

① Select the rows you want to move.

② Click the Cut button on the Standard toolbar.

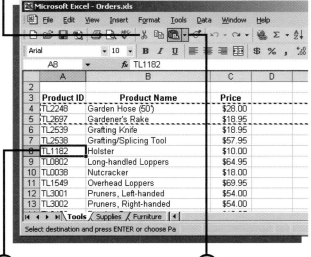

③ Click the first cell in the row where you want the rows to be moved.

④ Click the Paste button on the Standard toolbar.

Deleting Rows and Columns

Excel workbooks are a great place to store and manipulate your data, but there might be times when you no longer need to use a particular row or column. Whether you placed the extra column to add some white space between the main body of data and a summary calculation or the row holds the contact information of a customer who has asked to be removed from your list, you can delete a row or a column quickly and easily.

 SEE ALSO: For information about hiding rows or columns without deleting them, see "Hiding Rows and Columns" on page 85.

Delete Rows or Columns

1 Select the rows or columns you want to delete.

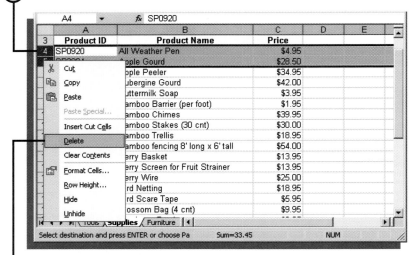

2 Right-click the selection, and choose Delete from the shortcut menu.

 CAUTION: Formulas that reference cells in the columns or rows you delete will no longer work. The Error smart tag will tell you there is an Invalid Cell Reference Error and give you options to fix the problem. #REF will appear in the damaged cell.

Outlining to Hide and Show Rows and Columns

When you develop worksheets, you'll probably try to keep similar entries together. For example, if you create a worksheet that lists all of the products you sell, you can group the products by category. In the case of a garden supply store, all of the tools would be together, then the furniture, and then a new category for each type of plant. If you want to hide the rows for one set of products, you can define the rows as a group and then you'll have the option to choose which rows you would like displayed.

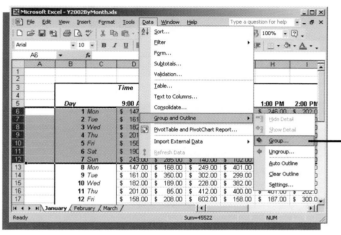

Group Rows and Columns

(1) Select the rows or columns you want to group.

(2) On the Data menu, point to Group And Outline, and choose Group.

Ungroup Rows and Columns

(1) Select the rows or columns you want to ungroup.

(2) On the Data menu, point to Group And Outline, and choose Ungroup.

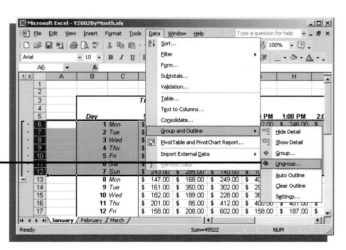

Hide Grouped Rows and Columns

1 Click the Collapse button next to the group you want to hide.

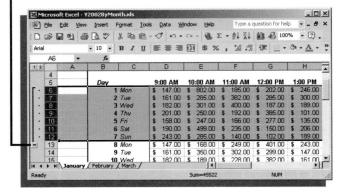

Show Grouped Rows and Columns

1 Click the Expand button next to the group you want to show.

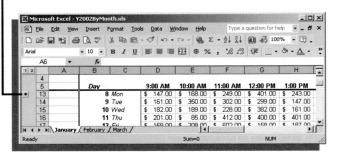

⚠️ **TIP:** To create a "group within a group," first group a set of rows, and then select the rows within that group that you want to make up the second group. Point to Group and Outline on the Data menu, and choose Group.

✅ **SEE ALSO:** For information about calculating subtotals for groups of rows, see "Summing with Subtotals and Grand Totals" on page 70.

Hiding Rows and Columns

If you're working with a worksheet that contains lots of data, you might need to refer to the contents of rows or columns that aren't close enough on the worksheet to appear on the same screen. Rather than scrolling back and forth to access the data you need, you can hide any intervening rows or columns so that everything you need to see is displayed on the screen at once. The rows you hide are only gone temporarily; the data hasn't been deleted, it's just been moved out of your way while you don't need it.

Hide Rows or Columns

1 Select the rows or columns you want to hide.

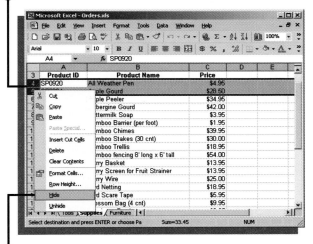

2 Right-click the selection, and choose Hide from the shortcut menu.

Unhide Rows or Columns

1 Select the row or column headers on either side of the hidden rows or columns.

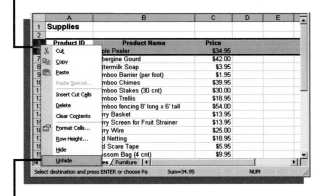

2 Right-click the selection, and choose Unhide from the shortcut menu.

! TIP: There are two ways you can tell there are hidden rows or columns in a worksheet. First, whenever rows or columns are hidden, there will be row numbers or column letters missing. For example, if row 2, row 3, and row 4 are hidden, the first two visible rows of the worksheet will be labeled row 1 and row 5. The other way you can tell that a worksheet contains hidden rows or columns is that a thick black line will appear on the border of the row header or column header where the rows or columns would otherwise appear.

Coloring Sheet Tabs ⊛ NEW FEATURE

A great way to make any worksheet element stand out is to change it to a color that contrasts with the other colors used in the worksheet. In Excel 2002, you can change the color of sheet tabs. For example, you can change the color of a sheet tab in a workbook where you track sales for a year, with a worksheet for each month.

Rather than move the current worksheet to the front of the list, which would put the worksheets out of order, you can change the color of the sheet tab to make it stand out. When the month ends, you can remove the color from that sheet tab and apply it to the new month's sheet tab.

Color a Sheet Tab

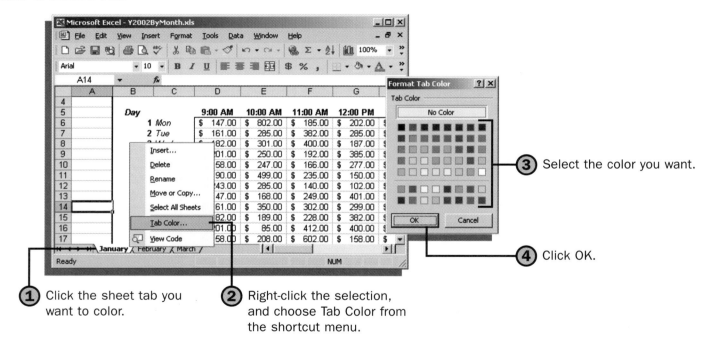

③ Select the color you want.

④ Click OK.

① Click the sheet tab you want to color.

② Right-click the selection, and choose Tab Color from the shortcut menu.

Setting Font Color

When you create labels to mark your text, you want the label text to stand out from the body of data. You can change the font or size of label text, and you can also change the color of the text to make it stand out even more. Red is a great color for cautionary text, and blue, which stands out from the standard black text color, works well for labeling explanatory text.

Change Cell Text Color

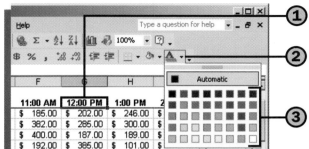

1 Select the cell in which you want to change the text color

2 Click the Font Color down arrow on the Formatting toolbar.

3 Select the font color you want.

> **CAUTION:** Remember that a little color on a worksheet goes a long way. You can easily get carried away when you first discover how simple it is to add color to your worksheet. Too much color on a worksheet can be a distraction.

Adding Cell Backgrounds and Shading

Just as you can change the color of text to make it stand out from the surrounding worksheet elements, you can also change the background color of cells to make those cells stand out. Although you should leave the cells containing your data with a white background, row or column headers will stand out from the data they describe if you add a light background color or change their shading.

Add Background Color

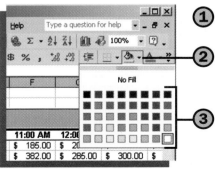

1 Select the cell in which you want to add a background color.

2 Click the Fill Color down arrow on the Formatting toolbar.

3 Select the background color you want.

Change Background Shading

(1) Select the cells you want to change.

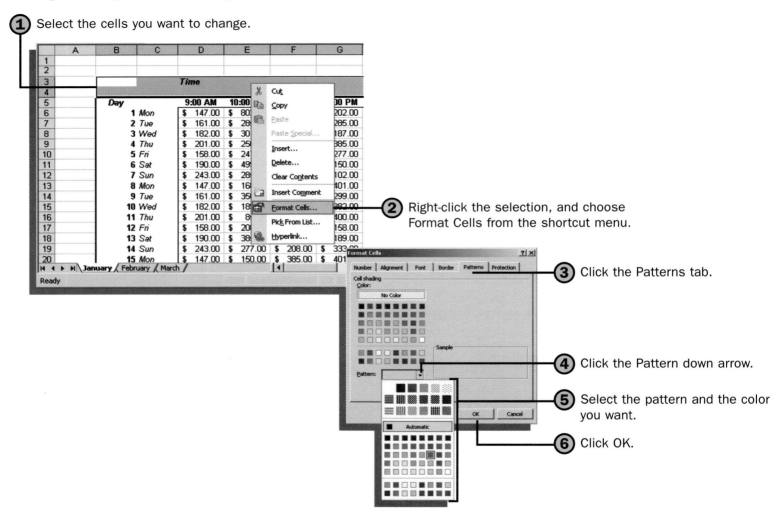

(2) Right-click the selection, and choose Format Cells from the shortcut menu.

(3) Click the Patterns tab.

(4) Click the Pattern down arrow.

(5) Select the pattern and the color you want.

(6) Click OK.

Formatting Cell Borders

The grid that appears on the standard worksheet uses light gray lines to mark cell boundaries, but those boundary lines don't distinguish one area of the worksheet from another. One way you can make a group of cells stand out from other groups is to draw a bor-

der on the edge of the cells. In Excel 2002, you can outline a group of cells or draw borders directly on the cells themselves. You can also change the color of any border you add to your worksheet.

Draw Borders ⊕ NEW FEATURE

① Click the Borders down arrow on the Standard toolbar.

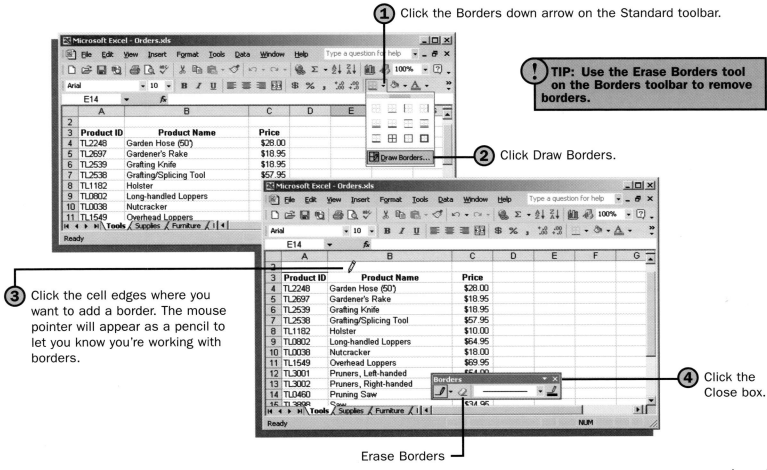

TIP: Use the Erase Borders tool on the Borders toolbar to remove borders.

② Click Draw Borders.

③ Click the cell edges where you want to add a border. The mouse pointer will appear as a pencil to let you know you're working with borders.

④ Click the Close box.

Erase Borders

Format Cell Borders

(1) Select the cells you want to format.

(!) **TIP: You can drag the mouse pointer over a group of cells to put a border around the edge of the group.**

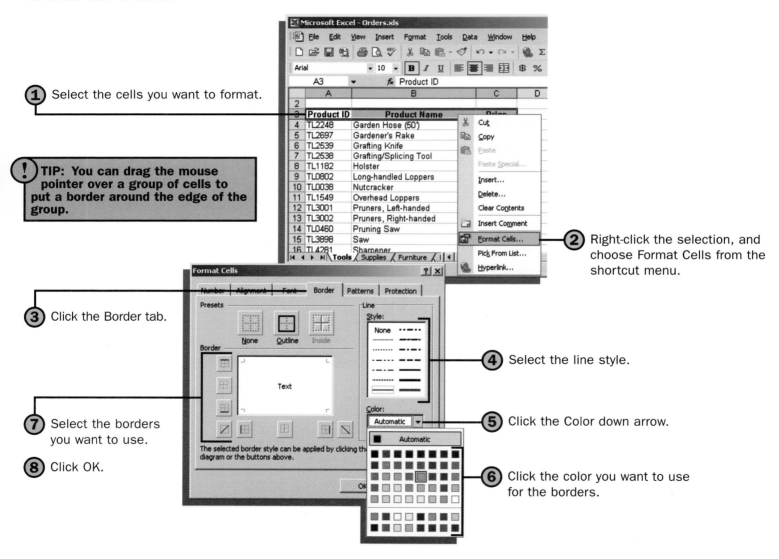

(2) Right-click the selection, and choose Format Cells from the shortcut menu.

(3) Click the Border tab.

(4) Select the line style.

(5) Click the Color down arrow.

(7) Select the borders you want to use.

(6) Click the color you want to use for the borders.

(8) Click OK.

Changing a Worksheet's Gridlines

Gridlines are the lines on your worksheets that define the cells formed by the intersections of rows and columns. In Excel 2002, the default gridline color is gray, but not all worksheets work well with this standard setting. Sometimes you'll want to change the color of the cell gridlines or even turn them off.

Change the Color of Cell Gridlines

① Choose Options from the Tools menu.

② Click the View tab.

③ Click the Gridlines Color down arrow.

④ Select the color you want to use for the gridlines.

⑤ Click OK.

Show or Hide Cell Gridlines

① Choose Options from the Tools menu.

② Click the View tab.

③ Select or clear the Gridlines check box.

④ Click OK.

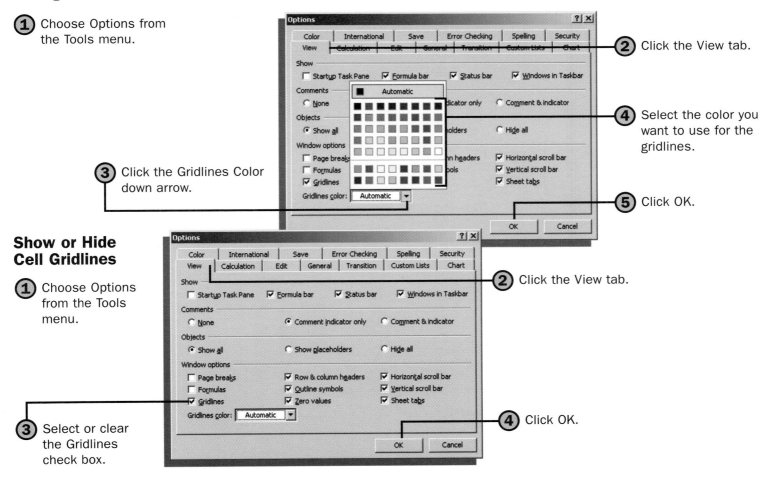

Formatting a Cell Based on Conditions

Another way you can make your data easier to interpret is to change the appearance of your data based on value. This kind of formatting is called *conditional formatting* because the data must meet certain conditions to have a format applied to it. For example, if you use a worksheet to track the credit lines of your customers, you could have a customer's outstanding balance appear in red if they are within 10 percent of their credit limit.

Change the Format of a Cell Based on Its Value

(1) Select the cells you want to change.

(3) Click the Condition Type down arrow.

(4) Click Cell Value Is.

(5) Click the comparison phrase down arrow.

(2) Choose Conditional Formatting from the Format menu.

(6) Click the comparison phrase you want.

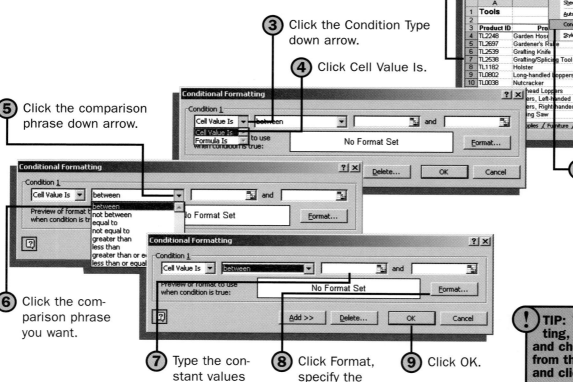

(7) Type the constant values or formulas you want evaluated.

(8) Click Format, specify the formatting you want, and click OK.

(9) Click OK.

> **!** **TIP:** To remove conditional formatting, select the formatted cells and choose Conditional Formatting from the Format menu. Click Delete, and click OK.

Change the Format of a Cell Based on the Results of a Formula

1 Select the cells you want to change.

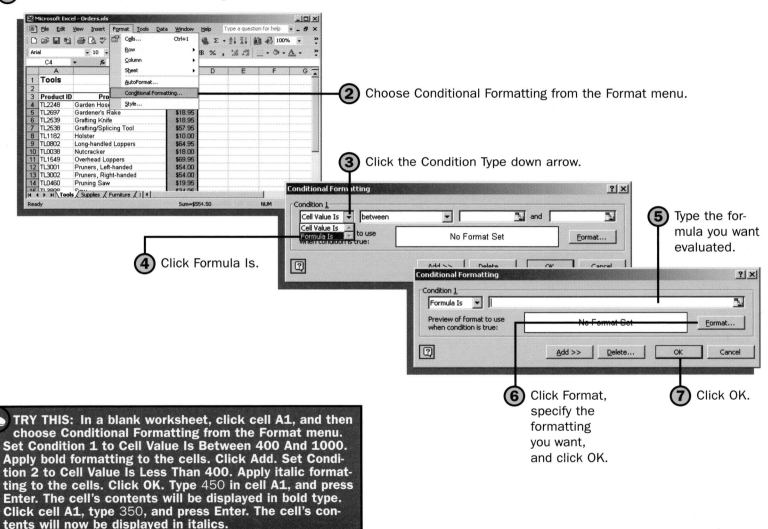

2 Choose Conditional Formatting from the Format menu.

3 Click the Condition Type down arrow.

4 Click Formula Is.

5 Type the formula you want evaluated.

6 Click Format, specify the formatting you want, and click OK.

7 Click OK.

> **TRY THIS:** In a blank worksheet, click cell A1, and then choose Conditional Formatting from the Format menu. Set Condition 1 to Cell Value Is Between 400 And 1000. Apply bold formatting to the cells. Click Add. Set Condition 2 to Cell Value Is Less Than 400. Apply italic formatting to the cells. Click OK. Type 450 in cell A1, and press Enter. The cell's contents will be displayed in bold type. Click cell A1, type 350, and press Enter. The cell's contents will now be displayed in italics.

Copying Formats with the Format Painter

After you create a format for a cell or group of cells, you can copy the format from one group of cells to another group of cells using the Format Painter. The Format Painter lets you copy the format quickly, saving you the time and effort it would take to copy the contents of another cell with the desired format and then change the data or formula.

! **TIP:** One great way to save time with the Format Painter is to keep a group of cells with formats you know you'll need later. Then, whenever you need to apply a format, you can just click the cell with the format, click the Format Painter button, and apply the format to the target cells.

Copy Styles with the Format Painter

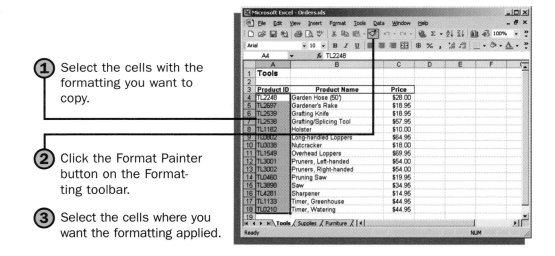

1 Select the cells with the formatting you want to copy.

2 Click the Format Painter button on the Formatting toolbar.

3 Select the cells where you want the formatting applied.

TRY THIS: Create a new workbook, type ProductID in cell A1, and type Price in cell A2. Click cell A1, click the Bold button on the Formatting toolbar, click the Font Size down arrow, and click 14. Make sure cell A1 is still the active cell, click the Format Painter button, and then click cell A2. The contents of cell A2 now have the same format as cell A1.

Protecting Worksheets from Changes

When you create a worksheet that contains sensitive data or data you don't want changed by anyone other than yourself, you can protect the worksheet from unauthorized changes. From within the Protect Sheet dialog box, you can choose the actions you want to allow all users to be able to perform on the worksheet. The options selected by default will allow anyone to select a cell, but will prevent them from deleting rows or columns, changing any formatting, or editing scenarios attached to the worksheet.

Protect a Worksheet

1 On the Tools menu, point to Protection and choose Protect Sheet.

2 Select the Protect Worksheet And Contents Of Locked Cells check box.

3 Select the protection options you want.

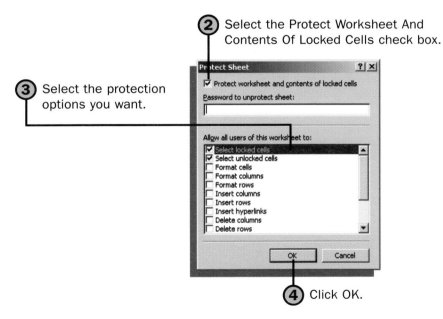

4 Click OK.

> **!** **TIP:** Specify a password in the Protect Sheet dialog box to restrict access to a workbook, a worksheet, or part of a worksheet. Once you've done this, only authorized users will be able to make changes.

Unprotect a Worksheet

1 Point to Protection on the Tools menu, and choose Unprotect Sheet.

> **!** **TIP:** You can protect chart sheets and other graphic objects in worksheets from unauthorized changes. Keep in mind that if the source data for a chart sheet changes, your chart sheet will also change, even if you have the chart protected.

Locking Cells to Prevent Changes

After you protect a worksheet, you can lock an individual cell to prevent it from being changed. This level of protection goes beyond simply protecting a worksheet—it prevents anyone using the worksheet from changing the contents or formatting of the cell.

Lock Cells

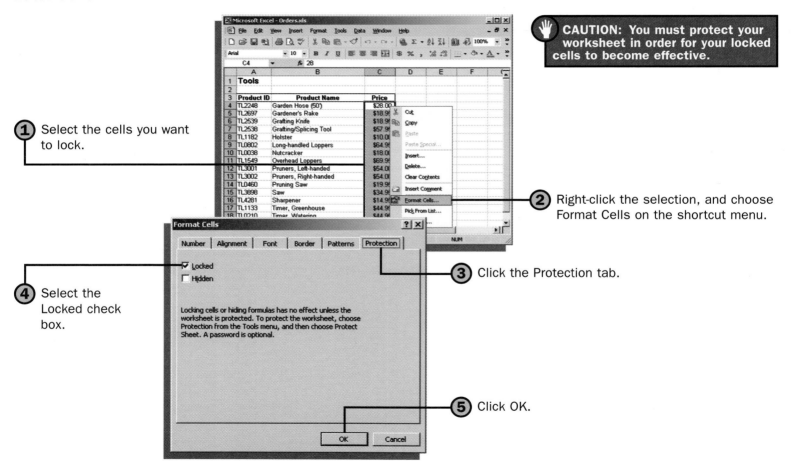

CAUTION: You must protect your worksheet in order for your locked cells to become effective.

① Select the cells you want to lock.

② Right-click the selection, and choose Format Cells on the shortcut menu.

③ Click the Protection tab.

④ Select the Locked check box.

Locking cells or hiding formulas has no effect unless the worksheet is protected. To protect the worksheet, choose Protection from the Tools menu, and then choose Protect Sheet. A password is optional.

⑤ Click OK.

Styling Cell Text

When you develop a worksheet, you will probably create a set of formats you want to apply consistently to certain parts of it. For example, you might always want your column headings to be slightly larger and in a different font than the body of the worksheet. You can save the formatting you want for a worksheet element and save it as a *style*, which you can then apply to appropriate parts of your worksheets.

Apply a Style

1 Select the cells you want to change.

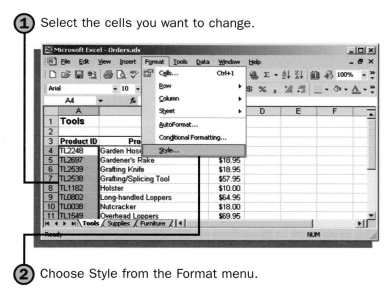

2 Choose Style from the Format menu.

3 Click the Style Name down arrow.

4 Click a style.

5 Click OK.

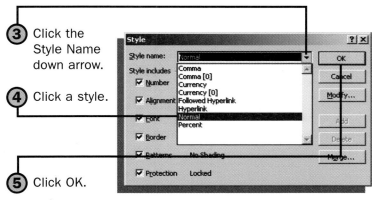

Create a Style

1 Choose Style from the Format menu.

2 Type a new style name.

3 Click Modify.

4 Specify the formatting you want this style to contain.

5 Click OK.

6 Click Add.

7 Click Close.

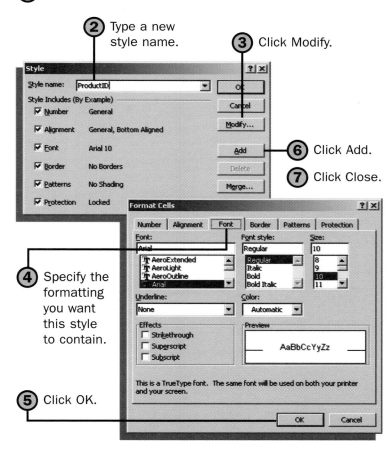

Delete a Style

1 Choose Style from the Format menu.

2 Click the Style Name down arrow.

3 Click a style.

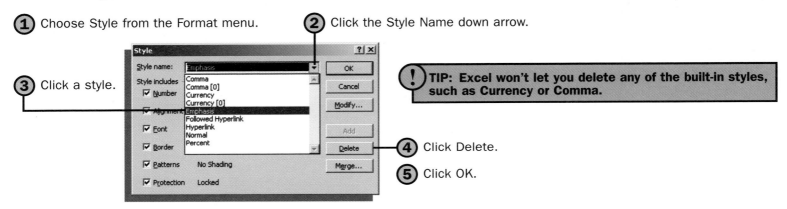

TIP: Excel won't let you delete any of the built-in styles, such as Currency or Comma.

4 Click Delete.

5 Click OK.

Modify a Style

1 Choose Style from the Format menu.

2 Click the Style Name down arrow.

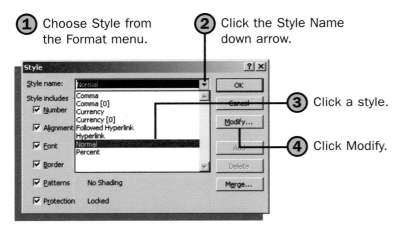

3 Click a style.

4 Click Modify.

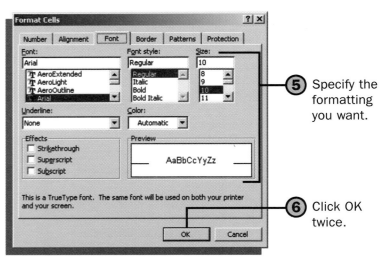

5 Specify the formatting you want.

6 Click OK twice.

Merging or Splitting Cells or Data

You can change a row's height or a column's width, but this might not be the best way to improve your worksheet's usability. For instance, a label might not fit within a single cell and increasing that cell's width, or every cell's width, might throw off the worksheet's design. One solution to this problem is to merge two or more cells. Merging cells allows you to treat a group of cells as a single cell as far as content and formatting go.

Merge Several Cells into One

① Select the cells you want to merge.

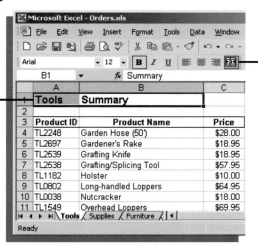

② Click the Merge And Center button on the Formatting toolbar.

● To split a merged cell into separate cells, click the merged cell and click the Merge And Center button.

> **TIP: If you do not want the merged data centered, click the Right Align or Left Align button on the Formatting toolbar.**

> **CAUTION: If more than one cell in the range of cells you selected contains data, only the data in the upper-left cell will remain after you merge the cells.**

Hiding or Showing a Worksheet

If you build a workbook that contains a lot of worksheets, you might find it easier to navigate the workbook if you can't see the worksheets you're not using. You can hide worksheets so that they don't appear in the Excel window, reducing the clutter and letting you find the worksheets you are using with no trouble.

Hide a Worksheet

(1) Hold down the Ctrl key, and click the sheet tabs of the worksheets you want to hide.

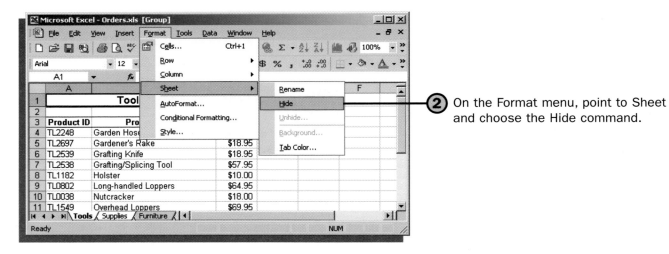

(2) On the Format menu, point to Sheet and choose the Hide command.

Unhide a Hidden Worksheet

(1) On the Format menu, point to Sheet and choose the Unhide command.

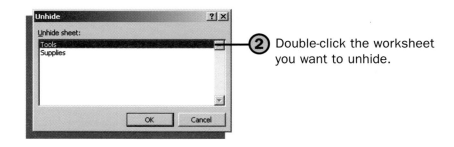

(2) Double-click the worksheet you want to unhide.

Printing Worksheets

Once you have created your worksheet, you can print a copy for reference, backup, or to distribute to your colleagues. Although you might be tempted to print your worksheet as soon as you have completed it, it's usually a good idea to check your work first. All you need to do to see how your worksheet will look when printed is to display the worksheet in Print Preview mode. If you want to change how your worksheet will appear on the printed page, you can do anything from changing the orientation of your worksheet to scaling it to fit within a specific number of pages. It's easy to fine-tune margins, adjust headers and footers, and customize a variety of other print options as well.

In this section, you will learn how to:

● Preview worksheets before printing.

● Choose a printer and printing media.

● Add headers and footers.

● Set margins and header and footer sizes.

● Print part of a worksheet.

● Change a worksheet's orientation.

● Set page breaks.

Previewing Worksheets Before Printing

Before you print a worksheet, it's helpful to take a step back and look at how your data will appear on the printed page. To do that in Excel, you display your worksheet in Print Preview mode. While you have your workbook open in Print Preview, you can zoom in to see cell contents clearly without altering printing size. You can also adjust the widths of any columns in Print Preview, saving you the trouble of switching between Print Preview and the standard Excel window.

View and Zoom Worksheets in Print Preview

1 Click the Print Preview button on the Standard toolbar.

2 Click any area of the worksheet to switch between magnified and full-page view.

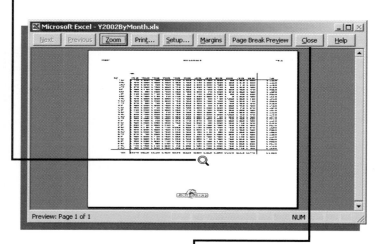

3 Click Close to return to the Excel window.

Change Column Widths in Print Preview

1 Click the Print Preview button.

2 If necessary, click Margins to display the margin lines.

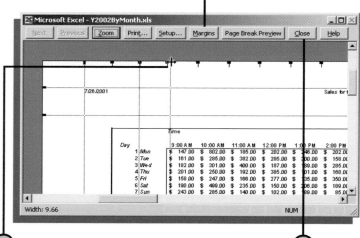

3 Hover the mouse over a column marker until the mouse pointer becomes a two-headed arrow. Drag the marker until the column is the desired size.

4 Click Close.

CAUTION: If you drag a column marker so far to the left that you overlap with or pass over another column marker, the column to the left of the marker will be removed.

Printing Worksheets with Current Options

After you've entered all of your data and formatted your worksheets so that the data is easy to read, you can print your worksheets for distribution to your colleagues, for example. Clicking the Print button on the Standard toolbar prints only the worksheet displayed on the screen—if you want to print more than one worksheet at a time, such as when you want to print out several months of sales results and each month is recorded on a separate worksheet, you can do that as well.

Print Multiple Worksheets from the Same Workbook

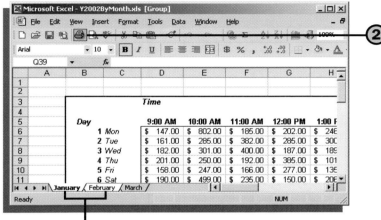

(2) Click the Print button.

> **CAUTION:** When you click the Print button, Excel prints the entire contents of the active worksheet, not just what you see on the screen. If your worksheet has a lot of data, you could use up a lot of paper you didn't have to!

(1) Hold down the Ctrl key and click the sheet tabs of the worksheets you want to print.

> **TIP:** If all of the worksheets in a workbook are adjacent, click the sheet tab for the first worksheet, hold down the Shift key, and click the sheet tab for the last worksheet. Click the Print button, and all the worksheets you selected will be printed.

Choosing Printers and Paper Options

You might not want to use the same printer and paper type for everything you print. Standard 8.5-by-11-inch letter size paper will be fine for printing some of your worksheets, but from time to time you'll probably need to use 8.5-by-14-inch legal size paper. You can also choose from a variety of media options that include materials other than the standard type of paper you would find in most homes and offices. For example, you might want to print on coated paper, transparencies, envelopes, or even T-shirt transfer paper.

Choose a Printer

1 Choose Print from the File menu.

2 Click the Name down arrow.

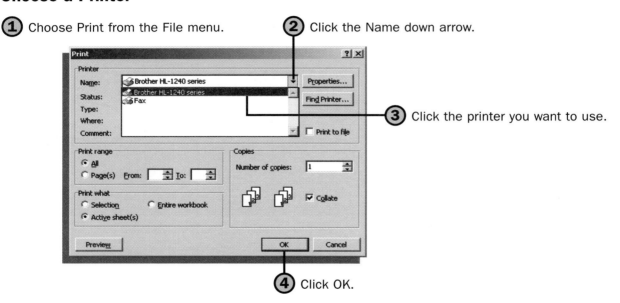

3 Click the printer you want to use.

4 Click OK.

> **! TIP:** If you work at a company with a large network and you can choose to use a printer at another location, you can use the network to deliver paper copies of your worksheets to anyone in your company as long as they have a printer nearby. With that flexibility, however, comes the extra responsibility to check that you have the proper printer selected whenever you want to print a worksheet.

Choose the Paper

1 Choose Page Setup from the File menu.

2 Click the Page tab.

5 Click Options.

3 Click the Paper Size down arrow.

6 Click the Paper/ Quality tab.

4 Click the paper size you want.

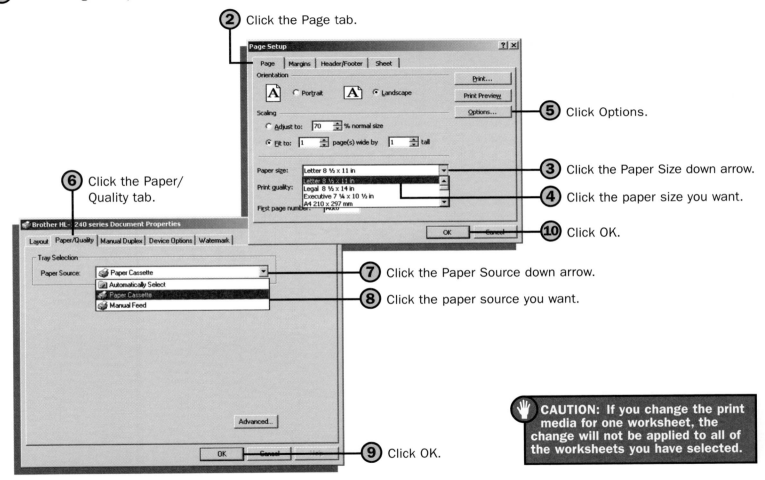

10 Click OK.

7 Click the Paper Source down arrow.

8 Click the paper source you want.

CAUTION: If you change the print media for one worksheet, the change will not be applied to all of the worksheets you have selected.

9 Click OK.

Printing Part of a Worksheet

When you create a worksheet containing lots of data, you might want to print the section of the worksheet with the data relevant to the point you're trying to illustrate. The good news is you can set a print area so that Excel will print as much or as little of your worksheet as you like. The print area is outlined with a dashed line, so you can tell which cells will be printed and which won't. When you set a Print Area, you can select cells in a single rectangle or select cells located in various areas of your worksheet.

> **(!) TIP:** Although setting a print area may be necessary in some situations, you should try to arrange your data so that the content you want to print is in the same part of the worksheet. If all of the data is together, you will not need to use print areas to select multiple parts of your worksheet.

Set a Print Area

(1) Select the cells you want to print.

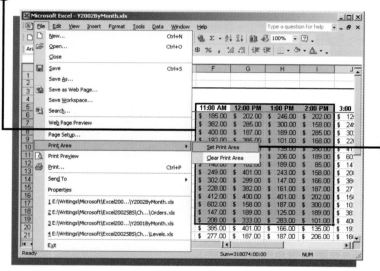

(2) On the File menu, point to Print Area and choose Set Print Area.

Remove a Print Area

(1) On the File menu, point to Print Area and choose Clear Print Area.

Printing Row and Column Headings on Each Page

When you print a worksheet in which the data doesn't fit on a single screen, you might have trouble remembering which data is stored in which column. Rather than make you look back to the top of the worksheet, or even type your headings where you guess the screen transitions occur, you can have Excel print your column and row headings at the top of every page. By printing the column and row headings on each page, you will save time, improve accuracy, and reduce frustration when dealing with large worksheets.

Identify the Rows and Columns to Repeat

(1) Choose Page Setup from the File menu.

(2) Click the Sheet tab.

(3) Click the Rows To Repeat At Top box.

(4) On your work-sheet, select the row headings you want to repeat.

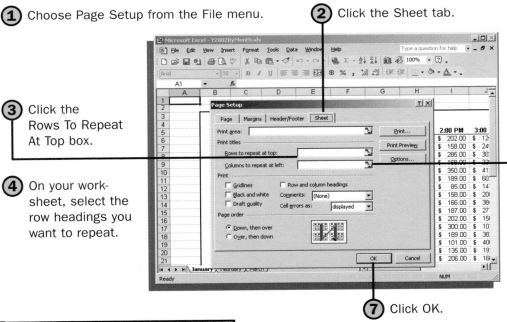

(!) TIP: Printing row and column headings on every page is useful when your worksheet contains frozen panes and you want to have the frozen panes appear on every page of the printout, just as they appear on the screen.

(5) Click the Columns To Repeat At Left box.

(6) On your worksheet, select the column headings you want to repeat.

(7) Click OK.

(✓) SEE ALSO: For more information about frozen panes, see "View Multiple Parts of a Worksheet by Freezing Panes" on page 57.

Setting and Changing Print Margins

Margins define the white boundary area of the page and provide a visual border around your printed data. Changing a worksheet's margins increases or decreases the amount of data displayed on a page, which allows you to make room for one last column of data, to divide your columns evenly be-tween two pages, or to allow for enough room at one edge for the page to be bound in a report or a three-ring binder. In Print Preview mode, margins appear as gray lines, which you can drag to the desired position.

Set Page Margins

(1) Choose Page Setup from the File menu.

(2) Click the Margins tab.

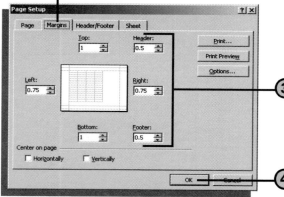

(3) Type new values for the worksheet's margins in the Top, Bottom, Left, and Right boxes.

(4) Click OK.

> **TRY THIS: Select multiple worksheets by holding down the Ctrl key and clicking the sheet tabs, and then choose Page Setup from the File menu. Click the Margins tab, type 1 in the Top, Bottom, Left, and Right boxes, and then click OK. All of the selected worksheets' margins will be changed to one inch.**

Adjust Page Margins

(1) Click the Print Preview button.

(2) If necessary, click Margins to display the margin lines.

(4) Click Close.

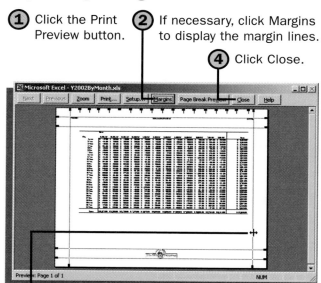

(3) Hover the mouse pointer over one of the gray lines until the mouse pointer becomes a two-headed arrow. Drag the line until the margin is set the way you want.

> **CAUTION: In Print Preview mode, it's some-times difficult to distinguish between margins and header or footer lines. Be sure to keep track of which is which.**

Setting Page Orientation and Scale

As you look at your worksheet and think about how you want it to appear on the printed page, be aware that you have the choice of printing in a vertical format (portrait mode) or a horizontal format (landscape mode). Landscape mode is particularly useful when you have a lot of columns in your worksheet, such as in a worksheet storing customer contact or product sales information. You can fit your worksheet onto a specific number of printed pages, which helps if you have been allotted a fixed number of pages in which to present your data in a typeset report.

Set Page Orientation

1 Choose Page Setup from the File menu.

2 Click the Page tab.

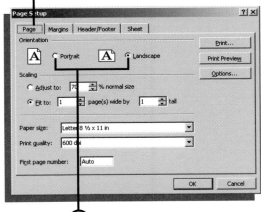

3 Select either the Portrait or Landscape option.

> **! TIP: Select Portrait orientation for long worksheets that are not very wide, and select Landscape orientation for worksheets with many columns.**

Scale the Printout to a Fixed Number of Pages

1 Choose Page Setup from the File menu.

2 Click the Page tab.

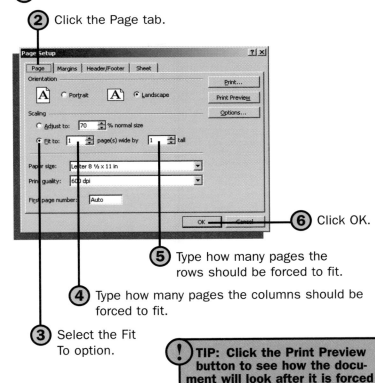

6 Click OK.

5 Type how many pages the rows should be forced to fit.

4 Type how many pages the columns should be forced to fit.

3 Select the Fit To option.

> **! TIP: Click the Print Preview button to see how the document will look after it is forced onto a fixed number of pages.**

> **✎ TRY THIS: Choose Page Setup from the File menu, click the Page tab, and then select the Fit To option. Type 1 in the Wide box, and delete the contents of the Tall box. The worksheet will now fit on a single page width, but will print on additional pages if necessary.**

Creating Headers and Footers

Headers and footers contain information that appears at the top and bottom of each page of your printed worksheet. You can select a premade header or footer that contains information about your file or you can create your own custom headers and footers using AutoText. AutoText is a list of expressions you can insert into your headers and footers to display certain information about your worksheet, such as page numbers or file names. Headers might include helpful information such as a workbook name, while footers can include page numbers, file names, or dates.

Add a Premade Header and Footer

1 Choose Header And Footer from the View menu.

SEE ALSO: For more information about how to change the size of your headers, see "Adjust Header and Footer Height" on page 112.

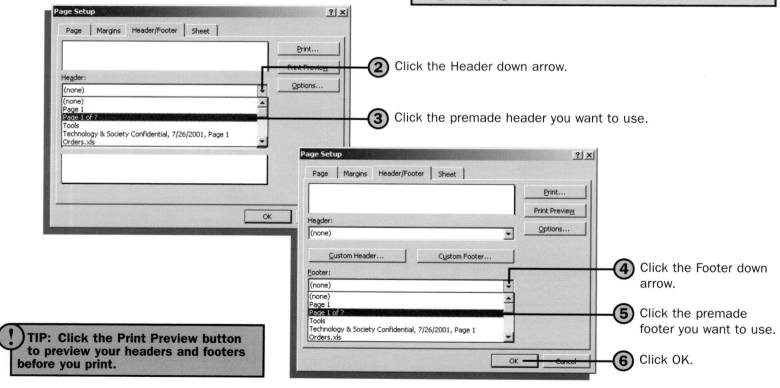

2 Click the Header down arrow.

3 Click the premade header you want to use.

4 Click the Footer down arrow.

5 Click the premade footer you want to use.

6 Click OK.

TIP: Click the Print Preview button to preview your headers and footers before you print.

Add AutoText to the Header or Footer

1 Choose Header And Footer from the View menu.

2 Click Custom Header or Custom Footer.

! TIP: You can change the font style by selecting the text and clicking the Font button.

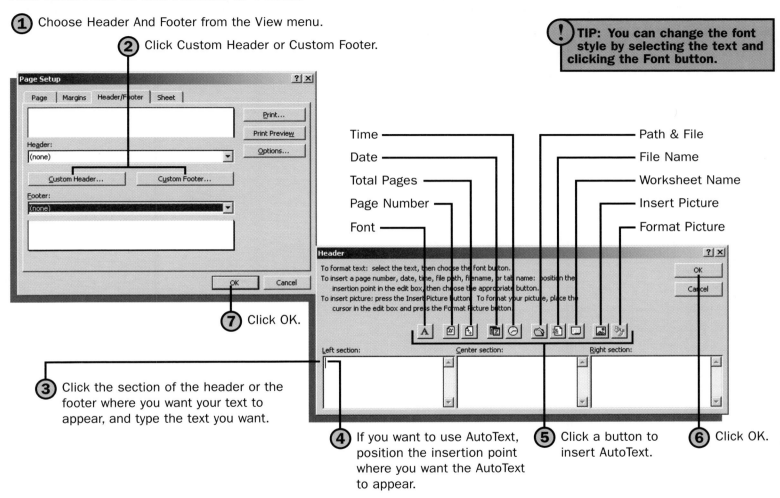

7 Click OK.

Time — Path & File

Date — File Name

Total Pages — Worksheet Name

Page Number — Insert Picture

Font — Format Picture

3 Click the section of the header or the footer where you want your text to appear, and type the text you want.

4 If you want to use AutoText, position the insertion point where you want the AutoText to appear.

5 Click a button to insert AutoText.

6 Click OK.

Adjust Header and Footer Height

① Click the Print Preview button.

② If necessary, click Margins to display the header and footer lines.

④ Click Close.

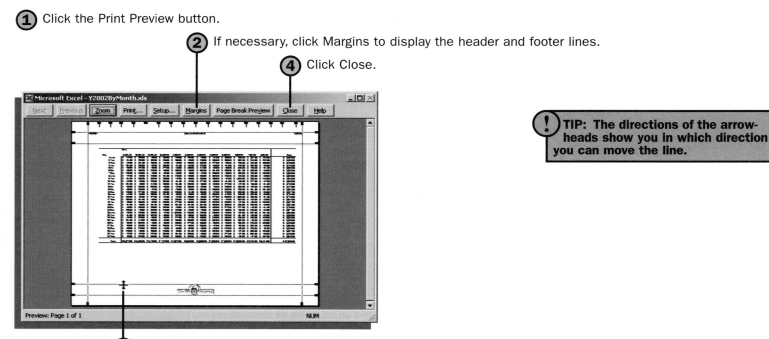

! TIP: The directions of the arrowheads show you in which direction you can move the line.

③ Hover the mouse over one of the gray lines until the mouse pointer becomes a two-headed arrow. Drag the line until the header or footer is the height you want.

Adding Graphics to a Header or a Footer

Creating attractive and professional looking printouts will help you communicate your message better. Often, the addition of a simple graphic to a header or a footer will give your worksheet a truly professional appearance. You might want to create printouts that include your company's letterhead or logo, or a graphic related to the information on your worksheet. An excellent way to include graphics on every printed page is to place them into the header and footer of your worksheet.

Include a Graphic in a Header or a Footer

(1) Choose Header And Footer from the View menu.

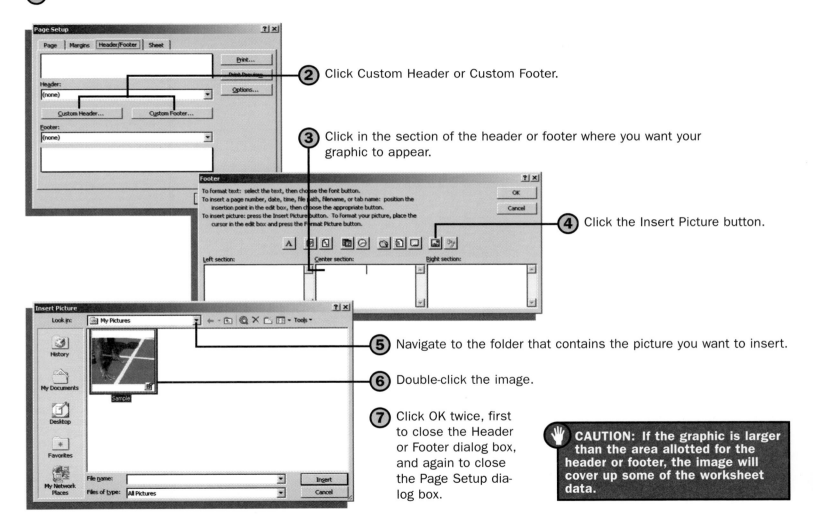

(2) Click Custom Header or Custom Footer.

(3) Click in the section of the header or footer where you want your graphic to appear.

(4) Click the Insert Picture button.

(5) Navigate to the folder that contains the picture you want to insert.

(6) Double-click the image.

(7) Click OK twice, first to close the Header or Footer dialog box, and again to close the Page Setup dialog box.

CAUTION: If the graphic is larger than the area allotted for the header or footer, the image will cover up some of the worksheet data.

Format a Graphic in a Header or a Footer

CAUTION: When using Format Picture, you cannot reverse your actions once they've been completed.

(1) Choose Header And Footer from the View menu.

(2) Click Custom Header or Custom Footer.

(3) Select the text &[Picture].

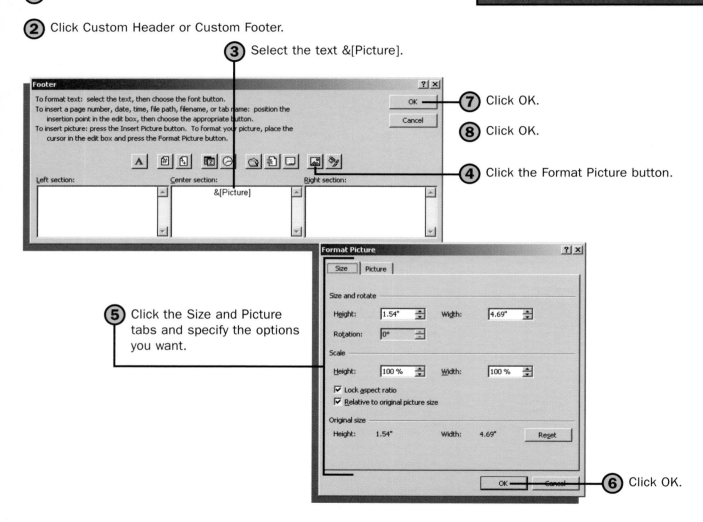

(7) Click OK.

(8) Click OK.

(4) Click the Format Picture button.

(5) Click the Size and Picture tabs and specify the options you want.

(6) Click OK.

Setting and Viewing Page Breaks

Excel determines where one printed page ends and the next begins based on your page size, margins, and orientation; however, the page breaks Excel sets might not work for a particular worksheet. You might want to have a chart or a table placed on its own sheet, or you might want to force two separate tables onto one page. You can display all existing page breaks by opening your worksheet in Page Break Preview mode, which displays the page breaks as blue lines. If the blue lines are dashed, they represent an automatic page break; if the blue lines are solid, they represent a manually set page break. While in Page Break Preview, you can change the location of any existing page breaks to ensure your worksheets print exactly the way you want.

View Current Page Breaks

① Choose Page Break Preview from the View menu.

Set Manual Page Breaks

① Click the cell below and to the right of where you want to insert a page break.

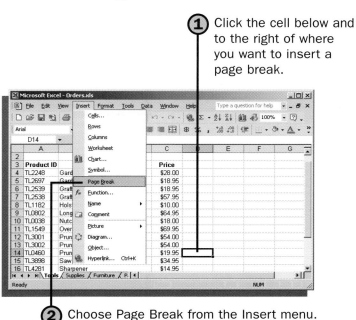

② Choose Page Break from the Insert menu.

Change Manual Page Breaks

① Choose Page Break Preview from the View menu.

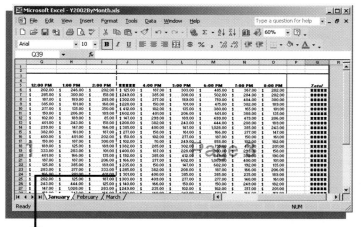

② Hover the mouse over one of the blue lines until the mouse pointer becomes a two-headed arrow. Drag the line until the page break is where you want.

Customizing Excel to the Way You Work

Microsoft Excel gives you lots of ways to work with your data, with dozens of menu items and toolbar buttons at your disposal. When you install Excel, the toolbars and menu system are set up so that you have easy access to the commands you'll use the most. These often-used commands are the ones that allow you to create, save, and print workbooks, and enable you to cut, copy, and paste worksheet contents. Excel is very flexible, and you can rearrange the toolbars and menus to meet your needs.

Two other ways you can customize Excel to make your life easier are to create *templates* and *workspaces*. A template is a workbook you use as a pattern for other workbooks. When you open a template, which is a separate Excel file type, you have the outline you need to create frequently used workbooks quickly. When you create a workspace, you identify several workbooks you often open together and save references to the files in a single Excel file. When you open the workspace, all the files appear, ready for use.

In this section, you will learn how to:

● Create and modify workspaces.

● Create and modify templates.

● Display and hide toolbars.

● Add buttons to existing toolbars.

● Add items to existing menus.

● Create a new toolbar.

Opening Several Related Workbooks

When you work with Excel for a while, you might find that you often work with a number of the same workbooks at a time. For example, you might open workbooks with your product information, inventory levels, and outstanding orders to determine whether you should reorder certain products immediately or return slow-moving products. If you want to open a number of workbooks simultaneously, you can define them as part of a workspace, which is a special Excel file that refers to several workbooks.

Create a Workspace

① Open the workbooks you want to include in your workspace.

② Choose Save Workspace from the File menu.

③ Navigate to the location where you want to save your workspace.

④ Type the file name you want.

Open a Workspace

① Click the Open button on the Standard toolbar.

② Navigate to the location of your saved workspace.

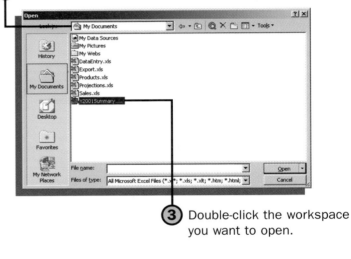

③ Double-click the workspace you want to open.

⑤ Click Save.

! TIP: If you want to include blank workbooks in your workspace, click the New button on the Standard toolbar before saving as a workspace.

Remove a File from a Workspace

1 Open the workspace you want to remove a file from.

2 Click the Close box on the file you want to remove.

3 Choose Save Workspace from the File menu.

4 Click Save.

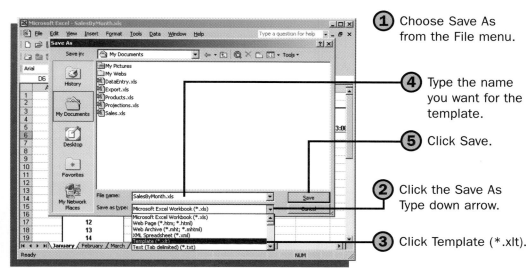

Creating Documents Using Templates

Once you have decided on the type of data you want to store in a workbook and what that workbook should look like, you will probably want to create similar workbooks without adding all the formatting and formulas again. For example, you might have settled on a design for your monthly sales tracking workbook. When you have settled on a design for your workbooks, you can save one of the workbooks as a pattern, or *template*, for similar workbooks you create in the future.

> ✋ **CAUTION: It's important to save your template in the Templates folder. If you save your template anywhere else, it won't show up in the list of available Excel templates.**

Save a Workbook as a Template

1 Choose Save As from the File menu.

4 Type the name you want for the template.

5 Click Save.

2 Click the Save As Type down arrow.

3 Click Template (*.xlt).

Create a Workbook from a Template

(1) Choose New from the File menu.

(2) Click General Templates.

(3) Click the General tab.

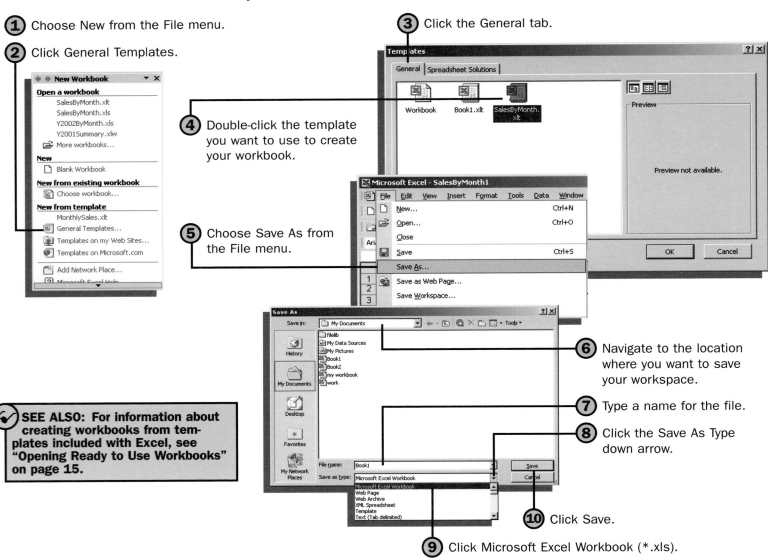

(4) Double-click the template you want to use to create your workbook.

(5) Choose Save As from the File menu.

(6) Navigate to the location where you want to save your workspace.

(7) Type a name for the file.

(8) Click the Save As Type down arrow.

(9) Click Microsoft Excel Workbook (*.xls).

(10) Click Save.

> **SEE ALSO:** For information about creating workbooks from templates included with Excel, see "Opening Ready to Use Workbooks" on page 15.

Modify a Template

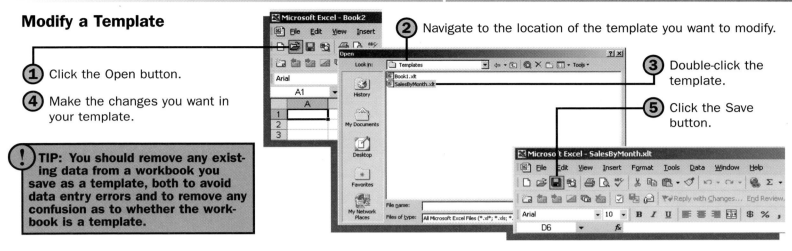

1 Click the Open button.

4 Make the changes you want in your template.

(!) TIP: You should remove any existing data from a workbook you save as a template, both to avoid data entry errors and to remove any confusion as to whether the workbook is a template.

2 Navigate to the location of the template you want to modify.

3 Double-click the template.

5 Click the Save button.

Displaying Additional Toolbars and Menus

When you work with Excel, you might find yourself performing tasks requiring you to dig into the menu system or use a toolbar not usually displayed in the Excel window. If so, you can display toolbars and menus that put additional capabilities in easy reach. If you add a graphic to a worksheet, for example, you can add the Picture toolbar to the menu bar so that the tools you use to work with pictures are within easy reach. Every toolbar, menu, and submenu available in Excel can be found in the Customize dialog box.

Show or Hide a Toolbar

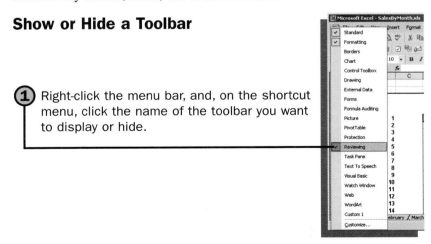

1 Right-click the menu bar, and, on the shortcut menu, click the name of the toolbar you want to display or hide.

(!) TIP: A check mark will appear next to the name of any toolbar that is already displayed.

Show a Menu

1 Choose Customize from the Tools menu.

2 Click the Commands tab.

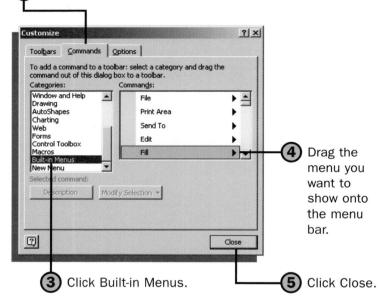

3 Click Built-in Menus.

4 Drag the menu you want to show onto the menu bar.

5 Click Close.

Hide a Menu

1 Choose Customize from the Tools menu.

2 Drag the menu you want to hide from the menu bar to the Customize dialog box.

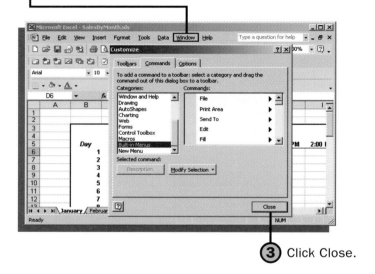

3 Click Close.

Customizing Toolbars

When you create and format your Excel workbooks, you'll find most of the toolbar buttons you need on the Standard and Formatting toolbars. When you work with existing workbooks, you might want to use one or two buttons from other toolbars. For example,

you could add the New Comment button, which is normally found on the Reviewing toolbar, to the Standard toolbar. When you review a workbook one of your colleagues created, the button will be within easy reach.

Add a New Toolbar Button

1 Choose Customize from the Tools menu.

2 Click the Commands tab.

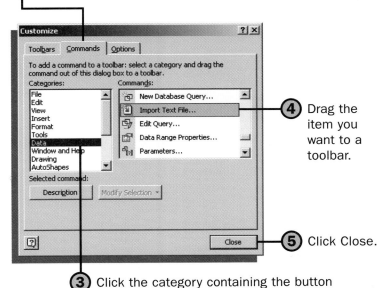

4 Drag the item you want to a toolbar.

5 Click Close.

3 Click the category containing the button you want to add to the toolbar.

Remove a Toolbar Button

1 Choose Customize from the Tools menu.

2 Drag the toolbar button you want to remove to the Customize dialog box.

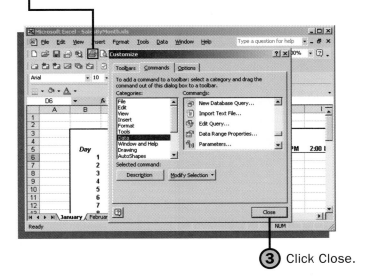

3 Click Close.

Customizing Menus

Just as you can add buttons from one toolbar to either the Standard or Formatting toolbars, you can add items to existing menus. For example, to make it simpler to import data from a series of text files one of your colleagues created, you can add Import Text File to the File menu. Once you've done this, you'll no longer need to point to Import External Data on the Data menu, click Import Data, and choose Import Data every time you want to import a file.

Add a Menu Item

(1) Choose Customize from the Tools menu.

(2) Click the Commands tab.

(3) Click the category containing the menu item you want to add.

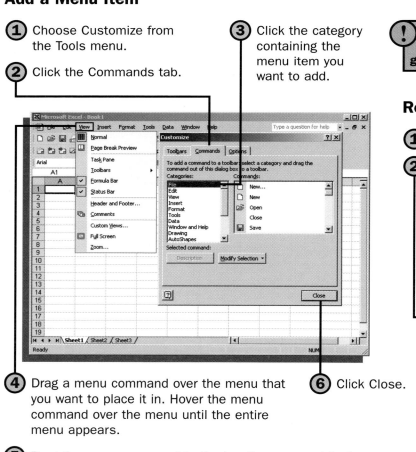

(4) Drag a menu command over the menu that you want to place it in. Hover the menu command over the menu until the entire menu appears.

(5) Drag the menu command to the location you want in the menu.

(6) Click Close.

> **TIP:** You can't place another toolbar on the same row as the menu bar, but if you add items to your menu bar, you can give yourself access to more commands on the same row.

Remove a Menu Item

(1) Choose Customize from the Tools menu.

(2) Drag the command you want to remove to the Customize dialog box.

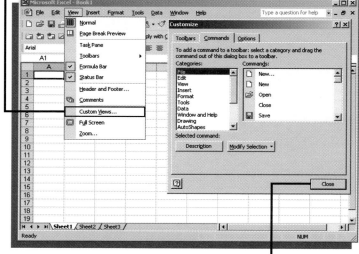

(3) Click Close.

Working with Custom Toolbars

After you've worked with Excel for a while, you might discover you use buttons from a number of toolbars. Adding all the toolbars you use would take up valuable screen space, but you can create a new toolbar and add buttons to it. For example, if you spend a lot of time working with PivotTables based on data from other sources, you could create a new toolbar with the Chart Wizard and Refresh Data buttons from the PivotTable toolbar and the Refresh All button from the External Data toolbar.

Make Your Own Toolbar

1 Choose Customize from the Tools menu.

2 Click the Toolbars tab.

3 Click New.

4 Type the name you want for your toolbar.

5 Click OK.

6 Click the Commands tab.

7 Click the category containing the item you want on the toolbar.

8 Drag the item you want to your toolbar.

9 Click Close.

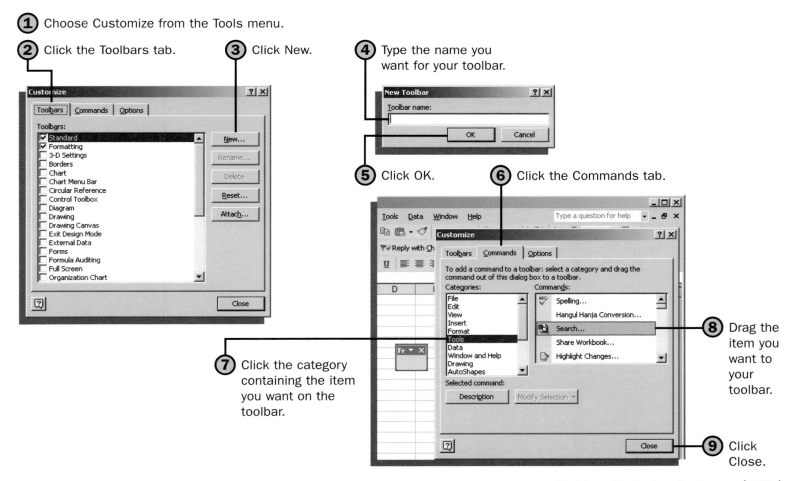

Delete a Custom Toolbar

1 Choose Customize from the Tools menu.

2 Click the Toolbars tab.

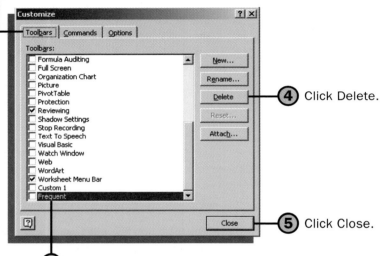

4 Click Delete.

5 Click Close.

3 Click the toolbar you want to delete.

9 Sorting and Filtering Worksheet Data

After you've added data to your worksheets, you might want to change the order in which the worksheet rows are displayed. For example, if you have a worksheet listing orders for a week, you might want to list the orders for each customer or perhaps reorder the rows in your worksheet so that the most expensive orders are at the top of the list and the least expensive at the bottom. You can also hide any rows that don't meet your criteria, which is particularly useful when you work with a large data set.

Just as you can change or limit how your worksheet data is displayed, you can control what type data is entered into your worksheets. By setting validation rules for groups of cells, you can check each value, and, if the value you or your colleagues enter falls outside the accepted range, you can instruct Microsoft Excel to display an error message that reminds the user what sort of value is acceptable in that cell.

In this section, you will learn how to:

● Sort worksheet data by the contents of a single column.

● Create multicolumn sorts.

● Define custom lists and sort using those lists.

● Limit worksheet data using filters.

● Guide data entry with validation rules.

Sorting Worksheet Data

You can sort a group of rows in a worksheet a number of different ways, but the first step, no matter how you sort, is to identify the column that will provide the values by which the rows should be sorted. Once you've selected the column you want to use, you can choose whether to display the sorted values in ascending or descending order. For example, if you have a list of products your company sells with each product's monthly sales in the same row, you can sort the worksheet by the contents of the sales column in descending order to discover which products generated the most revenue for your company. You can also sort the worksheet rows in ascending order to put the lowest-revenue products at the top of the list. If you want to sort by the contents of more than one column, you can create a multicolumn sort. One handy use for a multicolumn sort would be to sort your products by category, and then by total sales.

Sort Data in Ascending or Descending Order

1 Click any cell in the column by which you want to sort your worksheet.

2 Follow either of these steps:

Click the Sort Ascending button.

Click the Sort Descending button.

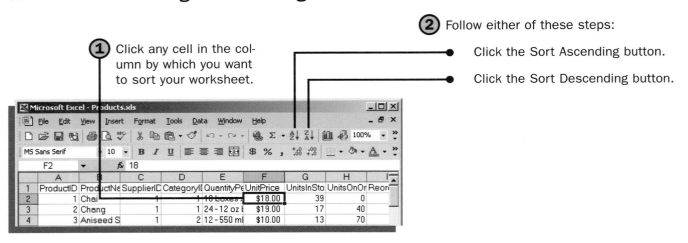

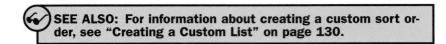

SEE ALSO: For information about creating a custom sort order, see "Creating a Custom List" on page 130.

Create a Multicolumn Sort

1 Select the cells you want to sort.

2 Choose Sort from the Data menu.

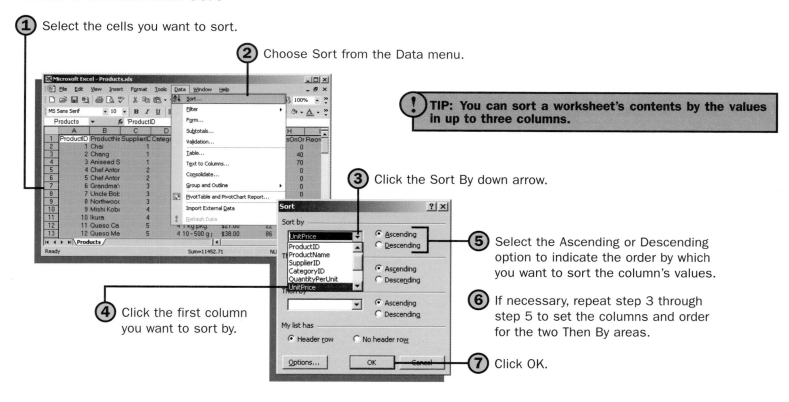

TIP: You can sort a worksheet's contents by the values in up to three columns.

3 Click the Sort By down arrow.

4 Click the first column you want to sort by.

5 Select the Ascending or Descending option to indicate the order by which you want to sort the column's values.

6 If necessary, repeat step 3 through step 5 to set the columns and order for the two Then By areas.

7 Click OK.

CAUTION: Excel doesn't remember the original order of rows in your worksheet. If you don't have a column with a unique value in each cell, such as a product number or customer identification number, you might not be able to put your worksheet back into its original order. You can click the Undo button to reverse a sort, but if you close a workbook after performing a sort, Undo won't be available when you reopen the worksheet.

Creating a Custom List

Excel sorts numbers according to their value and sorts words in alphabetical order. You'll find there are times when you need more alternatives for sorting your data than these two basic sort methods. For example, sorting the months of the year in alphabetic order would put February in front of January. To give you more sorting power, Excel provides four custom lists: days of the week, abbreviations for days of the week, months, and abbreviated month names. You can have Excel sort based on those lists or, if you want to create a custom list of your own, you can do so.

Define a Custom List of Values

1 Choose Options from the Tools menu.

2 Click the Custom Lists tab.

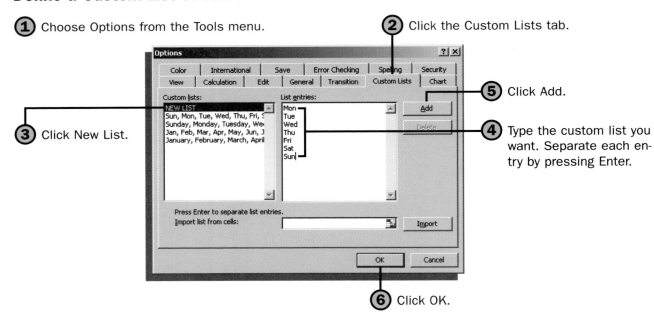

3 Click New List.

4 Type the custom list you want. Separate each entry by pressing Enter.

5 Click Add.

6 Click OK.

Sort by a Custom List

(1) Select the cells you want to sort.

(2) Choose Sort from the Data menu.

(3) Click the Sort By down arrow.

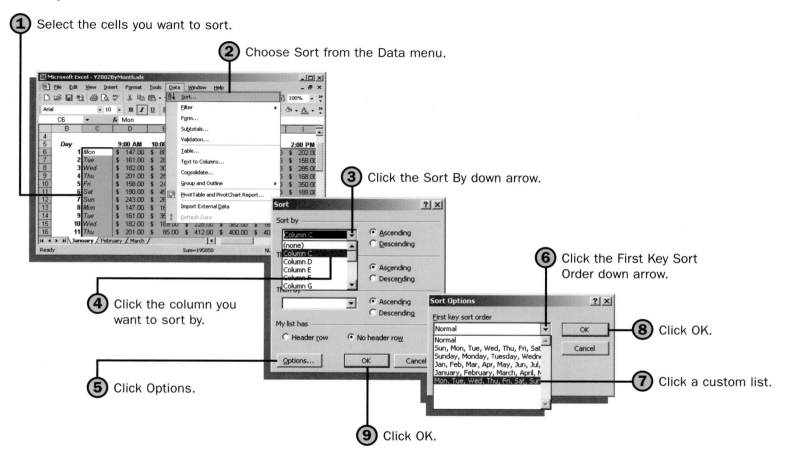

(4) Click the column you want to sort by.

(5) Click Options.

(6) Click the First Key Sort Order down arrow.

(7) Click a custom list.

(8) Click OK.

(9) Click OK.

> ✋ **CAUTION:** If you want to use a custom list in a multi-column sort, the custom list must be the primary sorting criteria.

Filtering Data Quickly with AutoFilter

An important aspect of working with large amounts of data is the ability to zero in on the most important data in a worksheet, whether that data represents the best 10 days of sales in a month or slow-selling product lines you might need to reevaluate. In Excel, you have a number of powerful, flexible techniques you can use to limit the data displayed in your worksheet. One of these techniques is to *filter* the contents of a workbook. Unlike sorting, which arranges worksheet rows according to rules you set, filtering a worksheet hides rows that don't meet the rules you define.

Create an AutoFilter

1 Select the cells you want to filter.

2 On the Data menu, point to Filter, and choose AutoFilter.

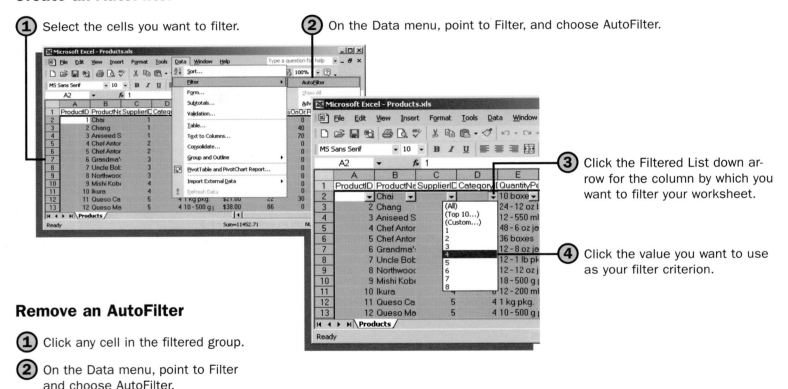

3 Click the Filtered List down arrow for the column by which you want to filter your worksheet.

4 Click the value you want to use as your filter criterion.

Remove an AutoFilter

1 Click any cell in the filtered group.

2 On the Data menu, point to Filter and choose AutoFilter.

Create a Custom AutoFilter

(1) Select the cells you want to filter.

(2) On the Data menu, point to Filter and choose AutoFilter.

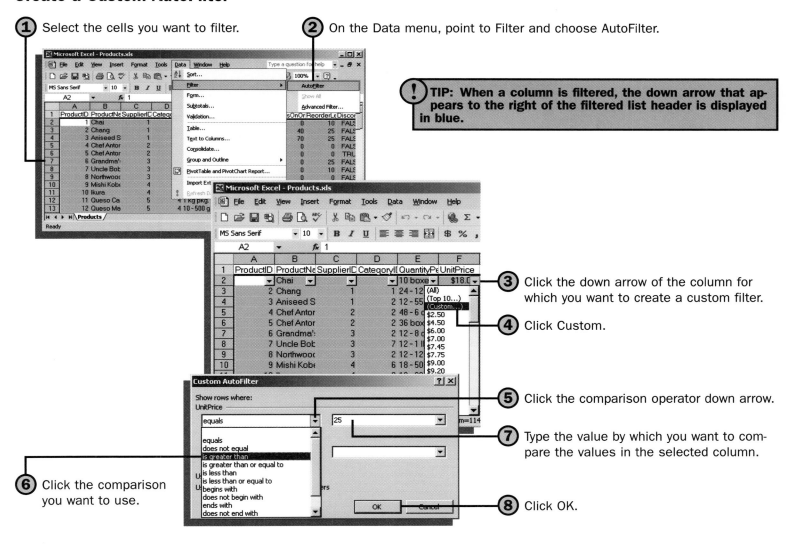

! TIP: When a column is filtered, the down arrow that appears to the right of the filtered list header is displayed in blue.

(3) Click the down arrow of the column for which you want to create a custom filter.

(4) Click Custom.

(5) Click the comparison operator down arrow.

(7) Type the value by which you want to compare the values in the selected column.

(6) Click the comparison you want to use.

(8) Click OK.

Creating an Advanced Filter

When you create a filter using AutoFilter, you can create complex rules to filter the contents of the worksheet. The limitation is that the rules used to filter the worksheet aren't readily discernible. If you want the rules used to filter a column's values to be displayed

in the body of the worksheet, you can write each rule in a cell and identify those cells so that Excel knows how to filter the worksheet. With the filtering rule visible in the body of the worksheet, you can change the rules used to filter your data by editing the cells with the filter criteria and re-applying the filter.

Build an Advanced Filter

① Copy the column titles of the list you want to filter.

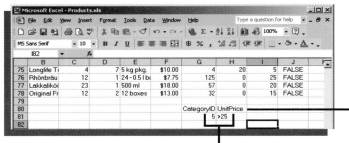

② Paste the titles in another spot on your workbook.

③ Under their respective titles, type what criteria you want met.

④ Select a cell in the list you want filtered.

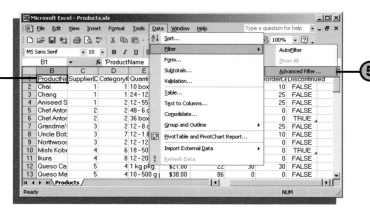

⑤ On the Data menu, point to Filter and choose Advanced Filter.

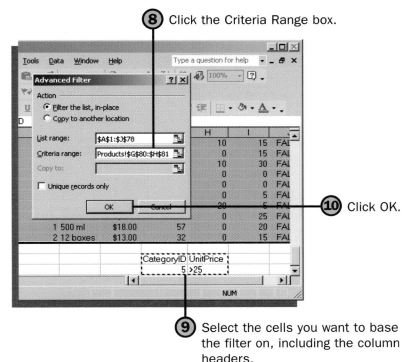

⑧ Click the Criteria Range box.

⑥ Click the List Range box.

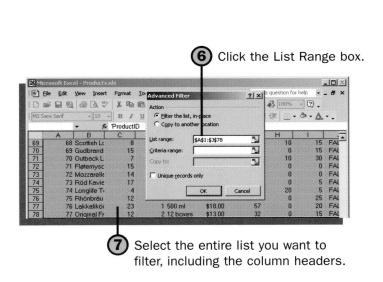

⑦ Select the entire list you want to filter, including the column headers.

⑩ Click OK.

⑨ Select the cells you want to base the filter on, including the column headers.

Remove an Advanced Filter

① Select the cells you want to remove a filter from.

② On the Data menu, point to Filter and choose Show All.

Validating Data for Correctness During Entry

Setting validation rules for data entered into cells lets you catch many of the most common data entry errors, such as entering values that are too small or too large or attempting to enter a word in a cell requiring a number. When you create a validation rule, you can also create a message to inform you and your colleagues what sort of data is expected for the cell.

Validate for Specific Requirements

1 Select the cells you want to validate.

2 Choose Validation from the Data menu.

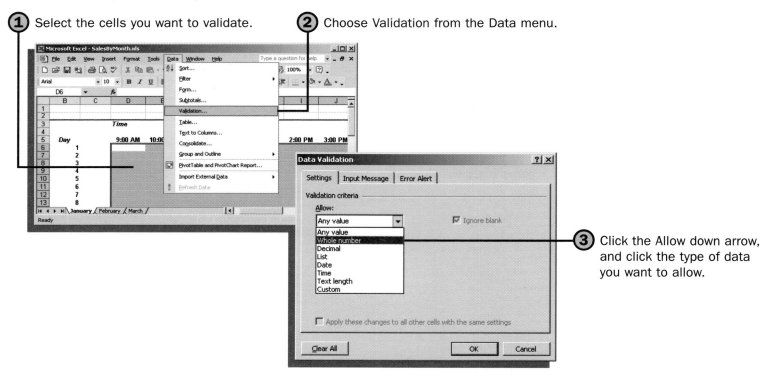

3 Click the Allow down arrow, and click the type of data you want to allow.

> **!** **TIP: If you want to display all of the cells in your worksheet with validation criteria, choose the Go To command from the Edit menu. Then click Special, and select Data Validation. Make sure the All option is selected, and click OK.**

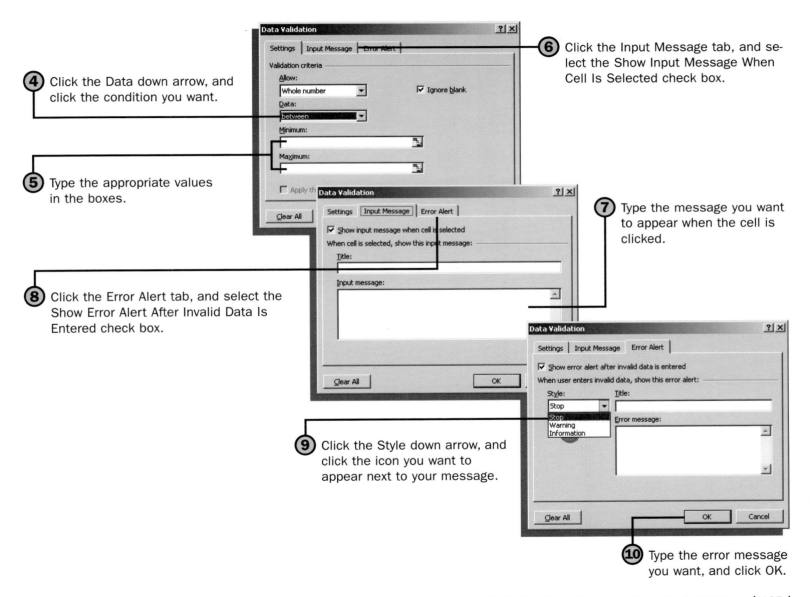

④ Click the Data down arrow, and click the condition you want.

⑤ Type the appropriate values in the boxes.

⑥ Click the Input Message tab, and select the Show Input Message When Cell Is Selected check box.

⑦ Type the message you want to appear when the cell is clicked.

⑧ Click the Error Alert tab, and select the Show Error Alert After Invalid Data Is Entered check box.

⑨ Click the Style down arrow, and click the icon you want to appear next to your message.

⑩ Type the error message you want, and click OK.

Validate Data According to a List in a Worksheet Range

1 Select the cells you want to validate.

2 Choose Validation from the Data menu.

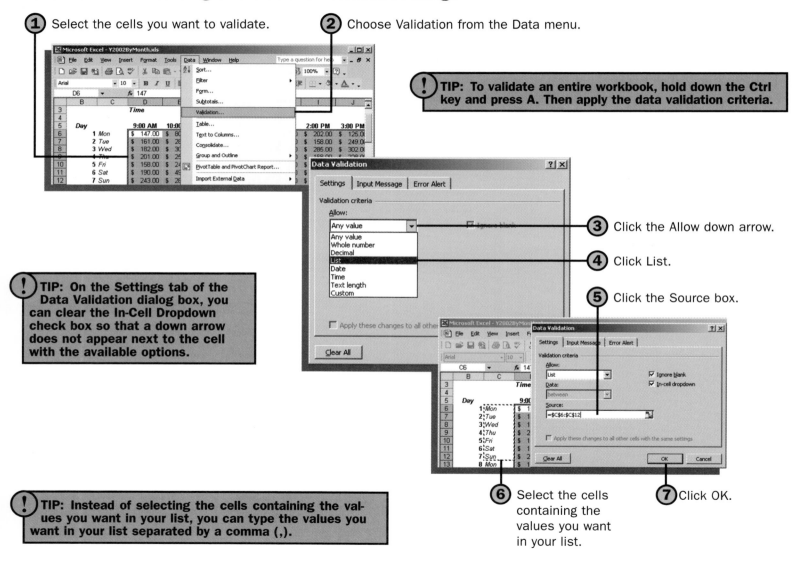

!TIP: To validate an entire workbook, hold down the Ctrl key and press A. Then apply the data validation criteria.

!TIP: On the Settings tab of the Data Validation dialog box, you can clear the In-Cell Dropdown check box so that a down arrow does not appear next to the cell with the available options.

3 Click the Allow down arrow.

4 Click List.

5 Click the Source box.

6 Select the cells containing the values you want in your list.

7 Click OK.

!TIP: Instead of selecting the cells containing the values you want in your list, you can type the values you want in your list separated by a comma (,).

Getting More out of Advanced Filters

You can use Advanced Filters to limit the rows that appear in your worksheet, but their utility doesn't stop there. In addition to setting multiple criteria to filter your worksheet, you can use Advanced Filters to locate unique values in your worksheets and copy the results to another group of cells on any Microsoft Excel worksheet.

When you have Excel locate unique values in a worksheet, you create an Advanced Filter that finds every value that occurs at least once in the single column you identify. For example, if you had a list of all sales on a given day, you could identify which sales

representatives had made at least one sale. One important limitation on finding unique values, however, is that identification only works on worksheets in which the data is limited to the columns in which you want to find unique values. For example, if you had a two-column worksheet listing the OrderID of an order and the sales representative who took the order, every row would have a unique combination of OrderID (which is different for every order) and sales representative. To find sales representatives who had made a sale on that day, you would need to delete the OrderID column.

Find Unique Rows

1 Select the cells in which you want to find unique values.

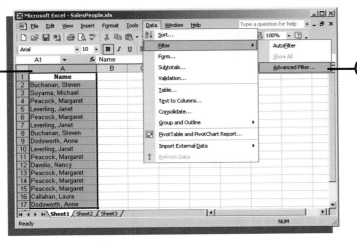

2 On the Data menu, point to Filter and choose Advanced Filter.

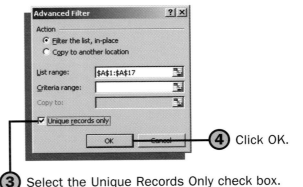

4 Click OK.

3 Select the Unique Records Only check box.

> **!** **TIP:** When you find unique values in a column, Excel returns only the first occurrence of each value.

Copy Filtered Rows to a New Location

1 Type the criteria to be used to filter the worksheet in a cell below the rows to be filtered.

3 On the Data menu, point to Filter and choose Advanced Filter.

4 Select the Copy To Another Location option.

5 Click in the Criteria Range box.

6 Select the cells with the filtering criteria.

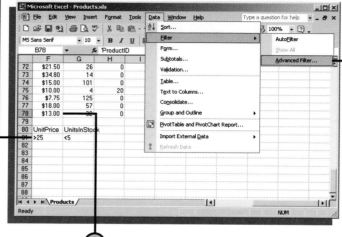

2 Click any cell in the range to be filtered.

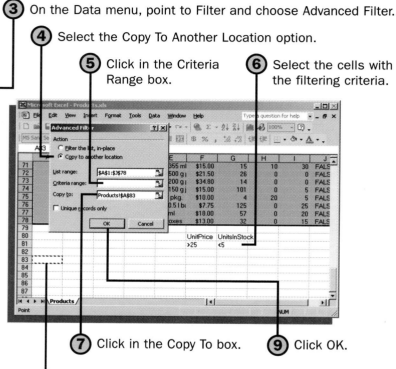

7 Click in the Copy To box.

9 Click OK.

8 Select the cell at the top left corner of where you want the filtered rows to be placed.

> **! TIP: Copying the results of an Advanced Filter saves you time by identifying where you want the results of your filter to be pasted. Rather than applying the filter and manually copying the results to the new location, you can identify the destination when you create the filter.**

> **SEE ALSO: For more information on assigning criteria for an Advanced Filter, see "Creating an Advanced Filter" on page 134 .**

Using Charts to Display Data

Excel gives you many ways to display your numeric data. You can change the color or font of data you want to emphasize, make labels bold to set them apart from the body of data in your worksheets, or add graphics to establish your corporate identity. You can use totals and subtotals to summarize your data, making it easier for you and your colleagues to compare values for entire categories of data.

One excellent way to present data—particularly large amounts of it—is by using charts. For example, when you present sales data to colleagues or potential investors who are less familiar with your business, you can use charts and graphs to visually summarize the information. By presenting your data this way, you will make it much easier to identify patterns and relationships at a glance.

In this section, you will learn how to:

● Create a chart using the Chart Wizard.

● Change a chart's type.

● Add or modify legends, titles, and annotations.

● Change a chart's scale.

● Customize a pie chart.

● Project future trends based on chart data.

Displaying Data Graphically

When you enter data into a Microsoft Excel worksheet, you can create a record of important information, whether they are individual sales, sales for an hour of a day, or the price of a product. What a list of values in cells can't easily communicate, however, are the overall trends in your data. A good way to communicate trends in large data collections is through charts and graphs, which summarize data visually.

As an example of how charts and graphs can help present your data more effectively, consider the selected cells in the following graphic, which list the sales at a garden supply store for the hour from 9:00 a.m. to 10:00 a.m. in January 2002.

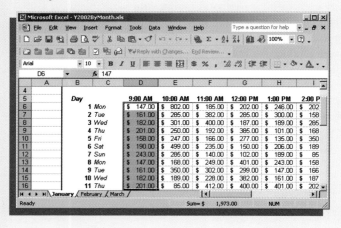

In a sense, the data does speak for itself. The total sales for each hourly period are listed so that you and your colleagues can compare them. However, each number must be comprehended, remembered, and compared to the other results individually. When you present the results in a chart or a graph, as is done with the following column chart, you can compare the values more readily.

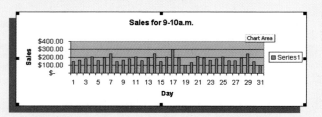

If you have trouble deciding which type of chart or graph to create, you can experiment while you build a chart with the Chart Wizard. The Chart Wizard explains what types of data each chart type represents most effectively. Experiment with different chart types to find one that works best with your data.

Standard Excel Chart Types and Uses

Chart Type	Use
Column	Compares data in a vertical format.
Bar	Compares data in a horizontal format.
Line	Compares data in a line format.
Pie	Compares the data in a percent format.
Scatter Plot	Compares pairs of values in a dot format.
Area	Compares the trend of values over time or across categories.
Doughnut	Compares multiple series of data in a percent format.
Radar	Displays changes in values relative to a center point.
Surface	Displays trends in values across two dimensions.
Bubble	Compares sets of three values.
Stock	Displays a chart for comparison of stock prices and quotes.
Cylinder	Same as a column or bar chart, but uses a cylindrical format.
Cone	Same as a column or bar chart, but uses a conical format.
Pyramid	Same as a column or bar chart, but uses a pyramid format.

Identify Chart Elements

The following graphic identifies the chart elements you'll set when you create your chart. You can modify any of these elements by double-clicking them and using the controls in the dialog box that appears.

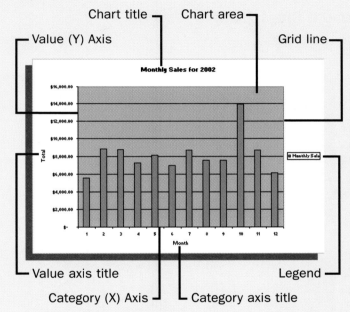

Creating a Chart Using the Chart Wizard

To present your Excel data graphically, select the cells you want to summarize and run the Chart Wizard. The cells with the data to be represented in the chart are part of one or more data series. A *series* is a collection of related data, such as all sales for a particular product or the sales for a day of the month. A bar chart could contain just one series; a line chart, which might display monthly sales for several years, could have many series. The Chart Wizard steps you through the process of creating a chart, letting you select the type of chart you want to create, set the chart's appearance, and decide whether you want to place the chart in an existing sheet or in a new sheet. As with all Excel wizards, you can step back through the wizard to change any of your choices before you finalize the chart.

Build a Chart Using a Wizard

(1) Select the cells you want to chart.

(2) Click the Chart Wizard button.

(3) Click the chart type you want.

(4) Click the chart subtype you want, and click Next.

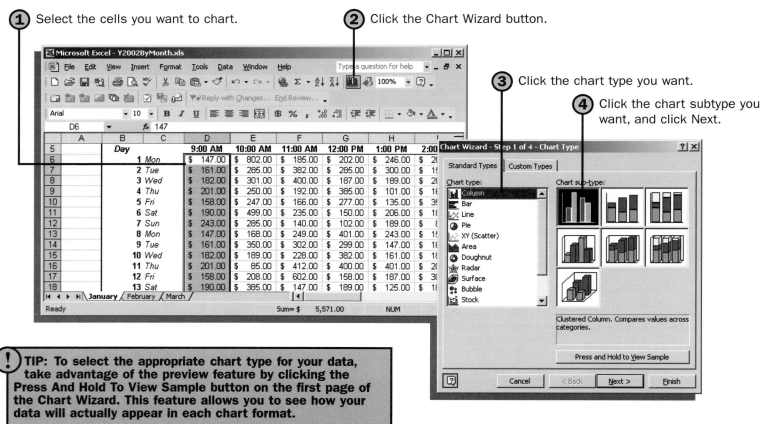

TIP: To select the appropriate chart type for your data, take advantage of the preview feature by clicking the Press And Hold To View Sample button on the first page of the Chart Wizard. This feature allows you to see how your data will actually appear in each chart format.

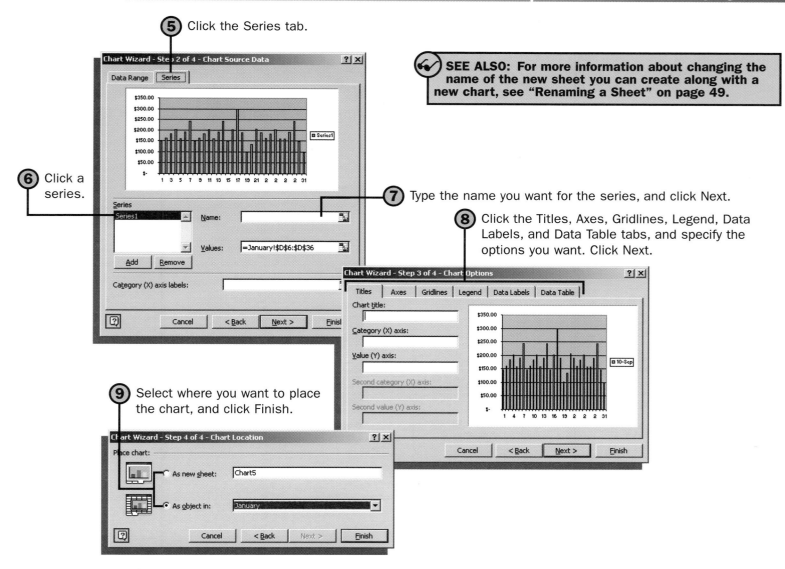

5 Click the Series tab.

Chart Wizard - Step 2 of 4 - Chart Source Data

Data Range | Series

☑ Series1

6 Click a series.

Series
Series1

Name:

Values: =January!$D$6:$D$36

Add | Remove

Category (X) axis labels:

Cancel | < Back | Next > | Finish

SEE ALSO: For more information about changing the name of the new sheet you can create along with a new chart, see "Renaming a Sheet" on page 49.

7 Type the name you want for the series, and click Next.

8 Click the Titles, Axes, Gridlines, Legend, Data Labels, and Data Table tabs, and specify the options you want. Click Next.

Chart Wizard - Step 3 of 4 - Chart Options

Titles | Axes | Gridlines | Legend | Data Labels | Data Table

Chart title:

Category (X) axis:

Value (Y) axis:

Second category (X) axis:

Second value (Y) axis:

☑ 10-Sep

Cancel | < Back | Next > | Finish

9 Select where you want to place the chart, and click Finish.

Chart Wizard - Step 4 of 4 - Chart Location

Place chart:

○ As new sheet: Chart5

● As object in: January

Cancel | < Back | Next > | Finish

Changing a Chart's Appearance

Once you've created a chart, you can change any part of its appearance, including the chart type! If you display monthly sales data as a series of columns and decide you'd rather show the data as a line rising and falling as it moves from month to month, it's simple to do so. You can also change the color, font, and other properties of any chart element. If you want your chart's title to be displayed in your company's official font, you can format the title easily.

Change a Chart Type

1. Click the chart you want to change.

2. Choose Chart Type from the Chart menu.

3. Click the type of chart you want.

4. Click the chart subtype you want.

5. Click OK.

Change the Formatting of a Chart Element

1. Double-click the chart element you want to change.

2. Click the Patterns, Font, and Alignment tabs, and select the formatting you want.

3. Click OK.

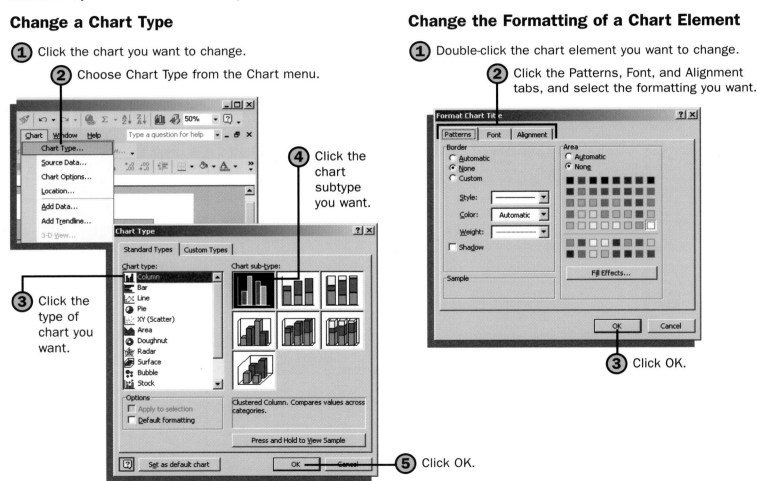

Formatting Chart Legends and Titles

An important part of creating an informative, easily read chart is to describe the contents of the chart with text. Some chart elements you can add to clarify your Excel charts are legends, titles, data labels, and annotations. A *legend* is a list of the categories in a chart and the color used to represent each one. For example, in a sales chart comparing monthly sales for several years, you might display the first year in yellow, the second year in blue, and the third year in red. The legend identifies those relationships so that you can read the chart easily and accurately. *Titles* and *data labels* describe specific parts of a chart. *Annotations* provide further information about the data the chart displays.

Show or Hide a Chart Legend

1 Click the chart you want to format.

2 Click the Legend button on the Chart toolbar.

Add Titles

1 Right-click the chart area of the chart you want to add a title to, and choose Chart Options from the shortcut menu.

2 Click the Titles tab.

3 Type the titles you want.

4 Click OK.

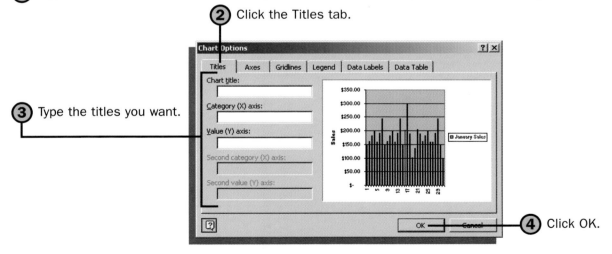

Add or Remove Data Labels

(1) Right-click the area of the chart you want to change, and choose Chart Options from the shortcut menu.

(2) Click the Data Labels tab.

(3) Select or clear the labels you want to show or hide.

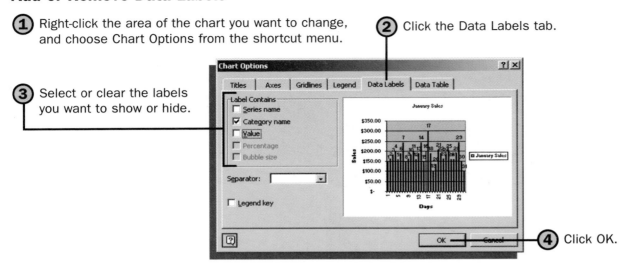

(4) Click OK.

Add Chart Annotations

(1) Click the chart you want to add annotations to.

(2) Type the text you want, and press Enter.

(3) Drag the annotations to the location you want.

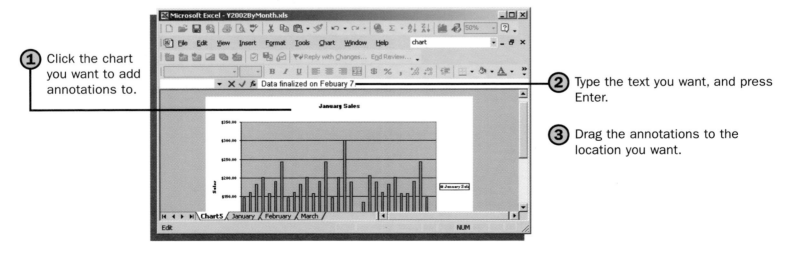

Changing the Body of a Chart

When you add labels, a legend, or annotations to a chart, you change the periphery of the chart but you don't affect how the data is displayed. If you do want to change how the data is displayed in the body of the chart, such as by showing or hiding gridlines or by changing the scale of the chart, you can do so. Adding gridlines can help viewers make fine distinctions between values, even if they're viewing the chart from the other end of a conference table. Changing the scale of a chart lets you highlight or downplay the differences among the chart's values.

Show or Hide Chart Gridlines

1 Right-click the area of the chart you want to change, and choose Chart Options from the shortcut menu.

2 Click the Gridlines tab.

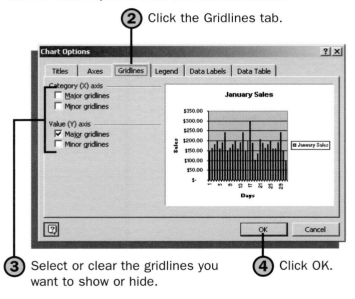

3 Select or clear the gridlines you want to show or hide.

4 Click OK.

Change the Scale on the Value (Y) Axis

1 Double-click the Value (Y) axis.

2 Click the Scale tab.

3 Type the value you want for the scale.

4 Click OK.

Change the Scale on the Category (X) Axis

(1) Double-click the Category (X) axis.

(2) Click the Scale tab.

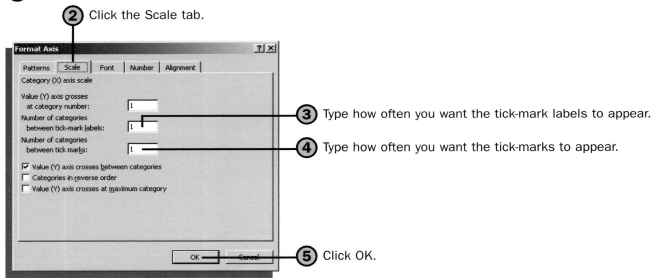

(3) Type how often you want the tick-mark labels to appear.

(4) Type how often you want the tick-marks to appear.

(5) Click OK.

> **TRY THIS:** Type scale in the Ask A Question box, and then press Enter. Click Change A Chart Category Axis from the list of help topics that appears to display the available help files for changing the category axis. The help files will show you how to change the number of categories between tick marks on the category axis, change where the value and category axes intersect, set display properties for multiple-level data, and change the category axis label.

Customizing Chart Data

When you create a chart for a business, there's always the possibility the data displayed in the chart will change. Whether those changes reflect continuing sales, updated values accounting for returns and inventory charges, or investment projections revised to match market conditions, you can update your chart by identifying a new data source. The data can be in any workbook on your computer or network—all you need to do is identify the cells with the data and Excel will do the rest.

Change the Source Data for Your Chart

(1) Right-click the area of the chart you want to change, and choose Source Data from the shortcut menu.

(2) Click the Data Range tab.   **(3)** Click the Collapse Dialog button.

(4) Select the cells you want as the new source data.

(5) Click the Expand Dialog button.

(6) Click OK in the Source Data dialog box.

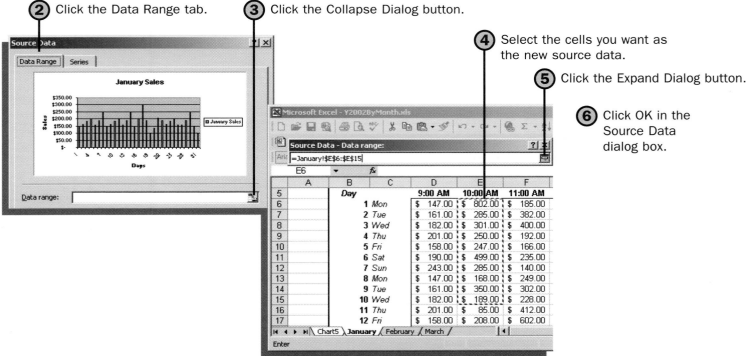

Add a New Series

(1) Click the chart you want to change.

(2) Choose Add Data from the Chart menu.

(3) Click the Collapse Dialog button.

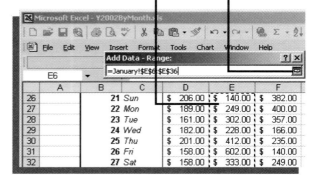

(6) Click OK.

(4) Select the cells you want to add.

(5) Click the Expand Dialog button.

> **! TIP:** If the data you want to display on your chart is on the same sheet as the chart, you can add the data to the chart. Select the cells with the data, hover the mouse pointer over an edge of the group until the mouse pointer changes to a four-headed arrow. Drag the cells onto the chart.

Delete a Series

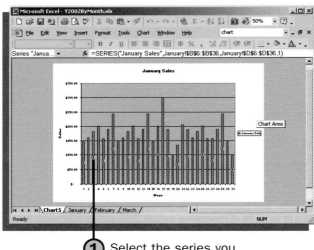

(1) Select the series you want to delete.

(2) Press the Delete key.

> **! TIP:** If you create a chart containing more than one data series, you can change the order in which the series appear on your chart by right-clicking any series, choosing Format Data Series from the shortcut menu, clicking the Series Order tab, and using the controls in the top section of the dialog box to reorder the series.

Working with Common Charts

One chart type you might use frequently is the pie chart, which displays the contribution of a series of values to the total of those values. Each section represents a category of data, such as a month in a year or a category of product. You can emphasize part of the data by pulling one section of the pie away from the rest of the chart, or you can pull all of the pieces away from the chart by exploding it. You can also change how you look at a 3-D chart, rotating the chart to change the perspective.

Pull out a Slice of a Pie Chart

(1) Click the data of the pie chart you want to change.

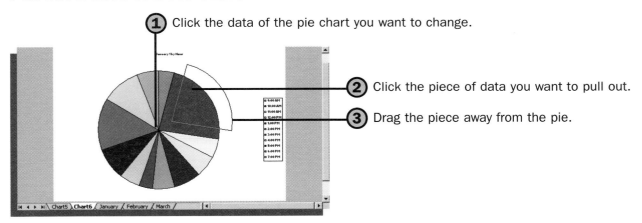

(2) Click the piece of data you want to pull out.

(3) Drag the piece away from the pie.

Explode a Pie Chart

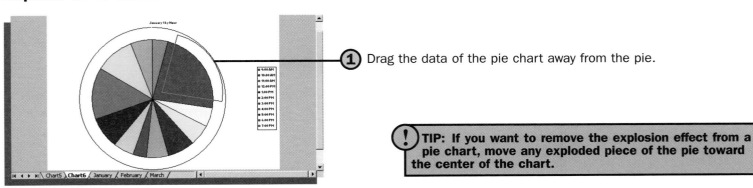

(1) Drag the data of the pie chart away from the pie.

> ! TIP: If you want to remove the explosion effect from a pie chart, move any exploded piece of the pie toward the center of the chart.

Change the Way You View 3-D Charts

(1) Right-click the chart you want to change and choose 3-D View from the shortcut menu.

(2) Type the elevation you want.

(3) Type the rotation you want.

(4) Select the additional 3-D options you want.

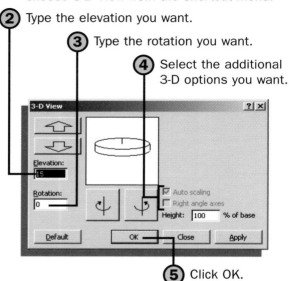

(5) Click OK.

(!) **TIP: You can preview the way your chart will look before you finalize it. Instead of clicking OK to accept your changes, click Apply to preview the changes without closing the dialog box.**

Working with Uncommon Charts

When you think about the types of charts or graphs available to present your data, the first few that come to mind will probably be the pie chart, line graph, and bar chart. Those chart types are used most often because of their familiarity and their straightforward presentation of the relationships between elements of a data series. However, there are other types of charts available to you, among them, the stock chart, which you can use to present stock market data.

Create a Stock Chart

(1) Select the stock data you want to chart. Be sure the data is formatted as shown in the figure.

(2) Click the Chart Wizard button.

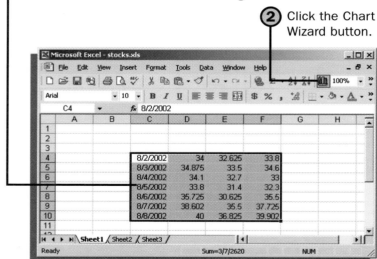

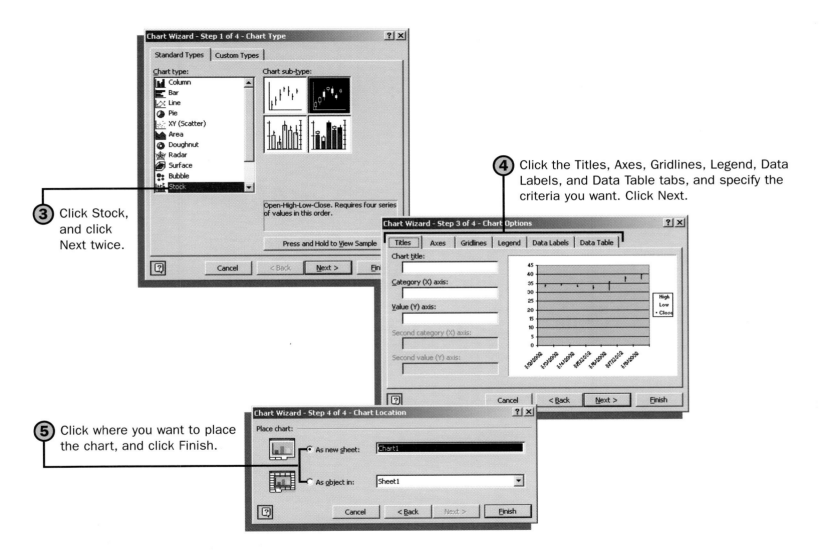

Chart Wizard - Step 1 of 4 - Chart Type

Standard Types | Custom Types

Chart type:
- Column
- Bar
- Line
- Pie
- XY (Scatter)
- Area
- Doughnut
- Radar
- Surface
- Bubble
- Stock

Chart sub-type:

Open-High-Low-Close. Requires four series of values in this order.

Press and Hold to View Sample

Cancel | < Back | Next > | Fin

(3) Click Stock, and click Next twice.

(4) Click the Titles, Axes, Gridlines, Legend, Data Labels, and Data Table tabs, and specify the criteria you want. Click Next.

Chart Wizard - Step 3 of 4 - Chart Options

Titles | Axes | Gridlines | Legend | Data Labels | Data Table

Chart title:

Category (X) axis:

Value (Y) axis:

Second category (X) axis:

Second value (Y) axis:

High Low Close

Cancel | < Back | Next > | Finish

(5) Click where you want to place the chart, and click Finish.

Chart Wizard - Step 4 of 4 - Chart Location

Place chart:

As new sheet: Chart1

As object in: Sheet1

Cancel | < Back | Next > | Finish

Performing a "What If" Analysis

You can use the data in your Excel workbooks to analyze past performance, but you can also have Excel make its best guess as to future performance if current trends continue. For example, if you create a chart that represents your company's sales for the past five years, you can have Excel analyze the data and add a trendline to the chart to represent how much sales would increase if the current trend holds true for the next year.

Add a Trendline to a Data Series

1 Right-click the data series that you want to add a trendline to, and choose Add Trendline from the shortcut menu.

2 Click the type of trendline you want.

3 Click the Options tab.

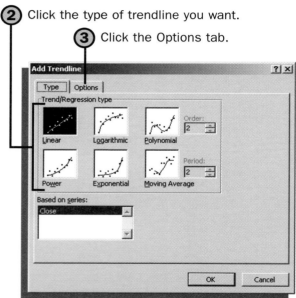

4 Select the Custom option.

5 Type the name you want for the trendline.

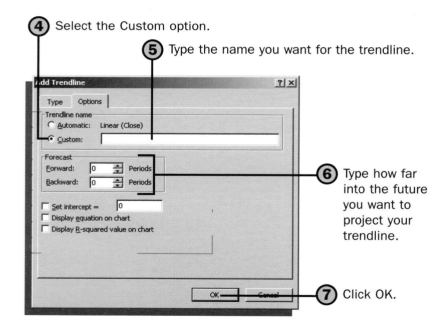

6 Type how far into the future you want to project your trendline.

7 Click OK.

✋ **CAUTION: Be sure to choose a linear regression analysis; the other types of analyses might not give you accurate results!**

Enhancing Your Worksheets with Graphics

When you create a worksheet, it's important to ensure that the data is stored in an understandable format and that all of the formulas produce the expected results. After you've taken care of these aspects of the worksheet's structure, you should also ensure that you and your colleagues can comprehend the data easily. One way to accomplish this is by adding drawing objects, such as boxes, stars, and banners, which will make your annotations and labels stand out.

Another way you can present business data in a Microsoft Excel worksheet is to create a *diagram*. In Excel, diagrams include common business items, such as Venn diagrams, which show the intersection of several data sets; and organization charts, which illustrate the hierarchy of a company or other organization.

In this section, you will learn how to:

● Add an image to a worksheet.

● Create and edit drawing objects.

● Add text to drawing objects.

● Change the appearance of drawing objects.

● Align and group drawing worksheets.

● Add Word Art and clip art to a worksheet.

● Create common business diagrams.

● Create an organization chart.

Working with Graphics in Your Worksheets

To add graphics to your worksheets, use the Drawing toolbar. The buttons on the Drawing toolbar let you add lines, shapes of many different types, and images to your worksheets. After you create a drawing object, you can change its line color or, if the object has an interior space, fill that space with a color or a pattern of your choosing. Another way you can make your images and drawing objects stand out is to add a shadow so that the objects appear to float above the surface of the worksheet. Hard shadows, which you create with black lines, mark the shadowed object as separate from the surrounding items. Softer shadows, created with a lighter shade of gray, make the shadowed object appear as part of the collection of objects on the worksheet.

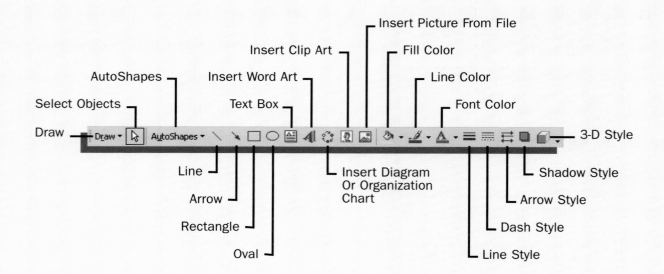

Adding Graphics to Worksheets

Once you've created a worksheet, you can add graphics to enhance the data. If your worksheet details the sales of a specific product, for example, you can add a photograph of the product. Adding a visual representation of the item described in the worksheet makes the results you offer much more memorable. You and your colleagues not only have numbers to work with, but also have a visual clue with which to associate the data.

Add a Picture

1 On the Insert menu, point to Picture and choose From File.

2 Navigate to the folder with the picture you want to insert.

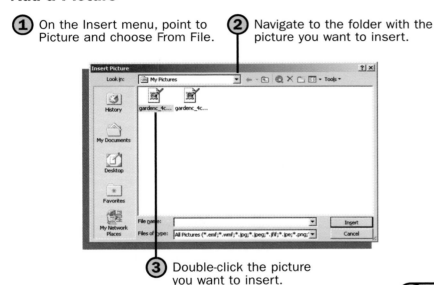

3 Double-click the picture you want to insert.

Delete a Picture

1 Click the picture you want to delete.

2 Press the Delete key.

> **SEE ALSO:** For information about adding a picture to a worksheet header or footer, see "Adding Graphics to a Header or Footer" on page 112.

Adding Drawing Objects to a Worksheet

Graphics or pictures of the items described in your worksheets make it easier to understand the data in those worksheets. Be aware, however, that you're not limited to the use of images from other sources. If you want, you can add drawing objects to your worksheets. For example, you can add shapes such as rectangles and circles, with the rectangles holding explanatory text and the circles displaying a one-word or two-word caption describing the contents of a cell.

Add a Simple Shape

(1) If necessary, right-click the menu bar and choose Drawing from the shortcut menu to display the Drawing toolbar.

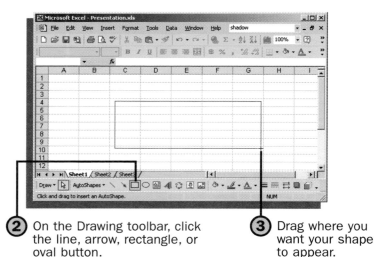

(2) On the Drawing toolbar, click the line, arrow, rectangle, or oval button.

(3) Drag where you want your shape to appear.

> **! TIP:** To create a circle or a square instead of a rectangle or an oval, hold down the Shift key and drag where you want the circle or square to appear.

Add Text to Any Shape

(1) In your worksheet, right-click the shape to which you want to add text and choose Add Text from the shortcut menu.

(2) Type the text you want in the body of the shape.

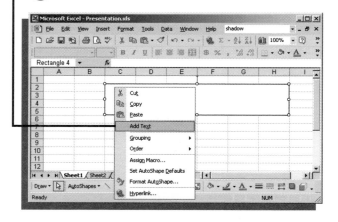

> **✋ CAUTION:** If the text you add to a shape doesn't fit in the shape, you'll only see the first part of the text you typed. To view the rest of the text, you must click the shape, click again to put the insertion point in the text, and then use the down arrow key to move through the text.

Adding Fills to Drawing Objects

Whenever you create a drawing object in Excel, you create a "blank" version of the object, meaning the object has no color or pattern filling its interior. You can add colors or patterns—referred to as *fills*—to bring the object's appearance into line with your company's color scheme, to make an object stand out from its surroundings, or simply to mask the gridlines behind the object.

Apply a Fill

(1) Double-click the object you want to fill.

> **!** **TIP: Textures are a great way to apply a pattern to an object without interfering with any text or image already positioned in the object.**

(6) Click the Gradient, Texture, or Pattern tab.

(7) Select how you want your fill to appear.

(2) Click the Colors And Lines tab.

(3) Click the Color down arrow.

(4) Click the color you want to fill the object.

(5) Click the Color down arrow again, and click Fill Effects.

(8) Click OK twice.

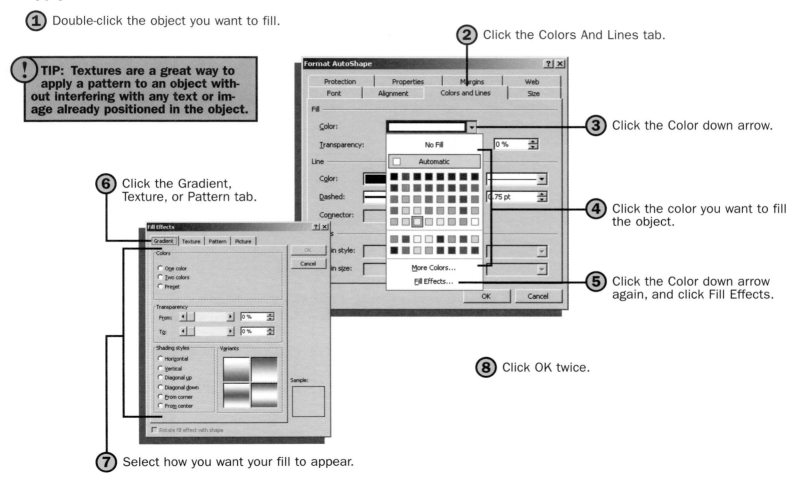

Fill an Object with a Picture

① Double-click the object you want to fill.

② Click the Colors And Lines tab.

③ Click the Color down arrow.

⑤ Click the Picture tab.

④ Click Fill Effects.

⑨ Click OK twice.

⑥ Click Select Picture.

⑦ Navigate to where the picture you want is located.

⑧ Double-click the picture.

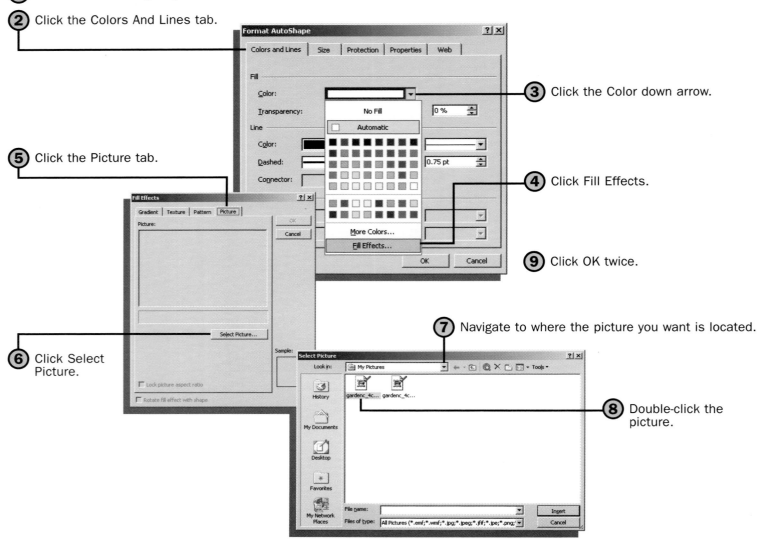

Adding Effects to Drawing Objects

When you add a drawing object to a worksheet, you can add text or color to the object to make it stand out from the rest of the worksheet's contents.

You can also add a shadow to the object, which makes it appear that the object is raised off the surface of the worksheet. If you want your drawing object to appear as a three-dimensional object (not just as a flat object that hovers over the worksheet) all you need to do is describe how you want the object to look!

Add a Shadow to an Object or Edit an Existing Shadow

① If necessary, right-click the menu bar and choose Drawing from the shortcut menu to display the Drawing toolbar.

② Click the object you want to edit or add a shadow to.

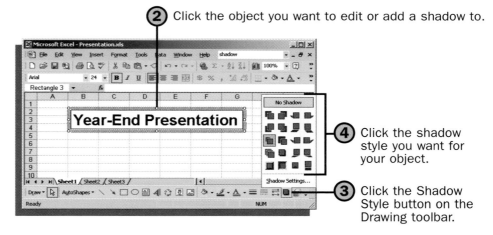

④ Click the shadow style you want for your object.

③ Click the Shadow Style button on the Drawing toolbar.

Add a 3-D Effect to an Object or Edit an Existing 3-D Effect

① Click the object you want to edit or add a 3-D effect to.

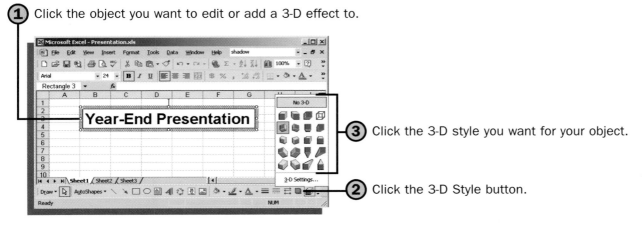

③ Click the 3-D style you want for your object.

② Click the 3-D Style button.

Customizing Pictures and Objects

You can change the size of pictures or drawing objects in your worksheets. You can also rotate objects to change their orientation on the page. Rotating an image a little to one side can indicate action or add a sense of fun, while turning an image upside down will indicate something a bit crazier. Of course, if your image is upside down when you add it to your worksheet and you don't want it to be, you can rotate it to its normal position.

Resize a Picture or Object

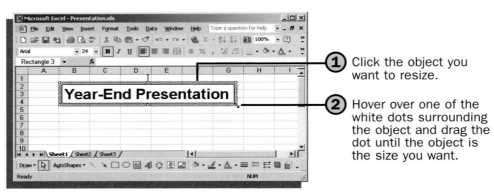

1 Click the object you want to resize.

2 Hover over one of the white dots surrounding the object and drag the dot until the object is the size you want.

Rotate a Picture or Object

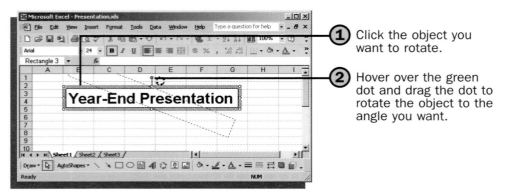

1 Click the object you want to rotate.

2 Hover over the green dot and drag the dot to rotate the object to the angle you want.

Aligning and Grouping Drawing Objects

One important design consideration is the proper alignment and order of the objects in your worksheet, both in relation to the edges of the worksheet and to any other objects. If you want your objects to be lined up with each other (for example, you want to align all objects with the left edge of the page) or if you want to order your objects behind and in front of other objects, you can do so. In a similar manner, if you want to work with a set of objects as a single unit, such as three text boxes you want to appear together, regardless of position, you can define the objects as a *group* and work with them as a single entity.

Align Objects

1 If necessary, right-click the menu bar and choose Drawing from the shortcut menu to display the Drawing toolbar.

4 Point to Align Or Distribute.

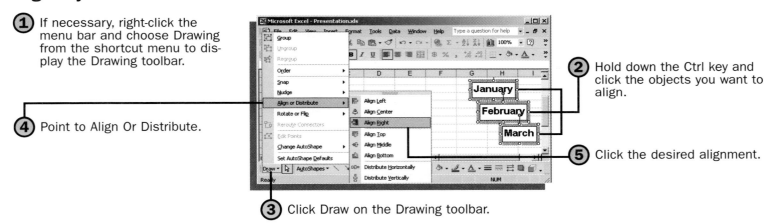

2 Hold down the Ctrl key and click the objects you want to align.

5 Click the desired alignment.

3 Click Draw on the Drawing toolbar.

> **! TIP:** If you have many objects grouped together and you then ungroup them, you may want to regroup them in the same way. You can do this quickly and easily by right-clicking one of the objects you want to regroup, pointing to Grouping, and clicking Regroup.

Group and Ungroup Objects

1 Hold down the Ctrl key, and click the objects you want to group.

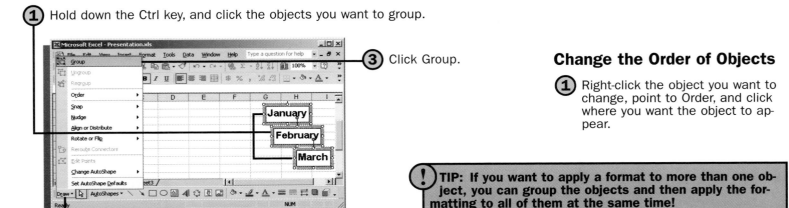

3 Click Group.

Change the Order of Objects

1 Right-click the object you want to change, point to Order, and click where you want the object to appear.

> **! TIP:** If you want to apply a format to more than one object, you can group the objects and then apply the formatting to all of them at the same time!

2 Click Draw on the Drawing toolbar.

Adding AutoShapes

If you want to add a drawing object to a worksheet, you're not limited to simple rectangles or circles. Excel has a wide range of AutoShapes you can add to your worksheet to get your message across. For example, you can add a star or a banner to a worksheet detailing the sales of your best-selling products, or perhaps add a cube, a crescent moon, or some other shape to add a bit of flair to your worksheet.

Add an AutoShape to a Worksheet

(1) If necessary, right-click the menu bar and choose Drawing from the shortcut menu to display the Drawing toolbar.

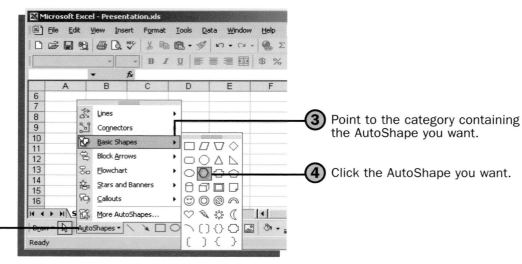

(3) Point to the category containing the AutoShape you want.

(4) Click the AutoShape you want.

(2) Click AutoShapes on the Drawing toolbar.

Connect AutoShapes with Attached Lines

(1) Click AutoShapes.

(2) Point to Connectors.

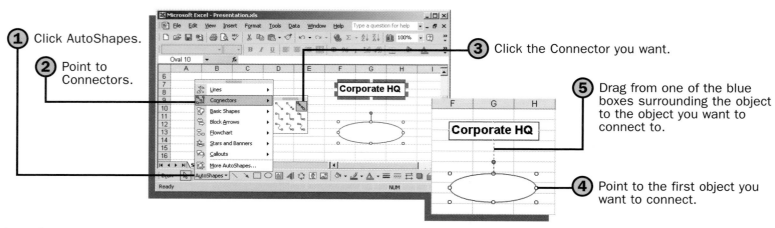

(3) Click the Connector you want.

(5) Drag from one of the blue boxes surrounding the object to the object you want to connect to.

(4) Point to the first object you want to connect.

Using WordArt to Create Text Effects in Excel

One of the benefits of working with Excel is that you can take advantage of the features of other Office programs to enhance your Excel worksheets. One of these features is WordArt, which lets you select from a wide range of styles to add exciting two-dimensional and three-dimensional text to your worksheets. Every style comes with a predefined color scheme, but you can change the color, size, and alignment of your WordArt by using the buttons on the WordArt toolbar.

Add WordArt Text

1 If necessary, right-click the menu bar and choose Drawing from the shortcut menu to display the Drawing toolbar.

3 Double-click the WordArt style you want.

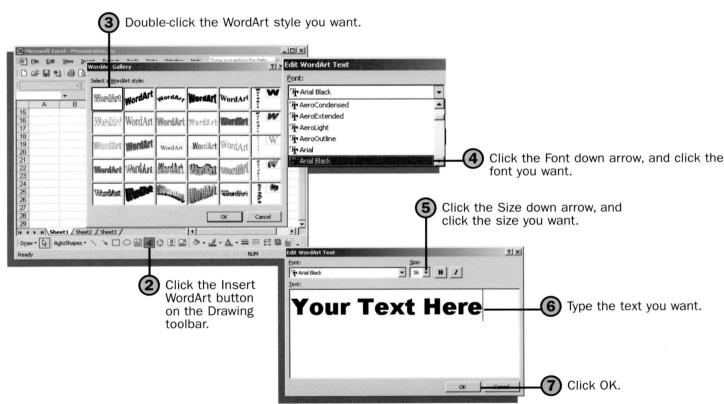

2 Click the Insert WordArt button on the Drawing toolbar.

4 Click the Font down arrow, and click the font you want.

5 Click the Size down arrow, and click the size you want.

6 Type the text you want.

7 Click OK.

Format WordArt

1 Click the WordArt you want to format.

3 Click the Colors And Lines, Size, Protection, Properties, and Web tabs to specify the formatting you want.

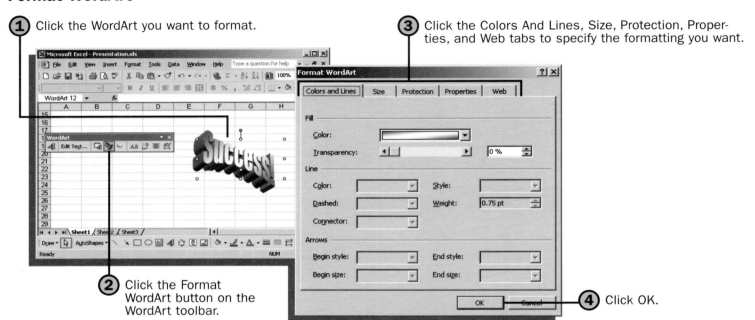

2 Click the Format WordArt button on the WordArt toolbar.

4 Click OK.

Change the Shape of Your WordArt

1 Click the WordArt you want to format.

2 Click the WordArt Shape button.

3 Click the WordArt shape you want.

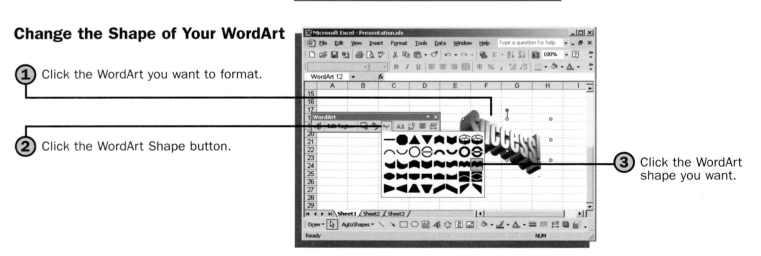

Inserting Clip Art into a Worksheet ⊕ NEW FEATURE

If you want to include a worksheet in a presentation you give to your colleagues or in a report you make available on your company's Web site, you can accent your worksheet with images from the clip art collection that comes with Microsoft Office. You can manage your clip art with the new Insert Clip Art task pane. You can search for clip art on your computer or on the Web.

Add Clip Art

1 If necessary, right-click the menu bar and choose Drawing from the short-cut menu to display the Drawing toolbar.

2 Click the Insert Clip Art button on the Drawing toolbar.

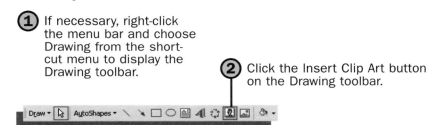

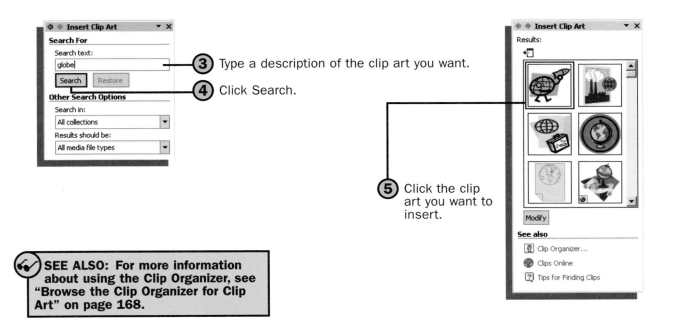

3 Type a description of the clip art you want.

4 Click Search.

5 Click the clip art you want to insert.

SEE ALSO: For more information about using the Clip Organizer, see "Browse the Clip Organizer for Clip Art" on page 168.

Browse the Clip Organizer for Clip Art

① Click the Insert Clip Art button.

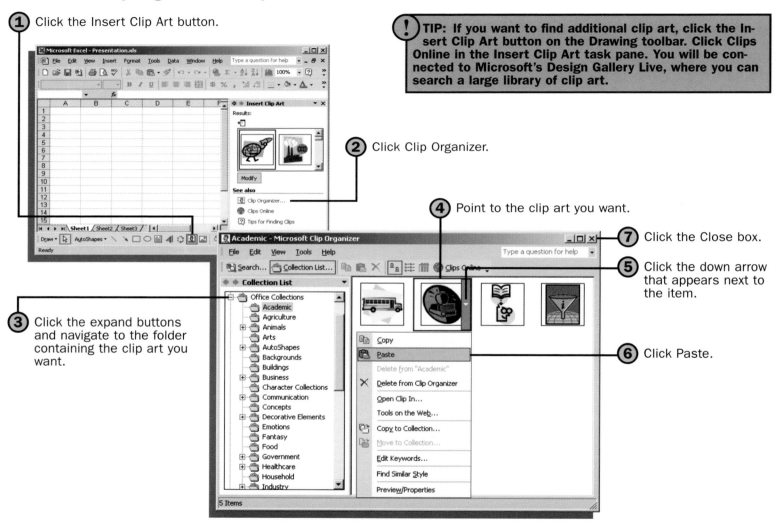

② Click Clip Organizer.

④ Point to the clip art you want.

③ Click the expand buttons and navigate to the folder containing the clip art you want.

TIP: If you want to find additional clip art, click the Insert Clip Art button on the Drawing toolbar. Click Clips Online in the Insert Clip Art task pane. You will be connected to Microsoft's Design Gallery Live, where you can search a large library of clip art.

⑦ Click the Close box.

⑤ Click the down arrow that appears next to the item.

⑥ Click Paste.

Inserting and Changing a Diagram

There are a number of diagram types that will probably be familiar to most businesspeople: the pyramid, which shows a hierarchical relationship; the target, which uses a ring of concentric circles to display the approach to a target; the Venn diagram, which shows the intersection of items in various sets; and the cycle, which dis-

plays the steps in a repeating process. Rather than create these diagrams on your own, you can have Excel create the basic diagram and then fill in the details yourself. Once you've created a diagram, you can apply an AutoFormat to alter its appearance.

Insert a Diagram and Enter Text and Change Colors

1 If necessary, right-click the menu bar and choose Drawing from the shortcut menu to display the Drawing toolbar.

2 Click the Insert Diagram Or Organization Chart button on the Drawing toolbar.

3 Double-click the type of diagram you want to add to your worksheet.

4 Click the area or areas labeled Click To Add Text to add text to your diagram.

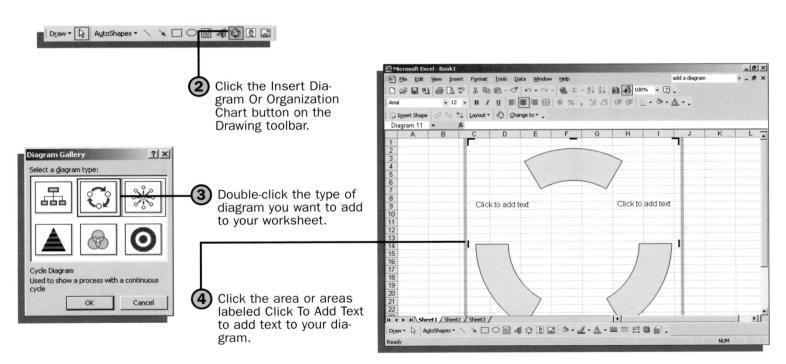

 TRY THIS: Type Add A Diagram in the Ask A Question box. Click Add A Diagram from the list of topics that appears to get more information on the types of diagrams available and how to modify them.

Change the Style of a Diagram

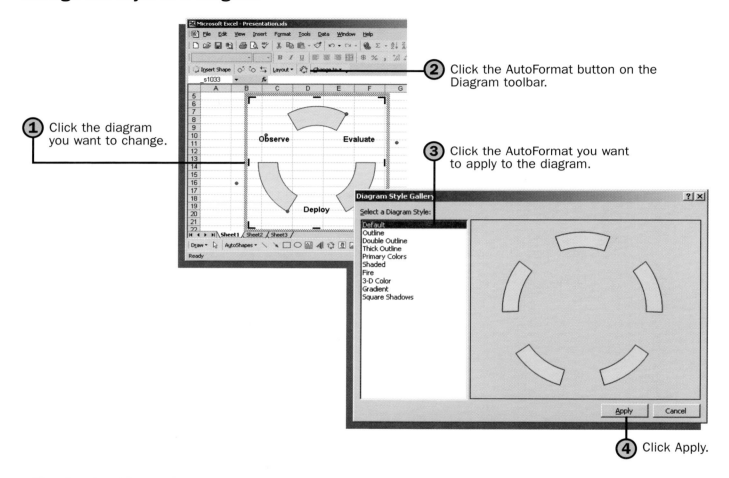

① Click the diagram you want to change.

② Click the AutoFormat button on the Diagram toolbar.

③ Click the AutoFormat you want to apply to the diagram.

④ Click Apply.

① TIP: A preview of the new format will appear in the Diagram Style Gallery dialog box. Feel free to experiment!

Creating an Organization Chart

One of the most important tools in any business is the organization chart, which shows the reporting relationships between employees and their supervisors. Creating the base of an organization chart is simple, as is adding employees to the chart. Once you've created

the chart, you can change the chart's direction so that the relationships run from left to right and not up and down, or you can apply an AutoFormat to the chart.

Create an Organization Chart

1 If necessary, right-click the menu bar and choose Drawing from the shortcut menu to display the Drawing toolbar.

2 Click the Insert Diagram Or Organization Chart button on the Drawing toolbar.

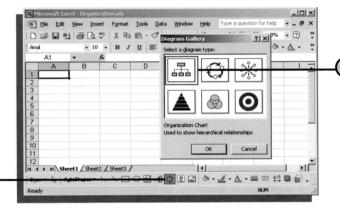

3 Double-click the Organization Chart button.

Add a Shape

1 Click the shape you want to enter a shape under or next to.

2 Click the Insert Shape down arrow on the Organization Chart toolbar.

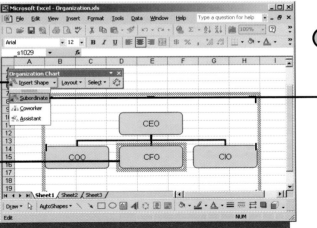

3 Do one of the following:

- Click Subordinate to place the shape below the current shape.

- Click Coworker to place the shape next to the current shape.

- Click Assistant to place the shape below the current shape with an elbow connector.

Alter the Layout of Your Organization Chart

1 Click the shape above the shapes whose layout you want to change.

2 Click Layout on the Organization Chart toolbar.

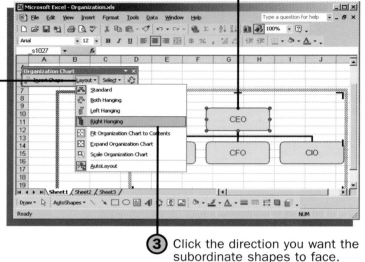

3 Click the direction you want the subordinate shapes to face.

TIP: To change the color of text in an organization chart, click the text box and then click the Font Color button on either the Formatting toolbar or the Drawing toolbar.

SEE ALSO: For information about adding a shadow or a 3-D effect to a shape in an organization chart, see "Adding Effects to Drawing Objects" on page 161.

Change the Design of Your Organization Chart

① Click the organization chart you want to change.

② Click the AutoFormat button on the Organization Chart toolbar.

③ Click the style you want.

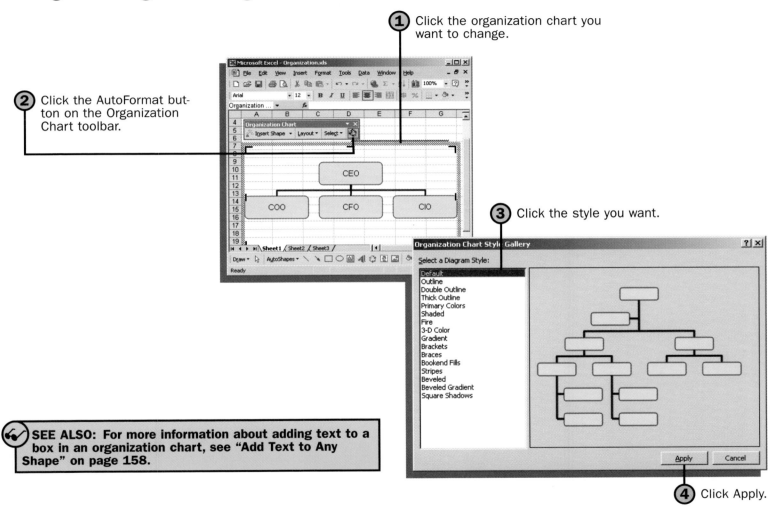

④ Click Apply.

SEE ALSO: For more information about adding text to a box in an organization chart, see "Add Text to Any Shape" on page 158.

12 Using Excel in a Group Environment

In this section

Sharing Workbooks in Excel

Commenting Cells

Tracking Changes in Workbooks

Accepting or Rejecting Changes

Merging Workbooks

Analyzing Alternative Data Scenarios

Combining Scenarios into One Worksheet

Even though one person might be in charge of managing a company's financial data and related information, there is often a group of people who either enter data into workbooks or have input into future sales or growth projections. You and your colleagues can add comments to workbooks to describe the contents and offer insights into how certain values were derived. If you and your colleagues need to open or edit a workbook at the same time but from different computers, you can enable workbook sharing, which allows more than one person to have the workbook open at the same time. You can view any changes your colleagues make and accept or reject those changes to produce the final version of the workbook.

Another aspect of using Excel workbooks in a group environment is in offering opinions regarding future sales and business goals that contain changing data. Rather than creating new worksheets for each of your colleagues' suggested values, you can define *scenarios*, or alternative data sets, to save each alternative with the original worksheet.

In this section, you will learn how to:

● Turn on workbook sharing.

● View and manage worksheet comments.

● Track workbook changes.

● Accept or reject workbook changes.

● Create scenarios.

● Copy scenarios from one worksheet to another.

Sharing Workbooks in Excel

The first step in making a workbook available to your colleagues is to turn on workbook sharing. When you turn on workbook sharing, you let more than one user work with a workbook simultaneously, which is perfect for mid-size businesses where employees need to look up customer, sales, and product data frequently. In larger companies, turning on workbook sharing makes it possible for co-workers at different offices to add values to a workbook used to develop a cost estimate or maintain expense reports.

Turn on Workbook Sharing

1 Choose Share Workbook from the Tools menu.

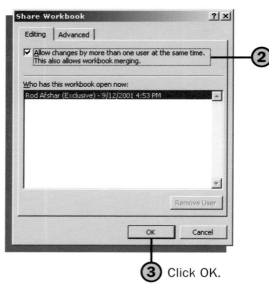

2 Select the Allow Changes By More Than One User At The Same Time... check box.

! **TIP: Excel has a toolbar created specifically for work-ing with comments and tracked changes easily. You can move between comments and changes, reject or accept them, and add new comments with little effort. To view the toolbar, point to Toolbars on the View menu and choose Reviewing. This will enable you to control com-ments and tracked changes easier.**

3 Click OK.

✋ **CAUTION: Prior to sharing your workbook, it must be saved first. Since the workbook will be used between multiple users, be sure to save the workbook that is shared over your network so that others may view it.**

Commenting Cells

When you and your colleagues share the responsibility for creating a workbook, you might want to add comments to some cells. You can suggest modifications to a formula, ask whether a cell's contents might be formatted differently, or provide an updated value for a workbook's owner to add after he or she verifies the data.

Cells with comments have a red flag at the top right corner, making it easy to identify which cells have additional information available. For example, you can add a comment to a sales worksheet explaining that two exceptionally large purchases pushed one hour's sales way beyond the norm.

Add a Comment

(1) Right-click the cell you want to add a comment to, and choose Insert Comment from the shortcut menu.

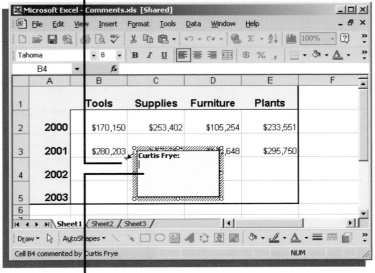

(2) Type the comment you want.

(3) Click anywhere outside the comment to stop adding text.

View a Comment

(1) Hover over a cell with a red triangle in the upper right corner.

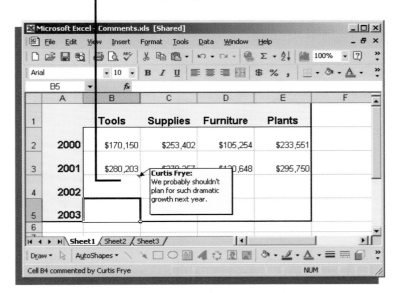

TIP: If you want a comment to be shown the entire time your workbook is open, right-click the cell with the comment and choose Show Comment from the shortcut menu.

Edit a Comment

1 Right-click the cell with the comment you want to edit, and choose Edit Comment from the shortcut menu.

Delete a Comment

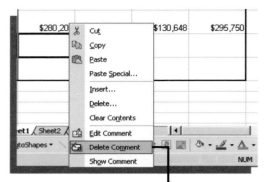

1 Right-click the cell with the comment you want to delete, and choose Delete Comment from the shortcut menu.

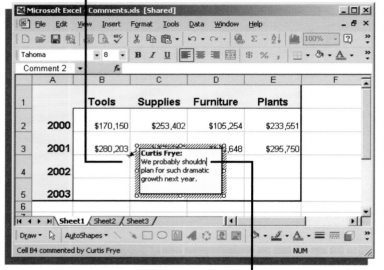

2 Edit the comment text.

3 Click anywhere outside the comment box to stop editing.

> **CAUTION:** Note that the name attributed to a comment might not be the name of the person who actually wrote it. Instead, a comment reflects the name of the person who was logged on to the computer when the comment was made.

Tracking Changes in Workbooks

Whenever you collaborate with your colleagues on a workbook, you should consider tracking the changes each user makes. When you enable change tracking, any changes made to the workbook are highlighted in a color assigned to the user who made the changes. One benefit of tracking changes is that if you have a question about a change, you can quickly identify who made the change and address your questions to the appropriate user.

Track Changes

(1) On the Tools menu, point to Track Changes and choose Highlight Changes.

(2) Select the Track Changes While Editing check box.

(!) TIP: If your workbook's changed cells aren't marked, you can retroactively have Excel display them by pointing to Track Changes on the Tools menu, and choosing Highlight Changes. In the dialog box that appears, clear the When check box and click OK.

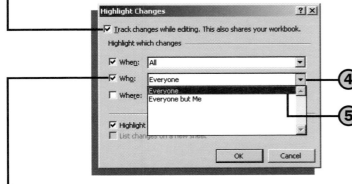

(4) Click the Who down arrow.

(5) Click Everyone.

(3) Select the Who check box.

(6) Click OK twice to close the dialog box and save your workbook.

Accepting or Rejecting Changes

Once you and your colleagues have made your changes to a workbook, you can go through the workbook and accept or reject those changes. The best way to accept or reject changes is to move through them one at a time. Although examining each change in a large document can be tedious, it can be far less work to take an hour to finalize a workbook than it is to spend a day reconstructing a workbook after you accidentally accepted every change. If you want to keep track of every change, you can have Excel create a new worksheet, named "History," in which Excel lists every change made since you last saved the file. Whenever you save your workbook, Excel will delete the History worksheet.

View a Change

(1) Hover over a cell with a blue triangle in the upper left corner.

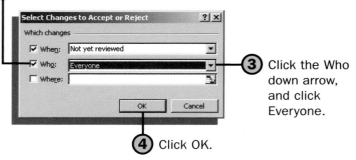

Review Changes

(1) On the Tools menu, point to Track Changes, and choose Accept Or Reject Changes.

(2) Select the Who check box.

(3) Click the Who down arrow, and click Everyone.

(4) Click OK.

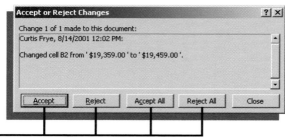

(5) Do one of the following:

- Click Accept to accept the current change.

- Click Reject to reject the current change.

- Click Accept All to accept all the changes.

- Click Reject All to reject all the changes.

Create a Change History

① On the Tools menu, point to Track Changes and choose Highlight Changes.

② Select the Track Changes While Editing check box.

③ Select the Who check box.

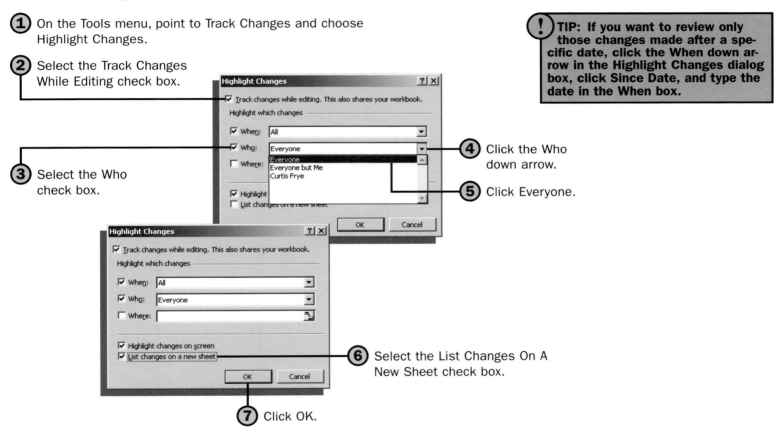

④ Click the Who down arrow.

⑤ Click Everyone.

⑥ Select the List Changes On A New Sheet check box.

⑦ Click OK.

! TIP: If you want to review only those changes made after a specific date, click the When down arrow in the Highlight Changes dialog box, click Since Date, and type the date in the When box.

! TIP: Consider making a backup copy of your workbook before accepting any changes. Having a record of the changes made in case something goes wrong is never a bad idea.

Merging Workbooks

Tracking changes lets you and your colleagues modify a document, maintain a record of the changes, and choose which changes to keep in the final version of your document. There will be times when every individual with input into a document won't be able to access the same copy of the workbook; for example, when a senior manager is away on a business trip. You can still allow your colleagues access to the final version of the document by sending them duplicates of the original document and later merging the changes from their copies into the original document.

Prepare a Workbook for Merging

(1) Ensure the files you want to merge meet these criteria:

- All distributed files must be copies of the same workbook, which must have had sharing, change tracking, and change history turned on when it was copied.

- All distributed files must have maintained a change history continuously since distribution (that is, never had sharing, change tracking, or change history turned off).

- All files must have different file names.

- All files must either have no password or have the same password.

Merge Workbook Changes

(1) Open the original file, and choose Compare And Merge Workbooks from the Tools menu.

(2) Hold down the Ctrl key, and click the files you want to merge into the original file.

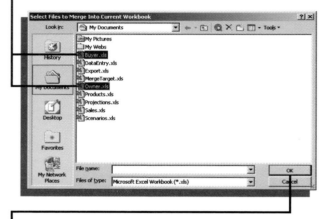

(3) Click OK. Changes from the merged workbooks appear as tracked changes.

> **!** TIP: If two workbooks will not merge, you can copy and paste data from one workbook to another.

④ On the Tools menu, point to Track Changes and choose Accept Or Reject Changes.

TIP: If there are conflicting changes for a cell, you will be able to select the value you want from a list displayed in the Accept or Reject Changes dialog box.

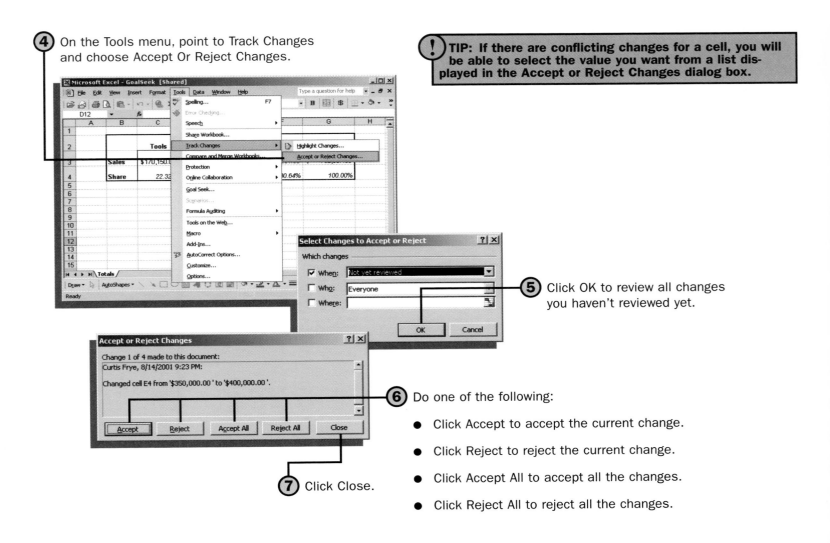

⑤ Click OK to review all changes you haven't reviewed yet.

⑥ Do one of the following:

- Click Accept to accept the current change.

- Click Reject to reject the current change.

- Click Accept All to accept all the changes.

- Click Reject All to reject all the changes.

⑦ Click Close.

Analyzing Alternative Data Scenarios

Every time you save data in an Excel worksheet, you create a record reflecting the characteristics of an event or an object. The data might represent an hour of sales on a particular day, the price of an item you just began offering for sale, or the percentage of total sales accounted for by a category of products. Once the data is in place, you can create formulas to find totals or averages or filter your worksheet to limit the data you see. You can also explore the impact that changes in your data would have on your formulas by creating a *scenario*, or alternative data set. When you create a scenario, you define alternative values for up to 32 cells in a worksheet. Displaying the scenario changes the data in your worksheet and causes Excel to recalculate formulas to reflect the new values.

Create a Scenario

1 Choose Scenarios from the Tools menu.

2 Click Add.

3 Type a name for the scenario.

4 Click the Collapse Dialog button.

5 Select the cells for which you want to define alternative values.

6 Click the Expand Dialog button.

7 Click OK.

CAUTION: It is not possible to create a scenario in a shared workbook.

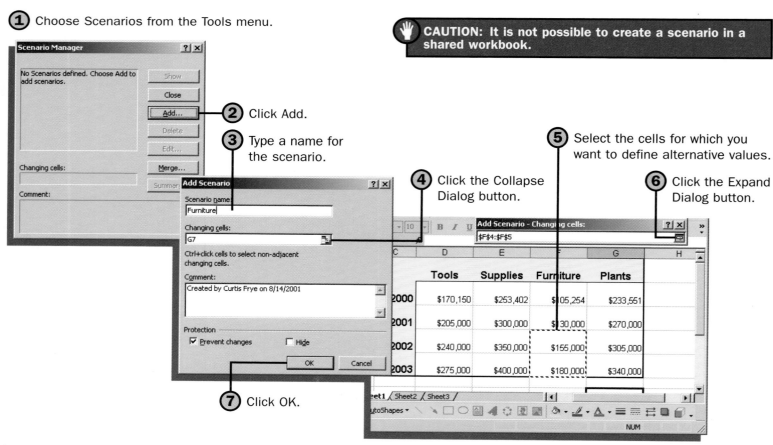

(8) Type values for each of the cells.

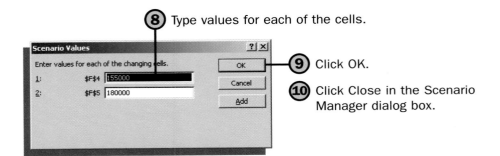

(9) Click OK.

(10) Click Close in the Scenario Manager dialog box.

View a Scenario

(1) Choose Scenarios from the Tools menu.

(2) Click the scenario you want to view.

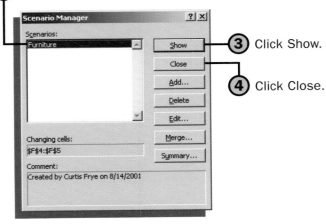

(3) Click Show.

(4) Click Close.

Delete a Scenario

(1) Choose Scenarios from the Tools menu.

(2) Click the scenario you want to delete.

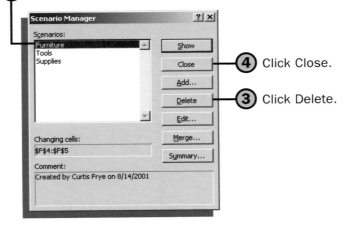

(4) Click Close.

(3) Click Delete.

 CAUTION: Once you delete a scenario, you cannot undo the action.

Modify a Scenario

1. Choose Scenarios from the Tools menu.

2. Click the scenario you want to edit.

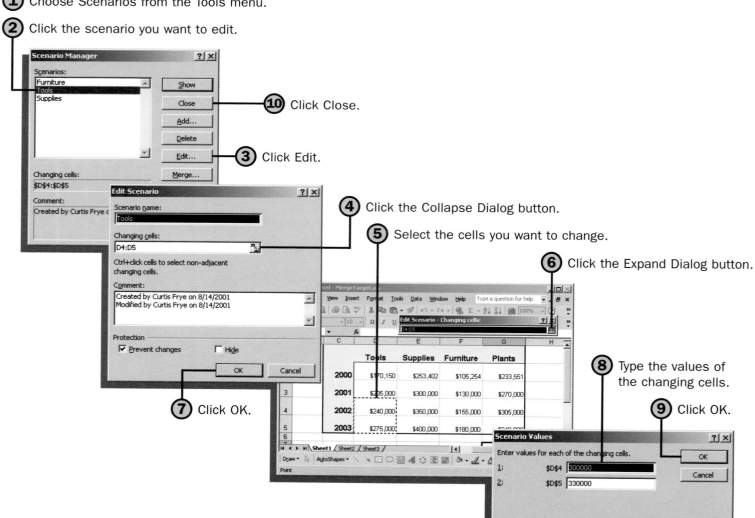

10. Click Close.

3. Click Edit.

4. Click the Collapse Dialog button.

5. Select the cells you want to change.

6. Click the Expand Dialog button.

7. Click OK.

8. Type the values of the changing cells.

9. Click OK.

Combining Scenarios into One Worksheet

You might very well create a scenario in one worksheet that can be used in another worksheet. For example, you can create a scenario projecting sales for a product category for the next three years and copy that scenario from the worksheet where you create it to other worksheets. In Excel, copying a scenario from one worksheet to another is called *merging*.

Merge Scenarios

1 Choose Scenarios from the Tools menu.

2 Click Merge.

SEE ALSO: For more information about projecting future values based on past performance, see "Performing 'What If' Analysis" on page 156.

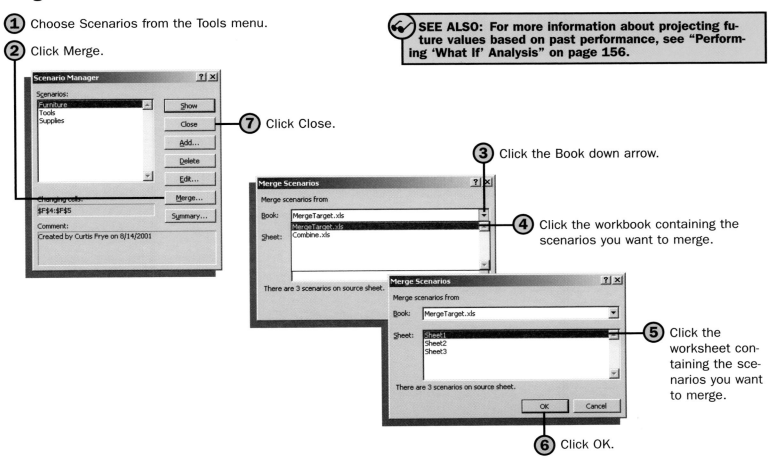

7 Click Close.

3 Click the Book down arrow.

4 Click the workbook containing the scenarios you want to merge.

5 Click the worksheet containing the scenarios you want to merge.

6 Click OK.

13

Web Linking and Publishing

✳ NEW FEATURE

One of the hallmarks of Microsoft Excel is that you can save your workbooks and worksheets as files that can be accessed and interacted with over the World Wide Web. Previous versions of Excel allowed you to bring data from the Web into your workbooks by creating queries, and Excel 2002 extends those capabilities in several ways, making the older tasks easier to perform.

Another new feature of Excel 2002 is its ability to create Extensible Markup Language (XML) spreadsheet files. XML is a content markup language, meaning that an XML file has information about the data contained within it, not just instructions for how the data should be displayed. Saving Excel workbooks as XML files means your Excel data will be readable by a wide range of programs, not only those programs listed in the Save As dialog box's Save As Type drop-down list. One application of XML is smart tags, a technology that recognizes certain types of information, such as stock symbols, and looks up related information on the Web.

In this section, you will learn how to:

● Save worksheets to the Web.

● Modify Excel data over the Web.

● Dynamically bring Web data into Excel.

● Use XML to exchange data over the Web.

● Use smart tags to get information from the Web.

Saving Worksheets to the Web

One of the easiest ways to communicate data to traveling colleagues is to make that data available on a Web page. Writing the data to a Web page means you don't have to send the entire workbook to the travelers. In fact, your colleagues don't even need Excel on their computers! Saving workbooks as Web pages is also a great way to make data available over a corporate network (an *intranet*). As long as your company's network supports Web connections, you can make your data available to any authorized user. You can also add a worksheet to an existing Web page instead of creating it as a separate file.

Save a Workbook to the Web

1 Choose Save As Web Page from the File menu.

2 Navigate to the folder where you want to save your workbook.

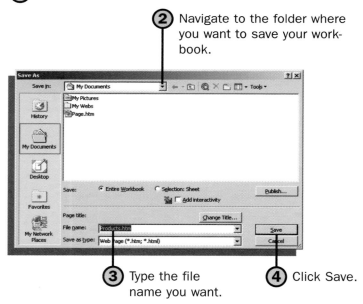

3 Type the file name you want.

4 Click Save.

Add a Worksheet to an Existing Web Page

1 Click Save As Web Page from the File menu.

2 Click the Selection: Sheet option.

3 Select the file to which you want to add the worksheet.

4 Click Save.

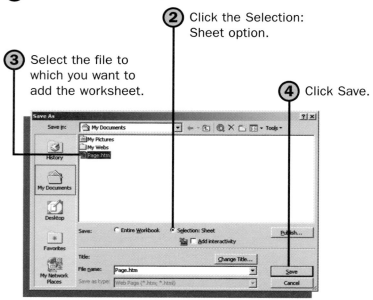

5 In the message box that appears, click Add To File.

! TIP: Excel saves each worksheet as a separate file. You can move from worksheet to worksheet using the representation of the sheet tabs at the bottom left of each page.

! TIP: You can change the text that appears on the title bar of the Excel document's Web page by clicking the Change Title button in the Save As Web Page dialog box.

Using Excel to Change Web Page Data

One advantage of working with Excel over the Web is that you and your colleagues can interact with Excel worksheets you have published on the Web. By adding interactivity to your worksheet, you and your colleagues can edit cell values, sort or filter the values in the worksheet, or create formulas. You can also use interactivity to update an Excel-based Web page whenever there is a change in the workbook on which the file is based.

Allow Users to Modify an Excel Document over the Web

1 Choose Save As Web Page from the File menu.

2 Navigate to the folder where you want to save your worksheet.

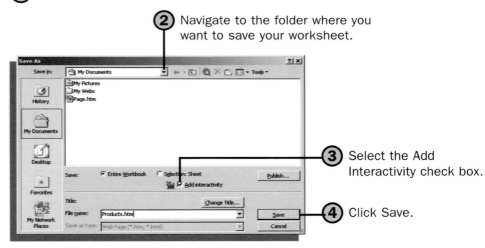

3 Select the Add Interactivity check box.

4 Click Save.

 **SEE ALSO:** For information about bringing Web data into Excel, see "Retrieving Web Data from Excel" on page 196.

TIP: It's a good idea to always keep a backup copy of any document that you allow other users to modify over the Web. With the backup in place, you can rest assured—no matter what mistakes you or a colleague makes, you will have the original copy of the data to work from.

Modify an Excel Document over the Web

① In Internet Explorer, choose Open from the File menu.

> **CAUTION: In order to modify an Excel file over the Web, you must have saved the file with interactivity turned on.**

② Click Browse.

③ Navigate to the folder with the file you want to open.

> **TIP: To change cell formatting while editing a worksheet over the Web, click the Commands And Options button to display the Commands And Options dialog box, and then make the changes you want.**

④ Double-click the file.

⑦ Click the Close box to save your work, and close Internet Explorer.

⑤ Click OK.

⑥ Modify the file in the Excel window that appears.

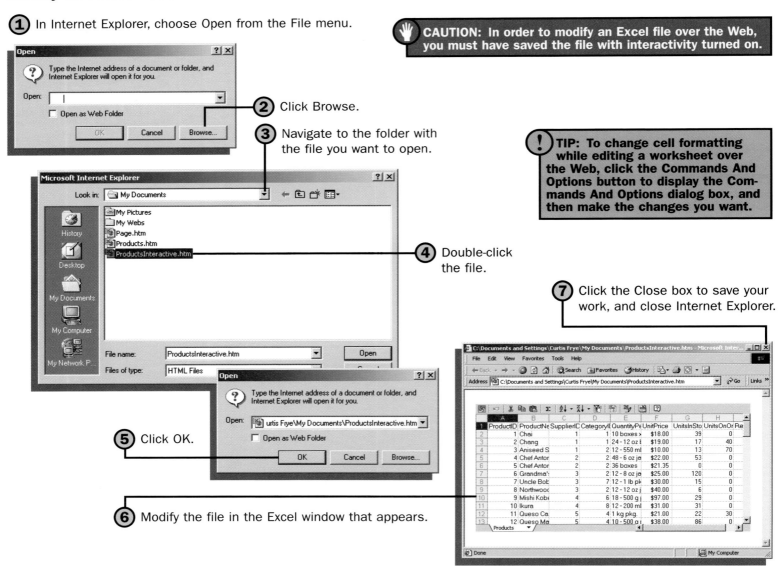

Dynamically Update Worksheets Published to the Web

① Click Save As Web Page from the File menu.

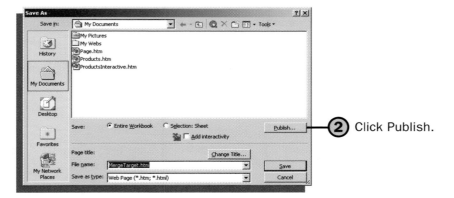

② Click Publish.

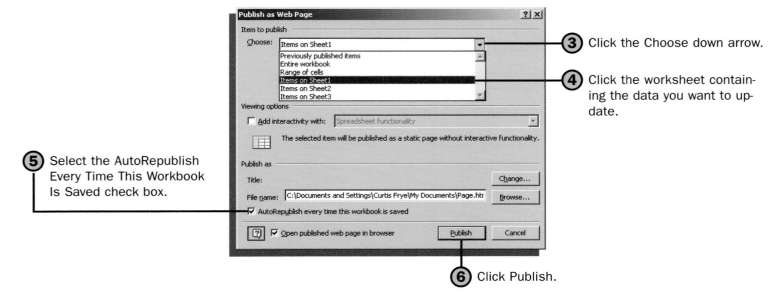

③ Click the Choose down arrow.

④ Click the worksheet containing the data you want to update.

⑤ Select the AutoRepublish Every Time This Workbook Is Saved check box.

⑥ Click Publish.

Retrieving Web Data from Excel

The World Wide Web is a great source of information. From stock quotes to product descriptions, many companies publish useful information on their Web sites. The most common structure used to present financial information is the table, which, like a spreadsheet, organizes the data into rows and columns. Excel makes creating a Web query easy by letting you copy data directly from a Web page into Excel and by creating a query to retrieve data from the table you copied.

Retrieve Data from a Web Page

(1) On the Data menu, point to Import External Data and choose New Web Query.

(2) Type the address of the Web page you want.

(3) Click Go.

(4) Click the yellow boxes with black arrows to specify which tables you want to import.

(5) Click Import.

(6) Click OK.

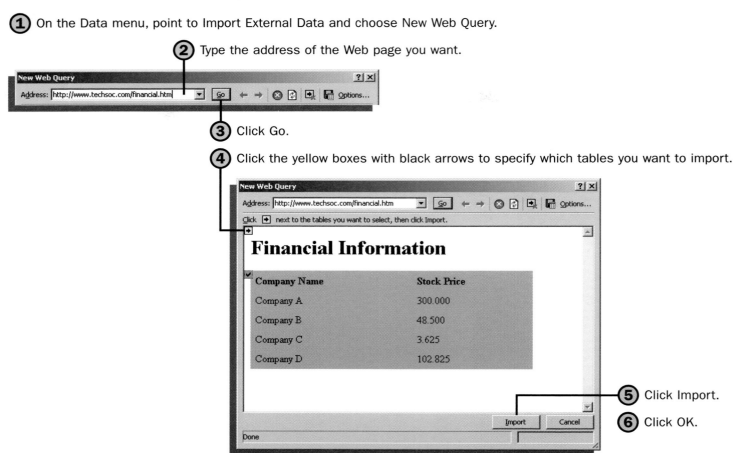

Copy Data from the Web to Excel

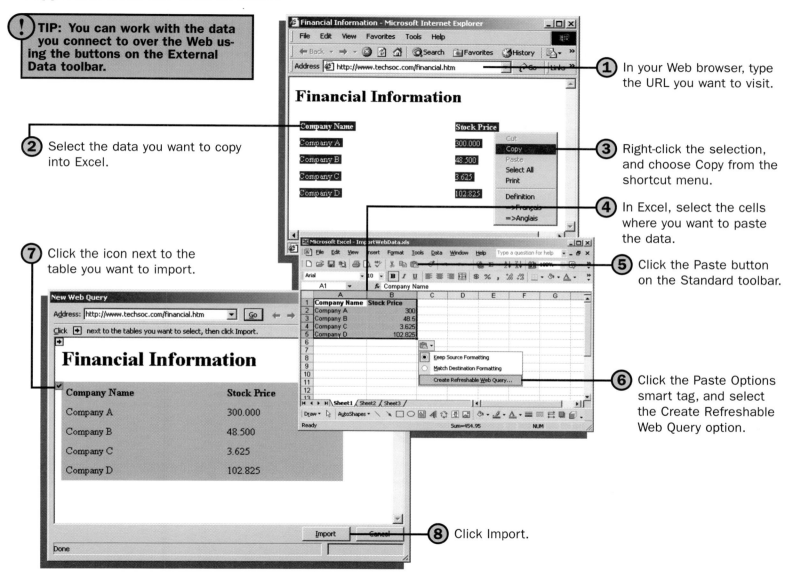

(1) In your Web browser, type the URL you want to visit.

(2) Select the data you want to copy into Excel.

(3) Right-click the selection, and choose Copy from the shortcut menu.

(4) In Excel, select the cells where you want to paste the data.

(5) Click the Paste button on the Standard toolbar.

(6) Click the Paste Options smart tag, and select the Create Refreshable Web Query option.

(7) Click the icon next to the table you want to import.

(8) Click Import.

Introducing XML

Hypertext Markup Language (HTML) is great for describing how a Web page should be displayed in a browser, but the language isn't designed to communicate anything about the contents of a document. For example, telling Internet Explorer to display a worksheet as an HTML table tells you nothing about the data shown on a Web page. When you save your worksheet data as an XML document, however, Excel annotates the data with tags describing which program generated the data, the name of the worksheet, and the data in each cell. With that information, Excel—or another spreadsheet program that understands XML data—can import your worksheet data and retain your original meaning.

While a full discussion of XML is beyond the scope of this book, the following bit of XML code shows how to identify an Excel workbook in XML.

```
<?xml version="1.0"?>
<Workbook xmlns="urn:schemas-microsoft-com:office:spreadsheet" xmlns:o="urn:schemas-microsoft-
com:office:office" xmlns:x="urn:schemas-microsoft-com:office:excel" xmlns:ss="urn:schemas-microsoft-
com:office:spreadsheet" xmlns:html="http://www.w3.org/TR/REC-html40">
```

Also, XML can identify rows and cells within the spreadsheet, as in the following example.

```
<Row>
<Cell><Data ss:Type="String">January</Data></Cell>
<Cell><Data ss:Type="Number">1</Data></Cell>
<Cell><Data ss:Type="String">Tue</Data></Cell>
<Cell><Data ss:Type="Number">2</Data></Cell>
<Cell><Data ss:Type="Number">9</Data></Cell>
<Cell><Data ss:Type="Number">161</Data></Cell>
</Row>
```

This XML code fragment represents the highlighted worksheet row in the following graphic.

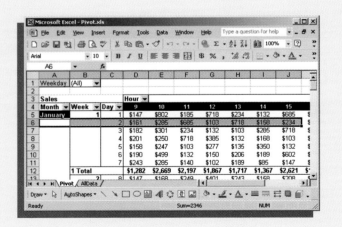

Interacting over the Web with XML

The goal of XML is to be a universal language, allowing data to move freely from one application to another. This means that saving an Excel worksheet as an XML document would allow any other spreadsheet program that supports XML to read the XML file, separate out the cell names and data, and use the annotations to recreate the worksheet. The reverse is also true: You can take a worksheet saved as an XML file and, regardless of the program used to create the file, import it into Excel.

Save a Workbook as an XML Document

(1) Click Save As Web Page from the File menu.

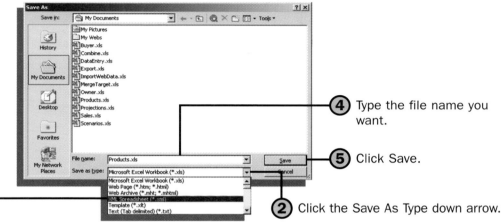

(3) Click XML Spreadsheet (*.xml).

(4) Type the file name you want.

(5) Click Save.

(2) Click the Save As Type down arrow.

Import an XML Document

(1) Click the Open button on the Standard toolbar.

(2) Navigate to the folder containing the XML document you want.

(3) Double-click the XML document you want.

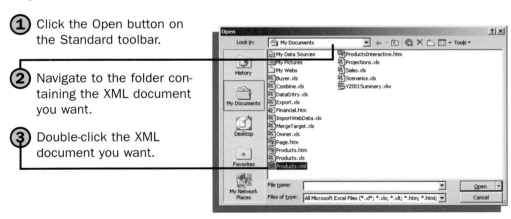

! TIP: If you don't see any XML documents listed in the Open dialog box, click the Files Of Type down arrow and click All Microsoft Excel Files.

Using Smart Tags to Dynamically Link Web Data to Excel ⊕ NEW FEATURE

Another new capability in Excel 2002 is the ability to capture information from the Web related to the contents of a worksheet cell. This new technology is called smart tags. The clearest example of how smart tags work is with stock symbols, the abbreviations of company names on stock market tickers. You can turn on smart tags, have Excel look for known stock symbols (such as Microsoft's stock symbol, *MSFT*), and then connect to a Web site with information related to that symbol.

Add Smart Tags to a Worksheet

1 Choose AutoCorrect Options from the Tools menu.

2 Click the Smart Tags tab.

3 Select the Label Data With Smart Tags check box.

4 Select the smart tags you want to use.

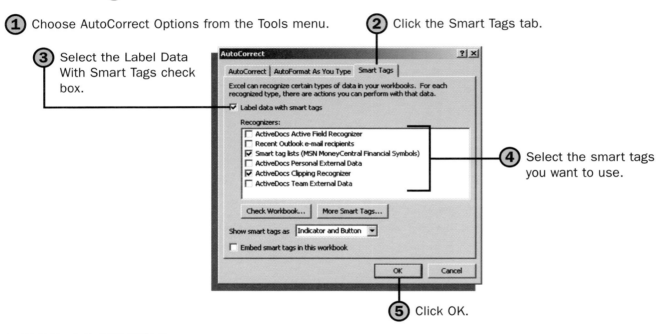

5 Click OK.

> **! TIP:** To turn off smart tags, clear the Label Data With Smart Tags check box.

> **! TIP:** More smart tags are available than the ones that come with Excel 2002. To find more smart tags, choose AutoCorrect Options from the Tools menu and click the Smart Tags tab. Click More Smart Tags, and your browser will open with Microsoft's Office Update page. If necessary, click the country you are located in and browse the site for the smart tags you want.

Change Smart Tag Options

1 Choose AutoCorrect Options from the Tools menu.

2 Click the Smart Tags tab.

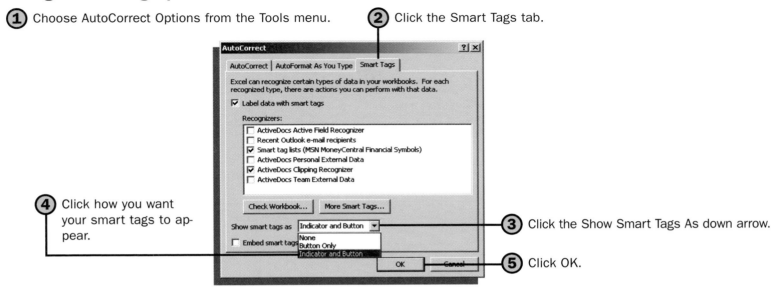

4 Click how you want your smart tags to appear.

3 Click the Show Smart Tags As down arrow.

5 Click OK.

Activate a Smart Tag

1 Hover the mouse pointer over a cell with a smart tag indicator (a purple flag at the bottom right corner of the cell).

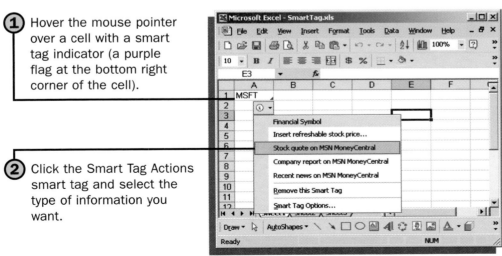

2 Click the Smart Tag Actions smart tag and select the type of information you want.

TRY THIS: Make sure your computer is connected to the Internet, and then create a blank workbook. Type MSFT in cell A1. If a smart tag indicator doesn't appear at the bottom right corner of cell A1, choose AutoCorrect Options from the Tools menu, click the Smart Tags tab, select the Label Data With Smart Tags check box, and click OK. After the indicator appears, hover the mouse pointer over cell A1, click the Smart Tag Actions indicator button, and click Stock Quote On MSN MoneyCentral. A Web page with a current stock quote for Microsoft appears in Internet Explorer.

Modifying Web Queries

When you create a Web query, you make it possible to use data from tables on your company's intranet or the Internet in your worksheets. Financial data can change, though, so you should use the buttons on the External Data toolbar to change how Excel deals with data drawn from other sources. One way you can ensure the external data is current is to have Excel refresh the data regularly.

Schedule Web Query Data Refreshes

(1) Right-click any toolbar, and choose External Data.

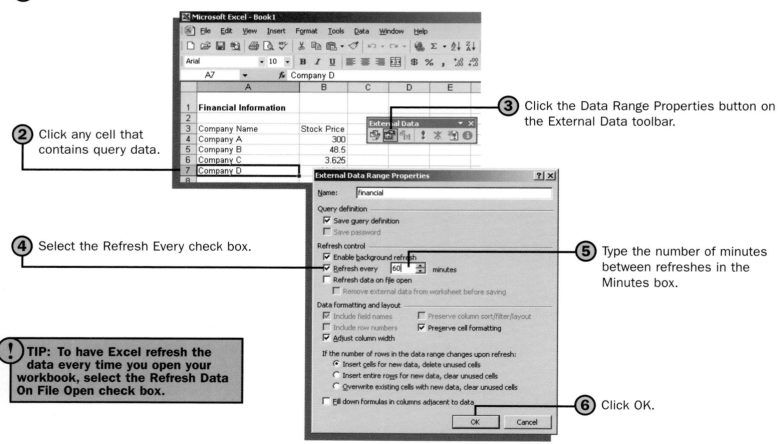

(2) Click any cell that contains query data.

(3) Click the Data Range Properties button on the External Data toolbar.

(4) Select the Refresh Every check box.

(5) Type the number of minutes between refreshes in the Minutes box.

(!) TIP: To have Excel refresh the data every time you open your workbook, select the Refresh Data On File Open check box.

(6) Click OK.

Using Excel with Other Progams

Microsoft Excel is a powerful program, but it doesn't try to do everything. Other programs in the Microsoft Office XP suite have complementary strengths: Microsoft Access is ideal for working with large data collections, Microsoft PowerPoint lets you create attractive presentations to print or project onto a screen, and Microsoft Word is great for creating text documents. You can include files created in other programs in your Excel workbooks or create links to them.

Excel is versatile when you're interacting with other companies or individuals who aren't using Excel. You can export your Excel data to many other file formats or import data from other programs. If you like, you can have Excel convert the text in your cells to speech, allowing you to examine the contents of a cell even if you can't see the screen. In this chapter, you'll learn how to:

● Convert text to speech.

● Link to and embed objects in Excel workbooks.

● Transfer data between Excel and Access, PowerPoint, or Word.

● Send an Excel worksheet as an e-mail message.

● Save Excel for Windows data as an Excel for the Macintosh file.

Turning Text into Speech

One of the ways Excel helps you and your colleagues interact with your worksheet data is by reading the contents of a cell aloud. How Excel reads the contents of your cell depends on how you're currently viewing the cell. If you're examining a formula, Excel reads the formula; if you're looking at the result of a calculation or a number entered into a cell, Excel reads the number.

> **! TIP:** You can find out more about converting text to speech by typing text to speech into the Ask A Question box, pressing Enter, and clicking About Speech Playback from the list of topics that appears.

Convert Text into Speech

① Right-click the menu bar, and choose Text To Speech from the shortcut menu.

② Select the cell you want to convert.

③ Click the Speak Cells button.

④ Click the Stop Speaking button to stop converting text to speech.

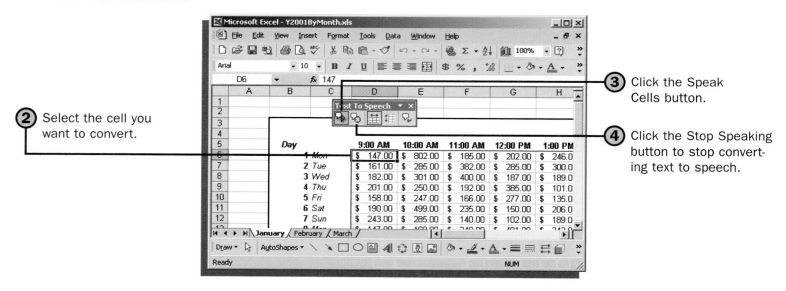

> **! TIP:** Click the Speak On Enter button on the Text To Speech toolbar to have each cell read to you after you press Enter.

> **! TIP:** Excel begins reading data in the active cell and continues by row. To have Excel read by column, click the By Columns button on the Text To Speech toolbar.

Introducing Linking and Embedding

Excel works wonderfully as a stand-alone program, but it really shines when you use it in combination with other programs. One way to use Excel in conjunction with other programs is to include in your worksheets files created in other programs, such as graphics, Word documents, or PowerPoint presentations. You can add these objects to your workbooks through *linking* and *embedding*.

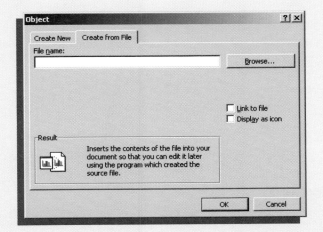

There are several important points to keep in mind when you're deciding whether to link to an object or to embed it in a worksheet. As the name implies, embedding an object in a worksheet stores a copy of the object within the workbook. For example, if you wanted to add a company logo to an invoice generated from table data, you can identify the graphic and indicate you want to embed it in the file. The advantage of embedding an object in an Excel file is that you won't have to worry about the graphic, chart, or image not being available because the person who created the workbook didn't include the graphic. If you create workbooks with embedded files, you can open your workbook anywhere and be certain your graphics will be available.

A disadvantage of embedding objects in workbooks is that the embedded files can be large and can dramatically increase the size of your workbooks. While a single, low-resolution logo meant to be viewed on a computer monitor probably won't have much of an impact on your file size, the same image rendered at a resolution suitable for printing might double the size of the workbook. If you embed more than one image, or more than one copy of the same image, you might make your file unworkably large.

When you want to include more than one image or external file in an Excel workbook, you should consider creating a link to the files. For example, rather than embed many copies of a high-resolution logo in your worksheets, you can save the file on your hard disk and use the linking and embedding dialog box to identify the file's location on your computer. Excel uses the reference to find the file and display it as part of a workbook. The workbook would be no larger than it was originally, and you wouldn't need to have multiple copies of the same file if you link to it more than once. The advantage of linking is that you save disk space, but the disadvantage is that moving the workbook from computer to computer can be difficult unless you have the extra files when you travel or distribute the workbook to colleagues.

In general, embedding an object in an Excel workbook works best if you only use the object once in the workbook and you have room to store the workbook, with the included objects, when you share the workbook. Otherwise, such as when you use the same file multiple times in the same workbook, link to the file instead.

Linking and Embedding Other Files

Excel workbooks can hold a lot of data, and you can make your data even more meaningful when you include files created with other programs. For example, you might have created a Word document with important background information or a PowerPoint presentation that puts your data into context for your colleagues. You can include those files in your worksheets by linking or embedding the files as *objects*.

Link to a File

1 Choose Object from the Insert menu.

2 Click the Create From File tab.

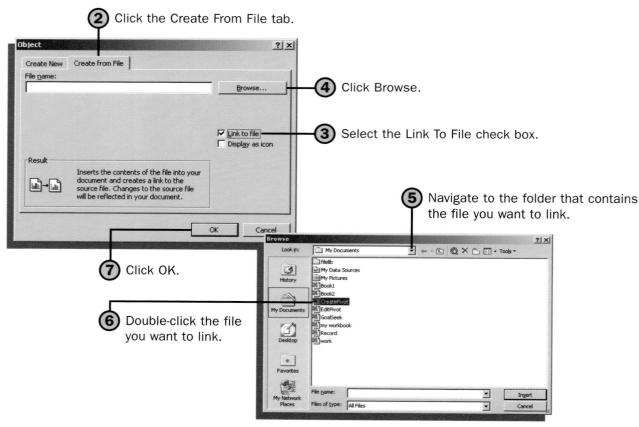

4 Click Browse.

3 Select the Link To File check box.

5 Navigate to the folder that contains the file you want to link.

7 Click OK.

6 Double-click the file you want to link.

Embed a File in a Worksheet

1 Choose Object from the Insert menu.

2 Click the Create From File tab.

3 Click Browse.

4 Navigate to the folder that contains the file you want to embed.

6 Click OK.

5 Double-click the file.

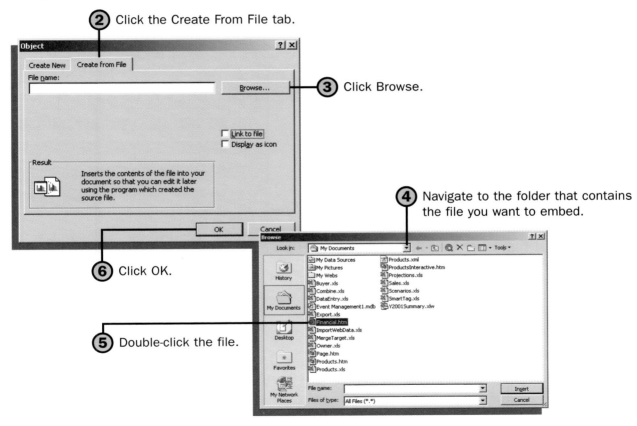

Exchanging Table Data Between Excel and Word

Just as you can create workbooks to store and manipulate financial and other data in Excel, you can use Word to create reports and other text documents to interpret and provide valuable context for your worksheet data. Word documents can also present data in tables, which are arranged in rows and columns like a worksheet. For example, if you receive a report from a traveling colleague in which she created a table listing the prices of popular products at a competitor's store, you can copy the data from the Word document to an Excel worksheet for direct comparison. You can also go in the opposite direction, copying Excel data to a table in Word.

Bring Word Data into Excel

② Click the Copy button on the Standard toolbar.

① In Word, select the table you want to import.

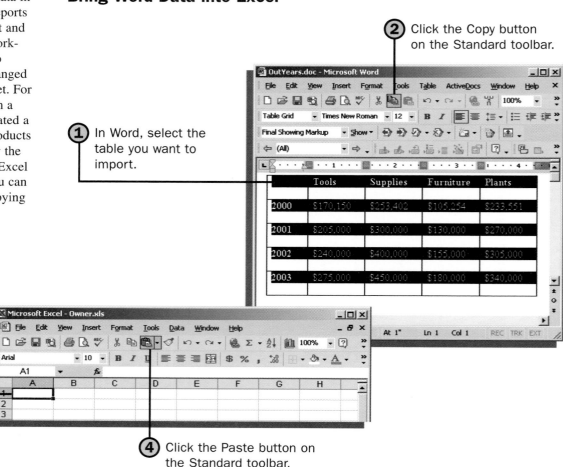

③ In Excel, click the cell where you want to import the data.

④ Click the Paste button on the Standard toolbar.

Copy Excel Data to Word

1 In Excel, select the cells you want to copy.

2 Click the Copy button.

! TIP: To establish a link to the source worksheet, which will update the table in Word if the contents of the source worksheet change, click Match Destination Table Style And Link To Excel.

3 In Word, click the Paste button.

4 Click the Paste Options smart tag and select the Match Destination Table Style option.

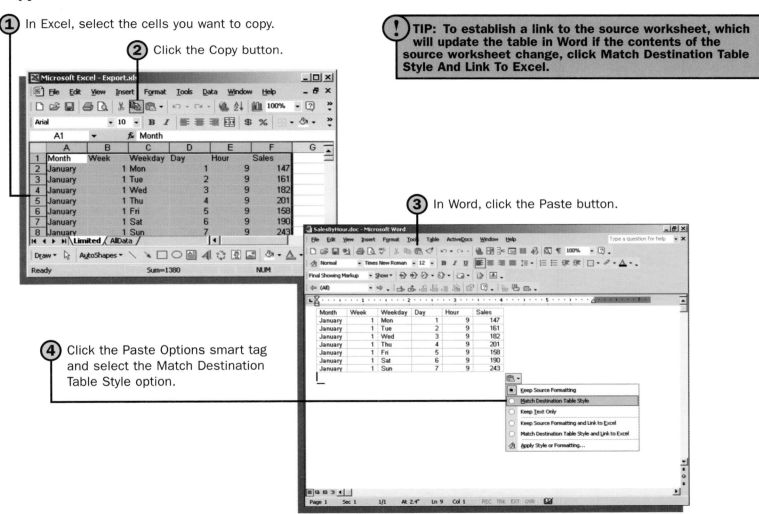

Copying Excel Charts and Data into PowerPoint

It's possible to present Excel data to your colleagues using Excel exclusively, but if you're developing a formal presentation, you might want to use PowerPoint. Because presentations often contain graphic representations of numerical data, it's easy to include your Excel data in a PowerPoint presentation.

Move Excel Data to PowerPoint

1 In PowerPoint, choose Chart from the Insert menu.

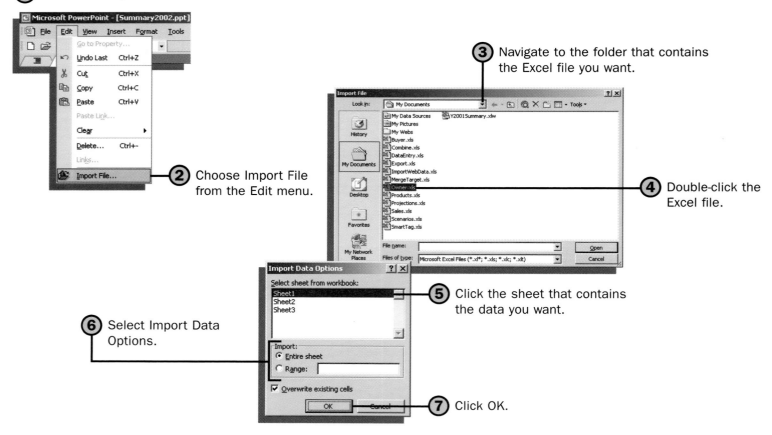

2 Choose Import File from the Edit menu.

3 Navigate to the folder that contains the Excel file you want.

4 Double-click the Excel file.

5 Click the sheet that contains the data you want.

6 Select Import Data Options.

7 Click OK.

Exchanging Data Between Access and Excel

No other Office XP programs have as much in common as Access and Excel, but each program has its unique strengths. Where Excel offers a wide range of data analysis and presentation tools you can use to summarize your data, Access is designed to let you store, manipulate, and ask questions of large data collections. You can also use Access queries to locate and summarize table data. While it is possible to look up data in an Excel worksheet, it's much easier to do in Access.

Bring Access Table Data into an Excel Worksheet

(1) In Access, on the Data menu, point to Import External Data and choose Import Data.

(2) Navigate to the folder that contains the database with the data you want to import.

TIP: You can have the imported data appear on a new worksheet by selecting the New Worksheet option in the Import Data dialog box.

(3) Double-click the database.

(4) Click the table or query with the data you want to import.

(5) Click OK.

(6) Click the Collapse Dialog button.

(7) In Excel, click the cell where you want the first cell in the group to appear.

(8) Click the Expand Dialog button.

(9) Click OK.

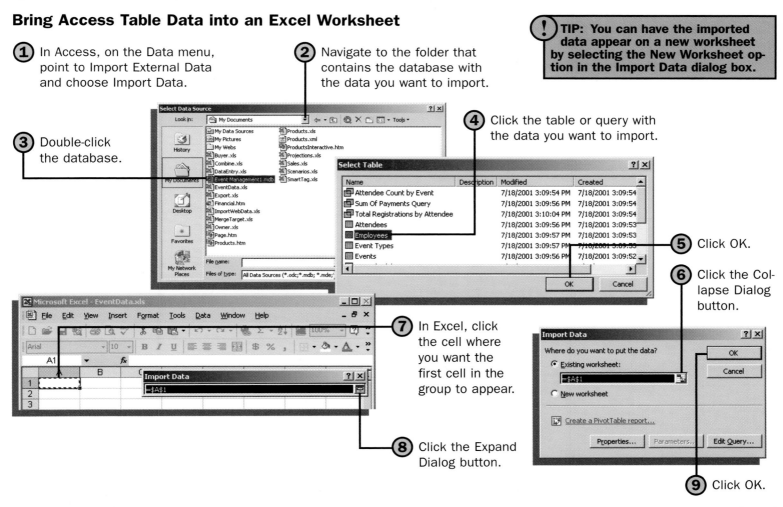

Send Excel Data to Access

(1) In Access, on the File menu, point to Get External Data, and choose Import.

(2) Click the Files Of Type down arrow.

(3) Click Microsoft Excel (*.xls).

(4) Navigate to the folder that contains the Excel file you want.

(5) Double-click the Excel file you want.

(6) Select the sheet or named range you want, and click Next.

(7) Select or clear the First Row Contains Column Headings check box, and click Next.

(8) Select whether you want to import the data into a new table or a currently existing table, and click Finish.

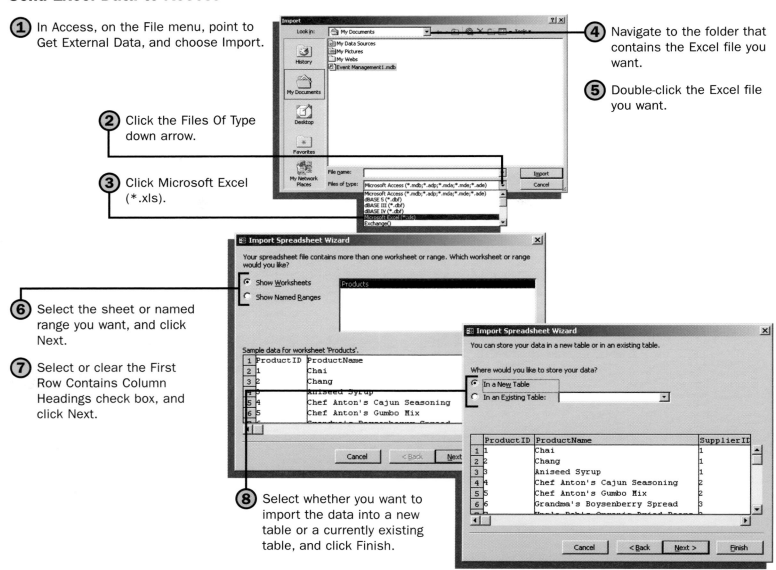

Sending E-Mail Directly from Excel

Sending an Excel worksheet by e-mail is easy when you use Microsoft Outlook or Microsoft Outlook Express as your mail program. All it takes is a single menu choice in Excel to create an e-mail message you can address and send quickly.

Share Workbooks Using E-Mail

! **TIP: Instead of sending your workbook as the body of an e-mail message, you can send it as an attachment. On the file menu, point to Send To, choose Mail Recipient (As Attachment), and then click Send.**

1 In Excel, click the E-Mail button on the Standard toolbar.

2 Type the recipient's e-mail address.

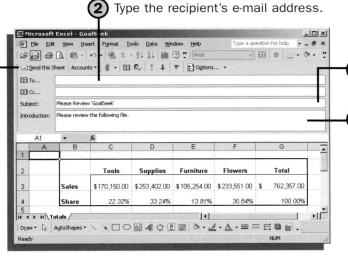

3 Type the subject of your e-mail.

4 Type the introduction message you want included with the e-mail.

5 Click Send This Sheet.

✋ **CAUTION: Some mail systems don't allow users to send or receive attached files by e-mail, or they limit the size of the files that can be sent or received. Check with your intended recipient to be sure the file you send will go through.**

Converting Files To and From Excel

When you collaborate with folks from outside your company, you might need to exchange worksheet data with colleagues who use programs other than Excel. Excel has built-in converters for other popular spreadsheet programs so that you can save your Excel data in the format of the program your colleague is using. You can even save your Excel for Windows files in Macintosh format!

Save Excel Files to Other Formats

(1) Choose Save As from the File menu.

(3) Navigate to the folder where you want to save your file.

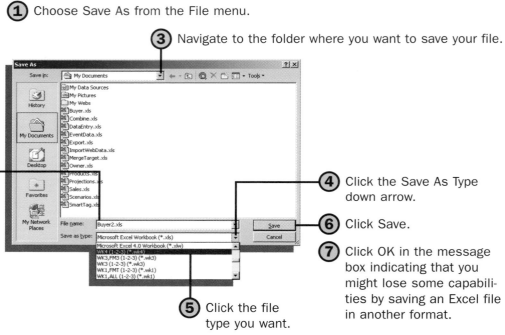

(2) Type the file name you want.

(4) Click the Save As Type down arrow.

(6) Click Save.

(5) Click the file type you want.

(7) Click OK in the message box indicating that you might lose some capabilities by saving an Excel file in another format.

 SEE ALSO: For more information about transferring files between Excel and other programs using text files, see "Importing A Text File" on page 216.

Open Other File Formats

(1) Click the Open button on the Standard toolbar.

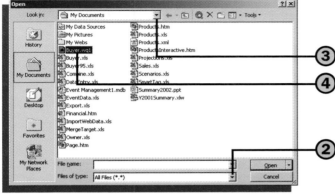

(3) Navigate to the folder that contains the file you want.

(4) Double-click the file you want.

> **(!) TIP:** When you install Excel, some but not all of the available file converters are installed. If you can't find the file type you want, you can install more converters using your Microsoft Excel 2002 CD-ROM.

(2) Click the Files Of Type down arrow, and click the file type you want to open.

Save an Excel Spreadsheet as a Macintosh File

(1) Choose Save As from the File menu.

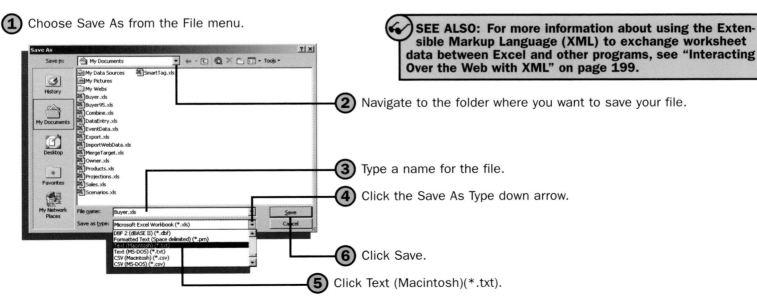

> **(✓) SEE ALSO:** For more information about using the Extensible Markup Language (XML) to exchange worksheet data between Excel and other programs, see "Interacting Over the Web with XML" on page 199.

(2) Navigate to the folder where you want to save your file.

(3) Type a name for the file.

(4) Click the Save As Type down arrow.

(6) Click Save.

(5) Click Text (Macintosh)(*.txt).

Importing a Text File

Excel can read data from quite a few other spreadsheet and database programs, but you may have a colleague who uses a spreadsheet or database program that creates files you can't read with Excel. If that's the case, you can ask your colleague to save the file as a text file, using a comma, tab, or other character (called a *delimiter*) to mark the end of each cell's data. Even if you're unable to transfer data any other way, you can always read spreadsheet data if it's presented to you in a text file. Any formatting or formulas will be lost, but the data will be there for you to analyze.

Bring Text Data into Excel

(1) Point to Import External Data on the Data menu, and choose Import Data.

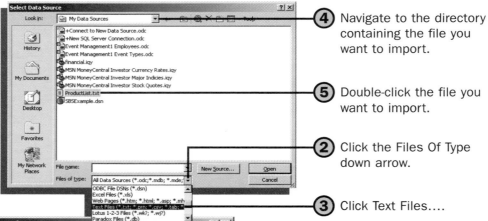

(4) Navigate to the directory containing the file you want to import.

(5) Double-click the file you want to import.

(2) Click the Files Of Type down arrow.

(3) Click Text Files....

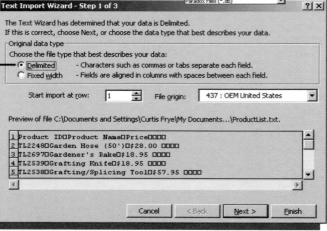

(6) Verify that Excel has correctly determined how the data in the text file is delimited, and click Next.

> **!** **TIP: Some databases create files in which each column takes up a set number of characters. If that's the case, the Fixed Width option will be selected.**

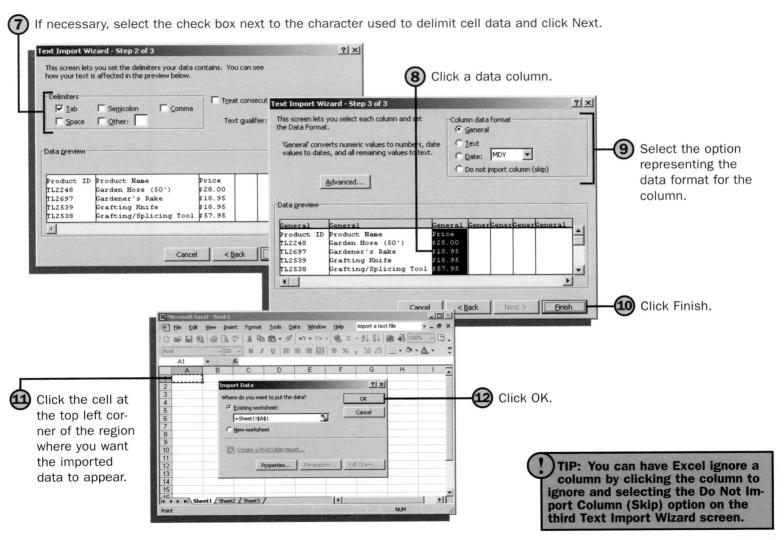

CAUTION: Using a comma as a delimiter can be a problem if the numbers in the text file use commas as thousands separators. If the data you're trying to import has commas in the numbers, ask your colleague to delimit cell data with a Tab character.

7 If necessary, select the check box next to the character used to delimit cell data and click Next.

8 Click a data column.

9 Select the option representing the data format for the column.

10 Click Finish.

11 Click the cell at the top left corner of the region where you want the imported data to appear.

12 Click OK.

TIP: You can have Excel ignore a column by clicking the column to ignore and selecting the Do Not Import Column (Skip) option on the third Text Import Wizard screen.

Introducing Advanced Excel Topics

The goal of *Microsoft Excel Version 2002 Plain & Simple* is to teach you everything you need to know to use Excel effectively, but there is a lot more to the program than can be covered in this book. This section introduces several of the more advanced features you can use to present your data and make Excel easier to use.

You can present your data effectively and make Excel easier to use by creating a PivotTable Report, which lets you dynamically reorganize your data. With PivotTables, you can emphasize different aspects of your data without having to create a separate worksheet for each arrangement, saving you both time and effort. Goal Seek, another of Excel's advanced features, lets you determine what input would be required for a formula to have a desired result. And finally, to make repetitive tasks easier to perform, you can record macros, which you can replay at your convenience.

In this section, you will learn how to:

● Create and modify PivotTables.

● Format PivotTables.

● Use Goal Seek to analyze your Excel data.

● Create and run macros.

Surveying PivotTables

There is a tool in Excel that you can use to reorganize and redisplay your data dynamically. You can create a *PivotTable*, or dynamic worksheet, that lets you reorganize and filter your data at any time. For instance, you can create a PivotTable in which the columns represent the month, week, and day and the rows represent hours in a day, as shown in the following graphic.

In this worksheet, every row represents a cell in the body of the finished PivotTable. The following graphic shows the first few lines of the list used to create this sample PivotTable.

Notice that every line of the list holds the month, week, weekday, hour, and sales for every hour in the month. Excel needs this data when it creates the PivotTable so that it can maintain relationships among the data. If you want to filter your PivotTable so that it shows all sales from 5:00 P.M. to 8:00 P.M. on every Thursday in January, Excel must be able to identify January 11 as a Thursday and then find the entries in the list representing sales for the hours beginning at 5:00 P.M., 6:00 P.M., and 7:00 P.M.

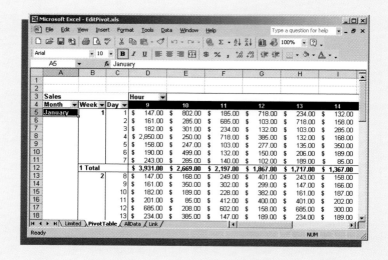

Formatting PivotTables

Once you've created a PivotTable, you can change the formatting of its cells, as on any other Excel worksheet. For example, if your PivotTable contains sales data, you can apply the Currency style to those cells by selecting them and clicking the Currency Style button on the Formatting toolbar. You can also distinguish cells with headings, subtotals, and totals by formatting the contents of those cells in bold, italic, or a larger type size.

Although you can apply your own formats to a PivotTable, Excel comes with a set of predefined formats, called AutoFormats, which you can apply to your PivotTable. To view the AutoFormats available in Excel and apply one to your PivotTable, click any cell in the PivotTable. Then, on the PivotTable toolbar, click the Format Report button to display the AutoFormat dialog box.

Preparing Worksheet Data for a PivotTable

Reordering worksheet data as a list might look daunting, but by using the FillSeries, AutoFill, and cut-and-paste techniques described in Section 2, "Getting Started with Excel 2002," it took only 15 minutes to reorder the contents of the three worksheets in Y2001ByMonth.xls into the data list used to create the PivotTable displayed here.

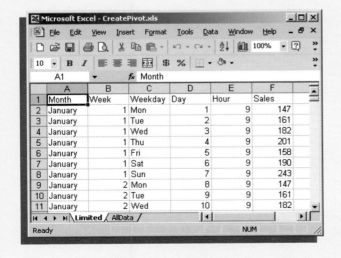

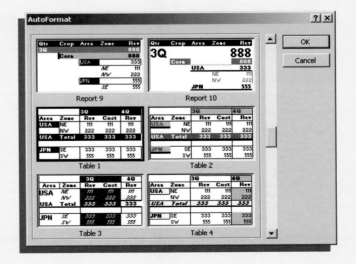

Building PivotTables

Excel worksheets let you gather and present important data, but the standard worksheets show only a list of values. Although you can organize your data to correspond to row and column values, you're limited to the original arrangement. PivotTables, by contrast, let you rearrange your data dynamically. If your PivotTable lists sales by category and you'd rather see the data organized by country, you can change the layout of your PivotTable quickly. Once you create your first PivotTable, you'll understand what powerful tools they are!

Make a PivotTable Using the PivotTable Wizard

(1) Choose PivotTable And PivotChart Report from the Data menu, and click Next.

(2) Select the cells you want to use in your PivotTable, and click Next.

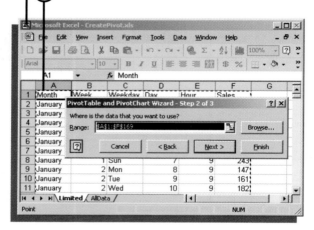

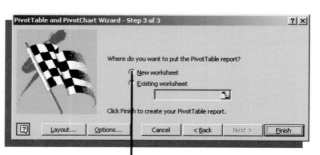

(4) Drag the fields with data you want to display in rows to the drop area labeled Drop Row Fields Here.

(5) Drag the fields with data you want to display across columns to the drop area labeled Drop Column Fields Here.

(6) Drag the fields containing the data you want to summarize to the area labeled Drop Data Items Here.

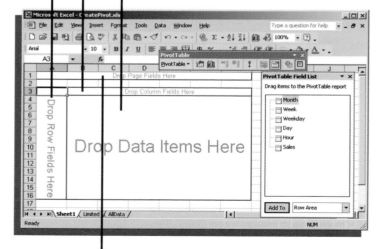

(3) Select where you want your PivotTable to appear, and click Finish.

(7) Drag the fields you want to use to filter the PivotTable to the area labeled Drop Page Fields Here.

Editing PivotTables

Perhaps the biggest benefit of presenting your data using PivotTables is that you can easily change the data's organization, creating literally dozens of different worksheets from a single data set! All you have to do is drag the header of the field you want to move to its new position—when you release the mouse button, Excel will examine the PivotTable's new structure and rearrange the data to match it. If you want to change the appearance of your PivotTable, you can do so by assigning an existing format.

Pivot a PivotTable

1 Drag the field name you want to move to a new location.

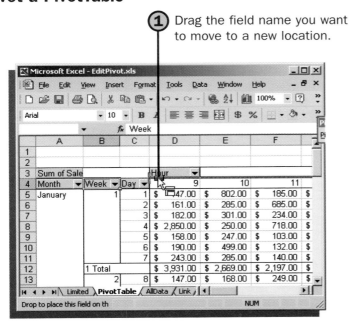

Format a PivotTable

1 Click any cell in the PivotTable you want to format, and choose AutoFormat from the Format menu.

2 Double-click the format you want.

Working with a PivotTable

When you create a PivotTable from the data in your tables or queries, you will often have several screens of data to move through. Reorganizing can help you interpret your data, but you can also filter your PivotTable by choosing the data you want to see. For example, if your PivotTable shows sales data for a series of products grouped by category, you can pick the categories for which you want to view data. You can also sort your data, perhaps alphabetizing all products within a category so that you can find the products you want more easily.

Sort a PivotTable

1 Click the field heading of the field you want to sort.

2 Click the Sort Ascending or Sort Descending button on the Standard toolbar.

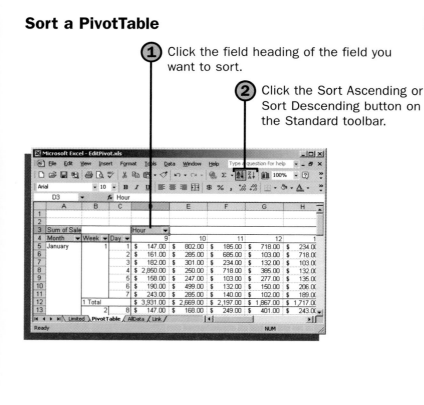

Filter a PivotTable

1 Click the down arrow next to the field you want to filter.

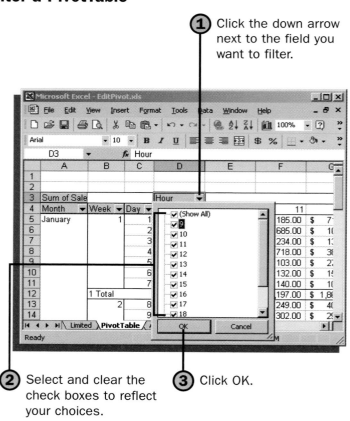

2 Select and clear the check boxes to reflect your choices.

3 Click OK.

Linking to PivotTable Data ⊛ NEW FEATURE

When you create a formula in Excel, you can create links to values in other cells. In Excel 2002, you now have the ability to create a link from a cell in your PivotTable to a cell on another worksheet or even in another workbook. When you click the PivotTable cell, a GETPIVOTDATA formula appears in the Formula Bar of the worksheet containing the PivotTable. Regardless of how you pivot the PivotTable, the cell's contents will be used in the formula.

Create a Link to a PivotTable Cell

① Click the cell in which you want to enter a formula.

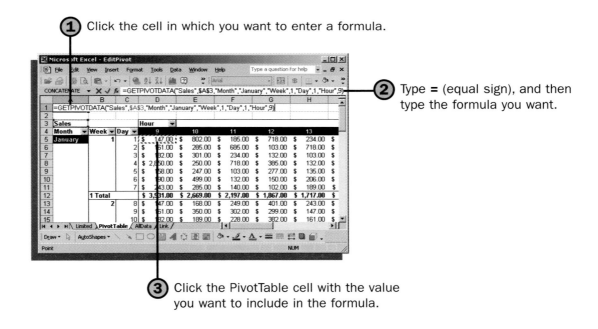

② Type = (equal sign), and then type the formula you want.

③ Click the PivotTable cell with the value you want to include in the formula.

> 🕹 **SEE ALSO: For more information about linking to a worksheet cell, see "Creating Formulas with Cells from Other Workbooks" on page 65.**

Publishing a PivotTable on the Web

When you publish an Excel workbook on the Web, you allow your colleagues to interact with the worksheets. You can make the data you publish to the Web even more useful to your colleagues by presenting it in the form of a PivotTable. When you do so, anyone viewing the PivotTable over your company's intranet or the Internet can rearrange the PivotTable data to emphasize an aspect of the data. You can also use PivotTables published on the Web in presentations you make while traveling. If the PivotTables contain sensitive data you don't want to carry with you on your laptop computer, you can connect the laptop to the network at your destination and view the data over the Web from that location.

Put a PivotTable on the Web

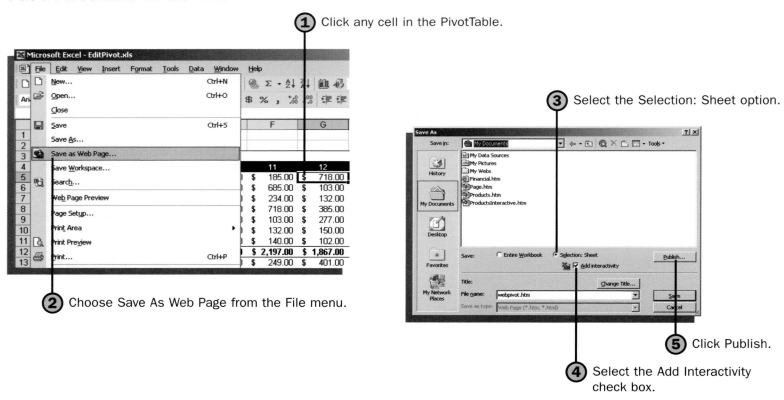

(1) Click any cell in the PivotTable.

(2) Choose Save As Web Page from the File menu.

(3) Select the Selection: Sheet option.

(4) Select the Add Interactivity check box.

(5) Click Publish.

6 Click the Choose down arrow, and click Items On PivotTable.

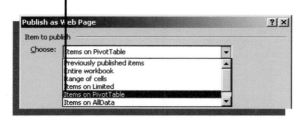

7 In the list below the Choose box, click the item beginning with PivotTable.

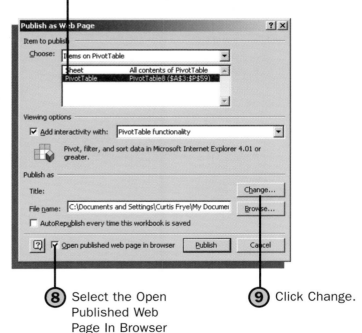

8 Select the Open Published Web Page In Browser check box.

9 Click Change.

10 Type a title for the Web page you are creating.

11 Click OK.

12 Click Publish in the Publish As Web Page dialog box.

> ✋ **CAUTION:** When you publish a PivotTable to the Web, Excel creates a folder named pivot_files in the directory to which you published the PivotTable. The pivot_files folder contains files you need for the PivotTable to work properly, so be sure you don't delete the folder!

> ❗ **TIP:** It is very important that you just publish the items on the PivotTable. If you publish the entire worksheet, rather than just the items on the PivotTable, viewers will not be able to interact with the PivotTable.

Using Goal Seek to Conduct a "What If" Analysis

When you create Excel formulas to summarize your worksheet data, you use known values, such as monthly sales and operating costs, to discover how much each element of your business contributes to your overall income and expenses. You can also analyze your data from the opposite direction, by having Excel find an input value that would cause a formula to produce the desired result. For example, you might run a garden supply company and want to have furniture sales account for 30 percent of your total revenue. Rather than performing the calculations on paper, you can use Goal Seek to have Excel determine what amount in furniture sales would be necessary to produce 30 percent of your revenue.

Define a Goal Seek Solution

(1) Choose Goal Seek from the Tools menu.

(2) Click the Set Cell box.

(3) Click the cell containing the formula you want to resolve.

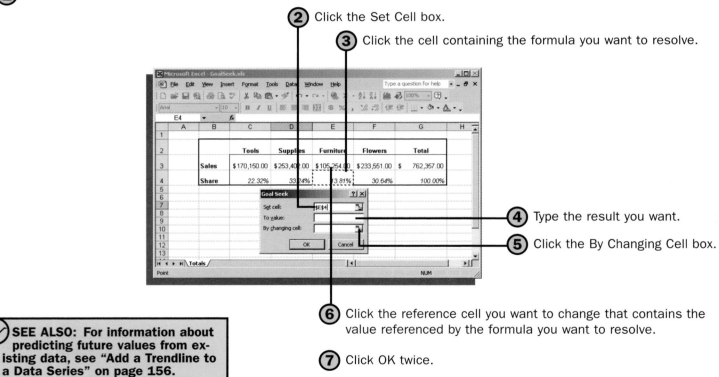

(4) Type the result you want.

(5) Click the By Changing Cell box.

(6) Click the reference cell you want to change that contains the value referenced by the formula you want to resolve.

(7) Click OK twice.

SEE ALSO: For information about predicting future values from existing data, see "Add a Trendline to a Data Series" on page 156.

Creating a Macro

After you have worked with your Excel documents for a while, you will probably discover some series of actions that you perform repeatedly. While many of these actions—such as saving your changes or printing—can be accomplished quickly, some sequences involve many steps and take time to accomplish by hand. For example, you might want to highlight a number of cells in a worksheet to emphasize an aspect of your data. Rather than highlight the cells by hand every time you present your findings, you can create a *macro,* or series of automated actions, to do the highlighting for you. Creating a macro is simple since you can actually record the actions you want. Whenever you start the recording process, the Stop Macro toolbar will appear automatically so that you can stop recording whenever you want. After you create your macro, you can run it as needed.

Record a Macro

1 On the Tools menu, point to Macro and choose Record New Macro.

2 Type the name you want for your macro.

3 Type the key or keys you want to press to run the macro.

5 Perform the actions you want recorded in your macro.

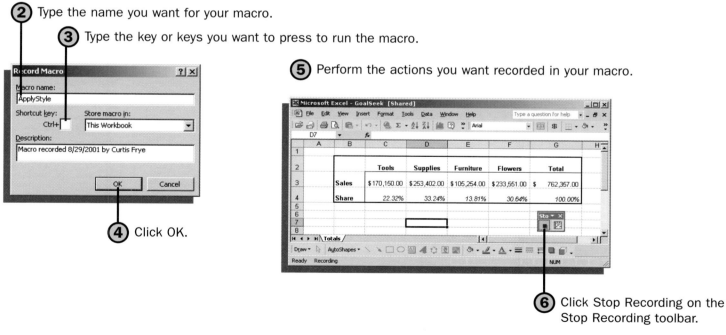

4 Click OK.

6 Click Stop Recording on the Stop Recording toolbar.

Run a Macro

1 On the Tools menu, point to Macro and choose Macros.

2 Click the macro you want to run.

3 Click Run.

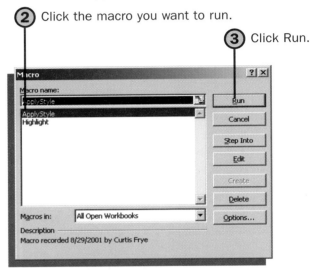

> **⚠ TIP: You can limit the macros shown by clicking the Macros In down arrow and clicking the workbook containing the macros you want to display.**

> **⚠ TIP: You can also run a macro by holding down the Ctrl key and pressing the key you assigned to the macro. This will allow you to execute the macro multiple times very easily.**

Setting Macro Security

Because viruses can sometimes be transmitted in a macro, Excel has a built-in functionality to help prevent data loss. There are three levels of *macro security* to choose from. The high security level allows only macros with digital signatures embedded in them to run on your computer. The medium level allows you to choose which macros to run; for instance, your colleague may not add a digital signature to his macros, but you know they are safe. The low level allows any macro to be run.

Set Macro Security Levels

1 On the Tools menu, point to Macro and choose Security.

2 Select the security level you want.

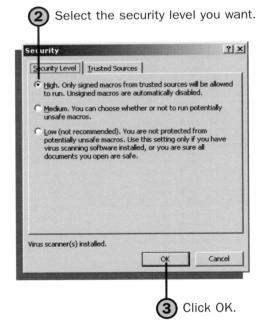

3 Click OK.

Index

Send feedback about this index to *mspindex@microsoft.com.*

Numbers

3-D
  charts, 154
  effects, 163

A

Access. *See* Microsoft Access
adding cells, 68
advanced filters, 134–35, 139–40
alignment
  cell contents, 36
  charts, 146
  drawing objects, 164–65
analyzing scenarios, 186–88
annotations, charts, 148
area chart, 143
arranging
  toolbars, 11
  windows, 17
  workbooks, 16, 56–57
art
  adding pictures, 159
  AutoShapes, 166
  clip art, 169–70
  Clip Art task pane, 9
  deleting pictures, 159
  diagrams, 171–72
  displaying data, 142–43

art, *continued*
  drawing objects, 160–66
  headers and footers, 112–14
  organization charts, 173–75
  overview, 158
  WordArt, 167–68
ascending order, sorting, 128–29
Ask A Question box, 20
audio, converting text to speech, 204
auditing formulas, 73, 74–75
AutoFill, 30
AutoFilter, 132–33
AutoShapes, 166
AutoSum, 69
AutoText, 110–12
axis, chart, 149–50

B

backgrounds, cell, 87–88
bar chart, 143
beginning Excel, 8
blank
  workbooks, opening, 8
  worksheets, inserting, 53
borders, cell, 89–90
breaks, printing, page, 115
browsing clip art, 170
bubble chart, 143
building PivotTables, 222
buttons, toolbar, 123

C

calculations. *See* formulas; functions
category axis, chart, 150
cells
  aligning contents, 36
  backgrounds, 87–88
  borders, 89–90
  building formulas, 63
  clearing contents, 41
  comments, 179–80
  conditional formatting, 92–93
  copying formatting, 94
  copying to multiple worksheets, 55
  copying values, 40–41
  cutting values, 40–41
  editing contents, 32
  editing formulas, 63
  entering dates and times, 29
  entering numbers, 28
  entering text, 27
  fills, 30
  formatting contents, 33–36
  formatting dates, 35
  formatting numbers, 34–35
  formulas using workbook links, 65–67
  gridlines, 91
  hyperlinks, 38–40
  linking to PivotTables, 225
  merging, 99
  orienting contents, 36

D

Q

R

text, *continued*
  importing files, 216–17
  styles, 97–98
  WordArt, 167–68
times, entering in cells, 29
titles, charts, 147
toolbars
  arranging, 11
  customizing, 123, 125–26
  Formatting, 7
  hiding, 11, 121
  overview, 7
  showing, 121
  Standard, 7
tracking changes, 181
trendlines, 156
type, charts, 143, 146
typing
  numbers in cells, 28
  text in cells, 27

 U

Undo, 43
unique rows, finding, 139
updating worksheets on Web dynamically, 195

 V

validating data, 136–38
value axis, chart, 149
values
  conditional formatting, 92
  converting to, 66
  filtering data, 139

values, *continued*
  sorting data, 130–31
  validating data, 136–38
viewing
  3-D charts, 154
  cell comments, 179–80
  changes, 182
  scenarios, 187
  worksheets, 48, 56–58
views, worksheets, 58
voice, converting text to speech, 204

 W

watch, formulas, 74–75
Web
  clip art, 170
  dynamically updating worksheets, 195
  help, 21
  hyperlinks, 38–40
  modifying worksheets, 193–95
  publishing PivotTables, 229–30
  queries, 202
  retrieving data, 196–97
  saving worksheets to, 192
  smart tags, 200–201
  XML, 198–99
What If analysis, 156, 226
width, column, 78–79, 102
windows
  arranging, 17
  size, 17
Wizard, Chart, 144–45
Wizard, PivotTable, 222
Word. *See* Microsoft Word

workbooks
  cell comments, 179–80
  change history, 183
  copying worksheets, 51–52
  creating new, 15
  embedding files, 206–7
  embedding objects, 205
  formulas, 65–67
  linking files, 206–7
  linking objects, 205
  merging, 184–85
  moving worksheets, 49–50
  multiple, 16, 118–19
  New Workbook task pane, 9
  opening, 8, 12–14
  saving, 19–20
  scenarios, 186–89
  sending by e-mail, 213
  sharing, 178
  templates, 15, 119–21
  tracking changes, 181
  validating data, 138
  viewing changes, 182
  XML, 199
workgroups
  cell comments, 179–80
  change history, 183
  merging workbooks, 184–85
  modifying worksheets over Web, 193–95
  scenarios, 186–89
  tracking changes, 181
  viewing changes, 182
  workbook sharing, 178
worksheets
  adding pictures, 159
  AutoShapes, 166

About the Authors

Curtis Frye

Curtis Frye is a freelance writer living in Portland, Oregon. This is his fourth book for Microsoft Press. Previously, he wrote *Microsoft Excel Version 2002 Step by Step*, *Microsoft Access Version 2002 Plain & Simple*, and co-authored *Microsoft Office XP Step by Step*. He is also the author of five other books (most notably *Privacy-Enhanced Business* from Quorum Books), three online courses for DigitalThink, and is the editor and chief reviewer of "Technology & Society Book Reviews." When he is not writing, and often when he is writing, he is a professional improvisational comedian with Portland's ComedySportz group.

epic software group, inc.

For the past eleven years, the artists, animators, and programmers at the epic software group, inc., have been helping their clients use the power of the computer to tell their stories in ways that are not possible with traditional media. epic creates applications such as multimedia presentations, electronic catalogs, computer-based training, interactive brochures, and touch screen kiosks. Their work is distributed on CD-ROM, disk, and the Internet.

In 1997, the epic software group entered the world of publishing when the company was chosen to create over one hundred 3-D illustrations for the "Happy and Max" series of children's books. In 2000, epic authored *Macromedia Flash 5 – From Concept to Creation*, followed by *Macromedia Director Game Development – From Concept to Creation*. Book projects currently in the works by the epic software group are titles on Flash 6, Director Shockwave 8.5, and LightWave 3D.

epic software group, inc.
701 Sawdust Road
The Woodlands, TX   77380
281-363-3742 (phone)
281-363-3742 (fax)

www.epicsoftware.com (web)
epic@epicsoftware.com (e-mail)

The manuscript for this book was prepared and submitted to Microsoft Press in electronic form. Text files were prepared using Microsoft Word 2002. Pages were composed by Microsoft Press using Adobe PageMaker 6.52 for Windows, with text set in Times and display type in ITC Franklin Gothic. Composed pages were delivered to the printer as electronic prepress files.

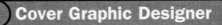

Cover Graphic Designer

Tim Girvin Design

Interior Graphic Designers

Joel Panchot, James D. Kramer

Interior Graphic Artists

Dan Latimer, James D. Kramer

Principal Compositor

Dan Latimer

Principal Copy Editor

Patricia Masserman

Indexer

Patti Schiendelman